TEACHING WITH
Voices of a People's History of the United States
by Howard Zinn and Anthony Arnove
SECOND EDITION

TEACHING WITH

Voices of a People's History of the United States

by Howard Zinn and Anthony Arnove

SECOND EDITION

Gayle Olson-Raymer
Humboldt State University

With selected chapters written by Humboldt County AP teachers:

Jack Bareilles (McKinleyville High School), Natalia Boettcher (South Fork High School), Mike Benbow (Fortuna High School), Ron Perry (Eureka High School), Robin Pickering, Jennifer Rosebrook (Arcata High School), Colby Smart (Ferndale High School), Robert Standish (South Fork High School), and Chapter 25 written by Humboldt State University history majors: Jeff Coomber, Adam Crug, Nicole Sinclair, Megan Watson

SEVEN STORIES PRESS
New York

Seven Stories Press
140 Watts Street
New York, NY 10013
www.sevenstories.com

College professors may order examination copies of all Seven Stories Press titles for a free six-month trial period. To order, visit www.sevenstories.com/textbook, or fax on school letterhead to 212-226-8760.

College professors who have adopted *Voices of a People's History of the United States* by Howard Zinn and Anthony Arnove as a course textbook are authorized to duplicate portions of this guide for their students.

Library of Congress Cataloging-in-Publication Data

CIP data on file.

ISBN: 978-1-58322-934-7

Design by Jon Gilbert

Printed in the U.S.A.

9 8 7 6 5 4 3 2 1

To Delores McBroome, Rodney Sievers, and Jack Bareilles—my
fellow travelers on the K–16 journey

and

to the teachers in the Teaching American History programs
in Humboldt County—my colleagues who made the journey
worth the effort.

Contents

Preface to the
Second Edition

Just over a year before the publication of the second edition of *Teaching with Voices of a People's History of the United States by Howard Zinn and Anthony Arnove*, the world lost one of its most vigorous voices for social justice. For decades, Howard Zinn's voice loomed large in classrooms across the United States where dedicated teachers committed to teaching for social justice used one or more of his many books and articles to inspire their students.

While Howard's voice will be sorely missed by teachers and students across the nation, he left a powerful legacy. Howard did not ask that we merely listen to and accept his voice and the voices of forgotten Americans woven throughout his writings. Rather, Howard wanted us to find *our own voices*; he wanted teachers and students to empower themselves by learning from the courageous examples of others. He believed youth yearned for stories of ordinary people like themselves who dared to demand and fight for change. As such, Howard was not a voice of pessimism, but rather of optimism—of an ordinary man and extraordinary scholar who believed in the goodness of the people, in hope for the future, and in the courage of convictions. As he wrote:

> It's clear that the struggle for justice should never be abandoned because of the apparent overwhelming power of those who have the guns and the money and who seem invincible in their determination to hold on to it. That apparent power has, again and again, proved vulnerable to human qualities less measurable than bombs and dollars: moral fervor, determination, unity, organization, sacrifice, wit, ingenuity, courage, patience . . .
>
> I have tried hard to match my friends in their pessimism about the world, but I keep encountering people who, in spite of all the evidence of terrible things happening everywhere, give me hope. Especially young people in whom the future rests . . . I try to tell each group that it is not

alone, and that the very people who are disheartened by the absence of a national movement are themselves proof of the potential for such a movement . . . We don't have to engage in grand, heroic actions to participate in the process of change. Small acts, when multiplied by millions of people, can transform the world . . .

An optimist isn't necessarily a blithe, slightly sappy whistler in the dark of our time. To be hopeful in bad times is not just foolishly romantic. It is based on the fact that human history is a history not only of cruelty but also of compassion, sacrifice, courage, kindness . . . If we see only the worst, it destroys our capacity to do something. If we remember those times and places—and there are so many—where people have behaved magnificently, this gives us the energy to act, and at least the possibility of sending this spinning top of a world in a different direction. And if we do act, in however small a way, we don't have to wait for some grand utopian future . . . And to live now as we think human beings should live, in defiance of all that is bad around us, is itself a marvelous victory.*

Howard Zinn believed in the power and courage of young people. The newest edition of this teaching guide is built upon this very foundation.

* Howard Zinn, "The Optimism of Uncertainty," 2004.

Acknowledgments

This guide materialized under the intellectual guidance and exceptional editorial suggestions of Ray Raphael, my friend and fellow historian. Chapters 1–11 were greatly improved by the creative touches of Bill Bigelow, my much-respected colleague in the K–16 world. The spirit of resistance was nurtured by the tutorial assistance of Anthony Arnove, the co-author of *Voices*.

Without the assistance of my colleagues—the eight Humboldt County high school educators who contributed seven chapters—the guide would lack the wisdom that can only come from a secondary and post-secondary collaboration. Many thanks to Jack Bareilles, Natalia Boettcher, Mike Benbow, Ron Perry, Robin Pickering, Jennifer Rosebrook, Colby Smart, and Robert Standish.

Four of the outstanding undergraduate history majors at Humboldt State University wrote Chapter 25: Jeff Coomber, Adam Crug, Nicole Sinclair, and Megan Watson. The contribution of these aspiring young teachers to the second edition was invaluable.

Introduction

> If history is to be creative, to anticipate a possible future without denying
> the past, it should, I believe, emphasize new possibilities by disclosing those
> hidden episodes of the past, when, even if in brief flashes, people showed
> their ability to resist, to join together, occasionally to win.
>
> —HOWARD ZINN[1]

In 2003, when *A People's History of the United States* sold its millionth copy, it was
clear that Howard Zinn had pioneered a new way of thinking about American
History. Americans everywhere gravitated to its message—that history is more balanced, relevant, and even empowering when examined from "the bottom up,"
rather than from "the top down." Educators throughout the nation who were disillusioned with traditional textbooks that told history solely from the voices of the
"important," "extraordinary" people embraced *A People's History* as a long-awaited
teaching tool that gave voice to the "unimportant," "ordinary" people whose courageous resistance helped shape modern America.

I was one of those educators. In the years before I adopted the "bottom up"
approach, it was painful to watch my students struggling with one-sided textbooks
about the great white men of America whose actions and voices did not speak to
them. I began asking the questions that form the foundation of Ronald Takaki's
study, *A Different Mirror*. "What happens when historians leave out many of
America's peoples? What happens, to borrow the words of Adrienne Rich, 'when
someone with the authority of a teacher' describes our society, and 'you are not in
it'"?[2] These questions led me to *A People's History*—the required text that has provided the intellectual forum for analysis, conceptualization, and debate in my
American History classes at Humboldt State University for the past ten years.

So, what are the benefits of using *A People's History*? What makes it different from
other history texts? It forces my students to actually THINK! It evokes visceral

responses. It forever changes the way they examine the voices of the past. And it forces my students to ask the all-important analytical questions: What perspective is clearly apparent in—or absent from—these pages? Why haven't we learned about this before now? What speaks to us and why? How much of this information is REAL and actually based upon primary documentation?

This last question is the one so many history teachers are eager to hear. For years, many of us have encouraged our students to read the words and examine the actions of the "ordinary" people who have shaped American history—de Las Casas, Nathaniel Bacon, Sojourner Truth, Black Hawk, Ida B. Wells, Emma Goldman. We have been thrilled when our students compared and contrasted these voices with the secondary analysis of historians who wrote about them. We have learned that when our students observe history through many personal lenses, they make intelligent observations about what Americans have done right, about what we have done wrong, and about what we still need to do; they critically examine the progress we have made, the consequences of such progress, and the prospects for even greater and more egalitarian progress in the future; and they walk away from our classrooms with a sense of optimism that we have indeed "come a long way" and that they can be involved in the next progressive steps forward. In short, the voices of the ordinary men and women of America encourage our students to find their own voices.

Today, all educators agree on the importance of using these historical voices—primary sources—in our classrooms. But we also face a daunting problem: it takes precious time and expense to locate and gather primary documents—especially those that deal primarily with resistance and the power of ordinary people to make positive change in society—and to find a way to make them readily available to our students. *Voices of a People's History of the United States* has solved this problem. Howard Zinn uses his encyclopedic knowledge of and first-hand involvement in people's history to bring these much-needed voices together into one easily accessible volume. Used in any social science course as a stand-alone textbook, in conjunction with another textbook, or in tandem with *A People's History*, *Voices* is designed to add rich primary source detail to our classes as well as to provide an incentive for students to recognize and utilize their own voices.

There is another critical reason for using *Voices* in classrooms across the nation—an enormous need that teachers are often afraid to address. As we enter the twenty-first century, it seems that dissent, resistance, and protest have become dirty words. Those who question government policies and actions increasingly are called "unpatriotic." Yet, as Howard Zinn reminds us, "One of the great mistakes made in discussing patriotism—a very common mistake—is to think that patriotism means support for your government. And that view of patriotism ignores the founding principles of the country expressed in the Declaration of Independence."[3] Indeed, some of the greatest American patriots have been the brave men and women who questioned government by resisting slavery, fighting for equal rights for all, and defying government policies when they violate civil rights. These are the ordinary people whose stories form the basis for *Voices of a People's History*. And their voices must be heard in today's classrooms.

How, then, can we best integrate *Voices* into our classrooms? *Teaching with Voices of a People's History of the United States* suggests varied and exciting ways to combine the use of secondary and primary historical materials in high school, college, and university classrooms. As such, it demonstrates how *Voices* may be used as a stand-alone text as well as in conjunction with *A People's History*. By using *Voices* or both books, our students will learn a more balanced story—a story that will challenge them to think about other viewpoints than those traditionally presented and to weigh such views against their own. Perhaps even more importantly, this story can empower our students as they listen to the words of ordinary people like themselves who used their voices throughout history to challenge the status quo, to ask the hard questions, and to demand and shape change.

Empowerment, then, is one of the primary philosophical forces behind this guide—a force that has not been of my own making, but rather is the result of input from thousands of students at Humboldt State University when leaving their semester-long experience with *A People's History* and the primary documents used to supplement its story. But this guide is not just an endorsement of what works in one university professor's history classroom. It is also a product of the hard work of several secondary educators in Humboldt County who have used all or parts of *A People's History* in their classrooms and who intend to begin using *Voices of A People's History* upon its publication. The contributions of my colleagues lend great credence to the belief that secondary and post-secondary educators can collaborate by using the same teaching sources and by agreeing that being good history teachers requires us to raise the intellectual bar in our classrooms—to ask our students to conceptualize, analyze, discuss, debate, and relate to what they read in either or both books. This guide would not be as useful without the input of these educators, eight of whom contributed chapters: Jack Bareilles, Natalia Boettcher, Mike Benbow, Ron Perry, Robin Pickering, Jennifer Rosebrook, Colby Smart, and Robert Standish.

How to Use *Voices of a People's History of the United States*

The decision to use *Voices* as a textbook in the classroom requires us to address at least two questions:

- How will I use *Voices*—as a stand-alone text, in tandem with *A People's History*, or together with another secondary source textbook?

- How will *Voices* supplement and strengthen my U.S. History curriculum?

USING *VOICES* AS A TEXTBOOK

The need for *Voices* is so great that there are almost unlimited ways that it can be used as a stand-alone textbook or with textbooks already used in secondary and post-secondary social science courses. As each of the twenty-five chapters in *Voices* will illustrate, each era of American history is represented through the voices of resistance. And because *Voices* is chronologically organized, it is easy to tailor reading, discussion, and research related to resistance to every important era in U.S. History. Thus, when you are teaching World War I, students can use Chapter 14, "Protesting the First World War" by:

- Reading the words of those who were opposed to "the war to make the world safe for democracy."

- Discussing how and why these voices influenced the antiwar movement as well as what their individual and collective messages contributed to the direction of American foreign and domestic policy.

- Researching the various U.S. Supreme Court decisions and Congressional laws that attempted to curb the antiwar movement during the time by drawing on the words from Chapter 14, as well as other primary and secondary resource documents that further explain governmental goals and accomplishments.

If you use *Voices* as your single textbook, it will reinforce classroom lectures and individual and group research projects that already form the core of your classes. If you use *Voices* to supplement an existing textbook, it will provide new perspectives about how ordinary people have shaped American history.

Using *Voices* together with this teaching guide provides examples of how the primary documentation in each chapter of *Voices* can be used to reinforce the important messages in *A People's History*. This marriage of primary and secondary resources, as each of the guide chapters illustrates, encourages students to critically compare and contrast what Howard Zinn has written about each era with what people who lived during the eras actually witnessed.

USING *VOICES* TO SUPPLEMENT AND STRENGTHEN THE U.S. HISTORY CURRICULUM

Voices does something that is different from other primary source compilations—it uses the voices of ordinary Americans to demonstrate how a more democratic understanding of American history can promote a more democratic society. This is the real beauty of *Voices*—we not only learn to think about the forgotten folks like ourselves who don't show up in traditional history books—we also enter into a relationship with them. By seeing history through the eyes of common people, by learning about their struggles for a more democratic nation, we refuse to marginalize them. And if students take ordinary people from the past seriously, they can learn to take ordinary people in their own lives just as seriously. This message is one that can easily be infused into any American history curriculum, especially through the use of overall themes.

Teaching thematically has changed the way many educators across the nation introduce history to their students. By identifying five to ten overall themes for each course, educators emphasize the really important, bottom-line messages that they want their students to remember after they leave their classrooms. *Voices* is a perfect vehicle for thematic teaching. While there are dozens of themes and sub-themes carefully interwoven throughout *Voices*, five are readily apparent and could easily be adopted as overall themes for an entire semester- or year-long American History class:

1. History matters. By studying the historic voices of all the people—the "important" and "unimportant" alike—Americans have a stronger foundation for understanding how and why the past tells us a great deal about the present and the future.

2. No telling of history is neutral or objective. By recognizing that all history, including that found in *Voices*, is selective and emphasizes some stories and some events more than others, we learn that history is really about making people think, ask questions, and demand answers.

3. History is usually told from the standpoint of the "victors." By focusing on history only as it is perceived by the "important" people—presidents, general, and other leaders—we do not learn the stories of the ordinary people—folks like you and I.

4. Ordinary people make history. By hearing the voices of "unimportant" people—workers, women, slaves, American Indians, migrant farm workers—we get a more complete understanding of how history unfolded and the role ordinary people played in its making.

5. Injustices are remedied when ordinary people speak up, organize, and protest. By learning about the actions of those who acted outside the bounds of, or in opposition to, "legitimate" political institutions, we get a better understanding of how they made democracy come alive.

Teachers should feel free to tweak these themes as they wish, but variations of these five messages should be well integrated into the course content. If *Voices* and *A People's History* are being used, the five themes are common to both books. Before students begin reading *Voices*, teachers should initiate a discussion about the themes. (See suggestions below.) As the course progresses and as the students become immersed in *Voices*, the themes should continue to provide a skeletal outline for most classroom discussions.

HOW TO INTRODUCE *VOICES* INTO THE CLASSROOM

An excellent introductory strategy to introduce students to *Voices*—whether it is used as the primary text or in conjunction with *A People's History* or another textbook—is the following two-pronged approach:

- Introduce the five overall themes from *Voices* (see above). Read and discuss each. Post them in a prominent place in the room—or put them online on your web site—and tell your students that they will be asked to refer back to themes as they progress through the course. Challenge them to find new themes or to revise these as the year continues.

- Assign the chapter "The Coming Revolt of the Guards" from *A People's History* as the first required reading for the class.

I have found that by requiring the last chapter to be read as an introduction to the class, students come to class ready and eager to learn because the story is evocative; some will love Howard Zinn's approach and his refreshing perspectives, while others will be skeptical. Regardless of the response, almost every student will be engaged and ready for a passionate discussion. Thus, this introduction through Howard Zinn's analysis and the voices of those in Chapter 24 allows the teacher to pose some important questions during the very first days of class:

- Given what you read in *A People's History*, what perspectives do you think will be reflected in *Voices*?

- What is different about reading a book that loudly proclaims its viewpoint, versus a more traditional book that presents the dominant narrative yet claims to be objective?

- When looking at the five themes we have identified for this course, which do you see reflected in "The Coming Revolt of the Guards"?

- In explaining his perspective and presenting voices to reinforce such perspectives, do you think you will examine Howard Zinn more critically as you begin to read *Voices*? Why or why not?

This discussion can be followed with a challenge—Tell students that they will be required at the end of the course to provide concrete evidence from *Voices* of how and where Howard Zinn supports his perspectives and when and where he might need greater support to convince them. Ask them to begin a journal in which they must explain at least one point that provokes their interest from each chapter, describe the way that point reinforces one or more of the overall themes expressed in the book, and discuss what other voices might be included to provide a greater understanding of the chapter's objectives. Journals will be reviewed periodically and turned in at the end of the course as part of their final exit requirements.

For several years, I have ended my introductory discussion with a quote from Howard Zinn's book, *You Can't Be Neutral on a Moving Train*. To be hopeful in bad time is not just foolishly romantic. It is based on the fact that human history is a history not only of cruelty, but also of compassion, sacrifice, courage, and kindness. What we choose to emphasize in this complex history will determine our lives. If we see only the worst, it destroys our capacity to do something. If we remember those times and places—and there are so many—where people have behaved magnificently, this gives us the energy to act, and at least the possibility of sending this spinning top of a world in a different direction. And if we do act, in however small a way, we don't have to wait for some grand utopian future. The future is an infinite succession of presents, and to live now as we think human beings should live, in defiance of all that is bad around us, is itself a marvelous victory.

We spend a few minutes discussing this quote, our own feelings about "this complex history," and our own perceptions of what "a marvelous victory" might entail. It's a perfect introduction to a year of provocative reading, respectful debate, and ultimately, empowerment and optimism.

How to Use *Teaching with Voices of a People's History of the United States*

Each chapter in the teacher's guide utilizes a format that focuses discussion questions, assignments, and evaluations around the major themes in *Voices of a People's History*—themes that are also reinforced in *A People's History*. Chapters are designed to provide an even flow for classroom use by following a standard organizational style:

1. Document-based-questions (DBQs). Document-based questions are included for each of the documents presented in *Voices*. Questions are analytical in nature, designed to get students to really think about what the author said, why they said it, the implications of the document on society as a whole, and how its contents relate to the major themes found throughout the book.

2. Chapter main points. While students are encouraged to find the main points within each chapter of *Voices*, we have included two lists of main points.

    *   The first list is for teachers who use *Voices* as their primary text. Each chapter list illustrates the threads that run through all the voices in the chapter.

    *   The second list is for teachers using the chapter in both *Voices* and *A People's History* and illustrates the issues common to both chapters.

3. Discussion questions for classroom conversations. Two sets of questions are included to help generate class discussions on each chapter:

    *   The first set of questions focus solely on issues that can be raised after

reading each chapter in *Voices*.

- The second set of questions combine issues relevant to each chapter for students who are reading both *Voices* and *A People's History*.

4. Three types of evaluation tools. In order to address a variety of evaluation methods, three types of evaluation tools have been included: suggested assignments, suggested essay questions, and simulations and other creative approaches.

- Suggested assignments. These assignments can be adapted to meet any classroom need—homework, short- or long-term research projects, and individual or group work. The end product in these assignments are designed to be flexible and should depend on teacher and student interest—papers, journals, oral reports, visual aides, etc.

- Suggested essay questions. These can be asked during in-class or take home examinations.

- Simulations and other creative approaches. These creative assignments can be used in various classroom settings.

NOTES

1   Howard Zinn, *A People's History of the United States: 1492–Present*, updated ed. (New York: HarperCollins/Perennial Classics, 2001).

2   Ronald Takaki, *A Different Mirror: A History of Multicultural America*. (Boston: Little, Brown and Company, 1993:16).

3   Interview with Howard Zinn on July 3, 2002, "Dissent In Pursuit Of Equality, Life, Liberty And Happiness" at http://www.theexperiment.org/articles.php?news_id=1821.

CHAPTER ONE

Columbus and Las Casas

The first chapter in *Voices* provides students with a perspective that many have never encountered. By reading the words of Columbus, de Las Casas, and Galeano, students experience a wide array of emotions. The ensuing discussions may be painful, yet they are also enlightening. These previously unheard perspectives tell them more about the Arawak[1] people and in so doing, encourage students to use their own voices by asking, "Why haven't I heard these voices before? Why have I only learned half of the story of Columbus and European contact? How could the Spanish have committed such atrocities?"

Some students insist that their previous teachers have "lied" to them. Others believe that their teachers may not have had a complete understanding of the story of Columbus or that they simply never learned the history. In the end, most students agree that an honest, balanced presentation of a diversity of voices is absolutely essential in classroom discussions at all levels of education—elementary, secondary, and postsecondary.

Document-Based Questions

CHRISTOPHER COLUMBUS

1. What new information did you learn about Columbus from these four diary entries? How does it differ from earlier opinions and images that you had of Columbus?

2. What does Columbus think of the native population in terms of its physical and mental conditions, its worth to the king and queen of Spain, and its relationship with the European explorers?

3. What is Columbus's plan for the island of Hispaniola? How does he explain how his plan will affect the native population? What do you think is missing from his plan?

BARTOLOMÉ DE LAS CASAS

1. Why do you think Bartolomé de Las Casas wrote these two accounts? To whom do you think he wrote them?

2. De Las Casas wrote these accounts fifty and sixty years respectively after Columbus initially arrived in Hispanola. Do you think the intervening years may have influenced his perceptions? How and why? What happens when someone writes down an account after most of the consequences of an event are known?

3. How do these two readings change your understanding of the consequences of European contact on the native people of the Western Hemisphere? Does this view make the Spanish explorers any less heroic? How and why?

4. Whose opinions do you think were most prominent during the late fifteenth century—those of Columbus or those of Las Casas? How and why?

5. Do you think that Las Casas's voice was heard at the Royal Council of Spain in 1550? Who do you think would have opposed him or supported him?

EDUARDO GALEANO

1. How did Eduardo Galeano use historical sources to support his re-imagining of the native experience after Columbus's "discovery"?

2. How does Galeano's description of the landing of Columbus compare and contrast with the descriptions given by Columbus and de Las Casas?

3. What does Galeano's account tell you about the fate of the enslaved Arawak/Tainos whom Columbus took to Spain?

4. How does Galeano describe the Pope? What, in his eyes, is the Pope's interest and complicity in both the goals and consequences of Columbus's voyages?

5. What does Galeano mean when he writes in his entry of 1493 on Santa Cruz Island that Columbus "has again planted the cross and gallows"? Do you agree or disagree? How and why?

Main Points in *Voices*, Chapter 1, "Columbus and Las Casas"

After reading Chapter 1 in *Voices*, students should be encouraged to identify what they believe to be the main points therein. Following are six possible main points.

1. Columbus's arrival in the Caribbean was an invasion of a very old world, not the discovery of a "New World."

2. Despite Euro-American claims to the contrary, Indian peoples were highly civilized before, during, and after contact.

3. Although the colonists believed they were helping native peoples progress from savagery to civilization, the end result was genocide.

4. The Americas were first explored and then colonized by the Europeans for economic gain and political conquest.

5. While the vast majority of Europeans supported the exploration, invasion, and colonization of the Americas, voices of dissent did exist.

6. The quest toward progress must be examined from different perspectives. Actions noted as "progress" by the conquering Europeans were believed to be destructive by the native populations.

Main Points in *Voices*, Chapter 1, "Columbus and Las Casas," and in *A People's History*, Chapter 1, "Columbus, the Indians, and Human Progress"

If your students are also reading *A People's History*, they should be encouraged to identify what they believe to be the main points in Chapter 1 in both books. Following are four additional points to be stressed when *Voices* and *A People's History* are used together.

7. To portray Columbus as a hero and his successors as discoverers and the rightful leaders of "civilized" peoples not only de-emphasizes their role in genocide but also justifies their actions and motives.

8. From the early days of colonization, Europeans used divide-and-conquer techniques to turn the Indians against one another.

9. Columbus planted the ideological seeds that came to characterize the European colonization of North America: the quest for wealth and power was noble and courageous; white domination of the nonwhite races was natural and inevitable; and Christians were superior to non-Christians.

10. Columbus introduced two tactics that influenced race relations in the Americas: taking land, wealth, and labor from indigenous peoples by force, and advancing the transatlantic slave trade.

General-Discussion Questions for *Voices*

While the following questions are designed for classroom discussion about all the voices read in Chapter 1, they can also be rewritten to be included as evaluation tools.

1. How would you contrast the viewpoints of Columbus and de Las Casas in regard to the "native people called Indians"? Do you think Columbus and de Las Casas agree or disagree about the goals of the Spanish explorers? How and why?

2. What does the fictional account of Galeano add to or subtract from your understanding of the Arawak/Taino people? How useful is historical fiction to your understanding of history in general?

3. Some historians have referred to the actions of Columbus and those who followed him as "genocidal." What is genocide? Using specific citations from at least two voices in this chapter, support or refute this accusation of genocide.

4. What do you think are the qualifications that are required before a nation can be considered "civilized"? Do you think the definition of "civilized" has changed in the last 400 years? If so, how? In reading the description of the Arawak/Taino in de Las Casas and Galeano, do you find any indication that these people were uncivilized? How and why do you think that Euro-American colonists thought that they were uncivilized?

5. Given the voices you have read in this chapter, how do you think we should commemorate Columbus Day?

6. What European cultural, political, economic, and spiritual values are exposed in these voices? How do you think they compared and contrasted with the values of the Arawak/Taino people?

7. How did the voices in this chapter reinforce any of the six themes listed in "Main Points in *Voices*"?

8. Which of the voices in this chapter did you find most powerful? Least powerful? How and why?

General-Discussion Questions for *Voices* and *A People's History*

These general-discussion questions are additional questions for students who have read the first chapter in both books. For all questions, discussion must focus on how the materials in both chapters help students to formulate and articulate their answers.

9. Of the voices in Chapter 1 in both books, who represents the one percent of the elite discussed in "The Coming Revolt of the Guards" in Chapter 24 of *A People's History?* Whose are the "unimportant" voices? Can you find quotes to support your positions?

10. In many traditional history books, the years between 1898 and World War I are known as "The Age of Imperialism." How would you define imperialism? Given what you have read in both first chapters in *A People's History* and in *Voices*, do you think imperialism first arrived in the Americas in the late nineteenth century? Why do you think textbooks refer to late nineteenth-century imperialism as a new type of foreign policy?

11. How do the voices in Chapter 1 of *Voices* reinforce the major points made in Chapter 1 of *A People's History?*

12. Given what you have learned about the cultural and economic values of the Arawak/Taino and the Spanish explorers, do you think there could have been a relationship different from that of victims and conquerors? Or do you think that such interaction was inevitable? How and why?

13. There is relatively little disagreement among historians about what happened to the Tainos. Why do you think this story is not more widely taught in school?

14. Given what you have learned in these chapters, why do you think Columbus Day is an official holiday for federal employees in the United States?

15. How did the colonists justify taking Indian land? How are their justifications similar and dissimilar to the justifications Columbus makes for his actions in Hispaniola?

16. What is "that special powerful drive born in civilizations based on private property" (p. 16) that Howard Zinn describes in "Columbus, the Indians, and Human Progress"? How will the issue of private property shape the ongoing battle between the Euro-Americans and the indigeneous peoples of North America?

17. Do you think it is "inevitable" that the writing of history take sides? Explain.

Evaluation Tools

SUGGESTED ASSIGNMENTS

These assignments can be adapted to meet any classroom need—homework, short- or long-term research projects, individual or group work. The end product should be flexible, depending on teacher interest and student abilities—papers, journals, oral reports, visual aides, and the like.

1. Using a search engine of choice, find a website that includes primary documents about early Spanish exploration in the Americas. Find at least one other primary document that provides more information about Spanish contact with American Indians. What new information did you acquire about early relationships between the Spanish and American Indians?

2. Using a search engine of choice, discover what you can about the descendants of the Arawak/Taino people. What new historical and contemporary information did you acquire about the people and their nation?

3. Justify the role of "progress" from the Spanish perspective, using specific phrases and explanations from any of the primary documents in Chapter 1. Then reverse your position and refute your justifications by using the phrases and words of those who suffered at the hands of such "progress."

4. Watch any feature-length movie that deals with the topics discussed in Chapter 1 in both *Voices* and *A People's History*. How did the movie(s) reinforce or refute the voices that you learned about in these chapters? What parts of the movie do you feel were historically accurate? Inaccurate? Why do you think the movie was made? Who do you think was its intended audience?

5. Recent scholarship has emphasized the role of the European explorers and settlers in the environmental degradation and destruction of the Caribbean and North America. In *The Conquest of Paradise: Christopher Columbus and the Columbian Legacy* by Kirkpatrick Sale (New York: Alfred A. Knopf, 1990), the author describes a "Columbian legacy" of environmental destructiveness. The Arawak/Taino people are characterized as living in perfect harmony with the environment, while Europeans are depicted as a people who are at war with nature. Find out more about this discussion of environmental degradation, especially in terms of its historical accuracy.

6. Much speculation exists about Columbus the man—his origins, religious beliefs, and goals—and what Columbus really hoped for from his voyages. Using this extensive website devoted to Columbus—www.win.tue.nl/cs/fm/engels/discovery/columbus.html—pick a few key sites to learn more about what Columbus hoped to gain from his voyages. Compare this information with what you have read in Chapters 1 in both *Voices* and *A People's History*.

7. Using excerpts from Columbus's journal and from José Barreiro's, "A Note on Tainos: Whither Progress?" (http://www.hartford-hwp.com/archives/41/013.html), write a diary entry from the point of view of a Taino during the first few days or weeks of their encounter with the Spaniards.

8. Read and critique together Jane Yolen's children's book *Encounter*. Discussion questions to ponder include: How does this story more or less accurately explain the first European/Taino encounter as told from a Taino boy's perspective? How does this story differ from traditional stories of contact? Is it important for young children to gain a more balanced perspec-

tive of the Columbus story that includes mention of genocide and violence, or is this story better left to the secondary schools to tell?

9. The Pledge of Allegiance was written in 1892 by Francis Bellamy to commemorate the 400th anniversary of Columbus's first voyage to the Americas. President William Henry Harrison proclaimed October 21, 1893, as the original Columbus Day—a national holiday—and designated schools to be the main sites of celebration. Research the original motivations behind creating the Pledge, as well as its original wording. Why was its creation tied directly to Columbus? What subsequent role did the Knights of Columbus have in making further changes to the Pledge? Who are the Knights of Columbus and what role do they play in keeping the legacy of Columbus alive in the United States today?

10. Read Howard Zinn's article, "Unsung Heroes" (www.theexperiment.org/articles.php?news_id=570). Who are some of his "unsung heroes"? Why does he feel that we should not be teaching about Columbus as a hero? Do you agree or disagree? Explain. Why does Zinn feel that it is important for students to learn about the unsung heroes in their classrooms? Do you think his advice is sound? How and why?

SUGGESTED ESSAY QUESTIONS

1. On page 29 in *Voices*, Howard Zinn writes, "Profit was the driving force behind Columbus's expedition and behind his actions after he landed." In the voices you read about in Chapter 1, what evidence can you find to support this statement? Do you agree or disagree? Why?

2. Do you think the actions of Columbus and other Spanish explorers referred to in these primary documents can be defined as acts of genocide? How and why?

3. Who do you think are the heroes in the primary documents you have read? If you were alive in the sixteenth or seventeenth centuries, do you think your answers would be any different? How and why?

4. Explain the ways in which Chapter 1 in *Voices* reinforces any of the overall themes we discussed in "Main Points in *Voices*."

5. How would you define progress? Do you believe that it was inevitable that

Euro-American progress be achieved at the expense of the Indian people of North America? How and why? In the twenty-first century, can you identify any group of people who may be achieving, or trying to achieve, progress at the expense of another group of people?

6. How has reading the voices in Chapter 1 broadened your understanding about early relationships between the Spanish explorers and the American Indians?

7. What voices in the first chapter in both *Voices* and *A People's History* were of most interest to you? How and why? Which did you find most compelling and why? Least compelling?

SIMULATIONS AND OTHER CREATIVE APPROACHES

1. Write a letter to one of the people you met in Chapter 1—Columbus, de Las Casas, King Ferdinand and Queen Isabella, Pope Alexander VI, and so forth. Tell your correspondent how you responded to his or her role in the "discovery" of the Americas by Columbus. Explain how you think he or she might have altered that role.

2. Imagine that de Las Casas has sent his observations about the effect of Columbus's expedition on the Arawak/Taino people to the Pope. Write a letter from the Pope to de Las Casas that represents not only the Pope's reaction to this information but also the Catholic Church's position on exploration and discovery in a "New World" populated by non-Christians.

3. Rewrite the portion of a traditional children's book to more accurately tell the story of the encounter between Columbus and the Arawak/Taino people.

4. Stage a trial of Christopher Columbus. Create a defense that bases its case on the traditional interpretations of Columbus and his goals for exploration and a prosecution that bases its case on the violation of human rights.

NOTE

1 Some debate continues about the use of the appellation Arawak or Taino for the people with whom Columbus initially came into contact. The dis-

tinction between the two is that Arawak refers to a linguistic group that spreads into South America, while the Taino are a cultural subset of the Arawak that include people living in what is now Puerto Rico, Cuba, Haiti, and the Dominican Republic. In *A People's History of the United States*, Howard Zinn uses Arawak—the term that was widely used in the 1980s and early 1990s. Today, Taino is the preferred usage for the people whom Columbus encountered.

CHAPTER TWO

The First Slaves

One of the problems with telling the history of slavery from the standpoint of the victors is that the stories often paint a benign picture of the "peculiar institution" of slavery. While most of our students are quick to condemn such an interpretation, very few know much about the way enslaved African Americans felt about bondage. Likewise, while most of our students know something about resistance to enslavement, they know little about the full extent of such resistance or the actual involvement in and commitment to resistance by the enslaved. They often know about the voices and actions of famous white abolitionists—John Brown, William Lloyd Garrison, Harriet Beecher Stowe—and a few important black abolitionists—Frederick Douglass and Harriet Tubman—but they are largely unfamiliar with the voices of ordinary African Americans—enslaved or free.

The documents in this chapter provide ample evidence that many of the ordinary men, women, and children who were enslaved drew upon vast resources of conviction, courage, and cunning to plan their escape, stage revolts, file petitions with colonial governors, and plead with the men in power to grant them their freedom. Most of the enslaved were neither passive nor pleased with their enslavement, neither cheerful about nor complacent with their living and working conditions. And when they did love their masters and the families they served, their affection was tinged with mistrust, uncertainty, and fear.

Document-Based Questions

THREE DOCUMENTS ON SLAVE REVOLTS

1. White men who discovered plans for rebellion wrote two of these documents, and an enslaved African American wrote the third document. Although they are written from different perspectives, enough similarities exist to provide information about the goals and grievances that motivated such

plans. What are they? Do the white authors appear to have any understanding of these grievances? How? Why, or why not?

2. What role does religion play in these documents? What does this tell you about the roles of religion in Euro-American colonial societies? In slave societies? How do you think the roles of religion in both societies were similar and dissimilar?

3. How do the authors of the first two documents describe the enslaved African Americans involved in the planned revolts? Do the contents of the third documents support these descriptions? How and why?

FOUR PETITIONS AGAINST SLAVERY

1. What similarities do these four petitions share in terms of their grievances, goals, and actual requests? How are they dissimilar?

2. Which of these petitions do you find most persuasive? How and why? Least persuasive? How and why?

3. What do these petitions tell you about their enslaved authors? About their conditions of servitude? About their family relationships?

4. How is the fourth petition, which was written after the signing of the Declaration of Independence and the beginning of the Revolutionary War, different from the other three in terms of its tone, goals, and grievances?

BENJAMIN BANNEKER'S LETTER

1. What are Benjamin Banneker's goals for writing this letter? What are the particular strengths of Banneker's letter to Jefferson? What are its weaknesses?

2. How do you think Jefferson responded to this letter? Why?

3. To what was Banneker referring when he wrote that at one time, Jefferson "publicly held forth" the "injustice of a State of Slavery"? (p. 60) Do you think Jefferson truly believed that "all men are created equal"? Why, or why not?

Main Points in *Voices*, Chapter 2, "The First Slaves"

After reading Chapter 2 in *Voices*, students should be encouraged to identify what they believe to be the main points therein. Following are four possible main points.

1. Enslaved African Americans persistently and courageously resisted slavery from the time it was institutionalized into colonial laws until it was abolished.

2. Enslaved African Americans clearly articulated their grievances; they were particularly eloquent in their arguments that slavery was antithetical to the goals of a "free and Christian people."

3. The fear of rebellion by the enslaved shaped the lives of white Americans in all the colonies.

4. In their petitions for freedom, ordinary enslaved African Americans were respectful and deferential to the "men of great Note and Influence" who controlled the political, economic, and social system of colonial America.

Main Points in *Voices*, Chapter 2, "The First Slaves," and in *A People's History*, Chapter 2, "Drawing the Color Line"

If your students are also reading *A People's History*, they should be encouraged to identify what they believe to be the main points in Chapter 2, "Drawing the Color Line." Following are five additional points to be stressed when *Voices* and *A People's History* are used together.

5. Within forty years after Africans arrived in British North America, slavery had become a legal, socially accepted institution.

6. Slavery was not simply a regional problem confined to the southern colonies; rather, it was a national problem that shaped the lives of all who lived in North America.

7. Most whites and black who shared common problems, common work, and common enemies treated each other as equals.

8. Despite the efforts of the slave system to destroy families, family ties and

hopes for reunification remained strong within the communities of enslaved African Americans.

9. The two greatest fears the colonial white establishment faced were the fear of black rebellion and the fear that discontented blacks and whites might unite to destroy the existing political, economic, and social order.

General-Discussion Questions for *Voices*

While the following questions are designed for classroom discussion about all the voices read in Chapter 2, they can also be rewritten and included as evaluation tools.

1. As slavery became more intimately embedded in American society, most southern colonies passed laws prohibiting anyone from teaching enslaved African Americans to read and write. How, then, can we account for such articulate and eloquent written pleas for freedom from the enslaved?

2. A contemporary political debate revolves around the issue of reparations for slavery. What are reparations? What specific arguments could be extracted from these documents to support reparations? What are the current arguments for and against reparations?

3. In colonial America, deterrence was believed to be the best way to prevent the colonists from committing crimes. What is deterrence? What methods of deterring the enslaved from rebelling are discussed in these documents? Which do you believe were most successful and why? Least successful?

4. Until the early 1960s, most history textbooks described slavery at its worst as a benign institution and at its best as a socially acceptable way to "civilize" an "uncivilized" race and to keep blacks happy and productive. What evidence to the contrary do you find in these documents? Why do you believe the horrors of slavery were not exposed or discussed in our schools prior to the 1960s? What changed in the 1960s?

5. What specific types of resistance by the enslaved are described in these documents? What other types of resistance do you know about? What others would you like to learn about?

6. How did the voices in this chapter reinforce any of the five themes listed in "Main Points in *Voices*"?

7. Several of these documents focus on the fact that many of the enslaved African Americans were "freeborn Pepel" (p. 56) and they were "unjustly dragged" (p. 57) from freedom into servitude. Is this an effective argument for emancipation? How do you think slave owners were able to counter these arguments? Do you think that arguments for freedom for those born in Africa changed after 1808 when the slave trade was prohibited and the vast majority of the enslaved were no longer freeborn, but rather, born into slavery? How and why?

8. Which of the voices in this chapter did you find most powerful? Least powerful? How and why?

General-Discussion Questions for *Voices* and *A People's History*

These general-discussion questions are additional questions for students who have read Chapter 2 in both books. For all questions, discussion must focus on ways the materials in both chapters help students formulate and articulate their answers.

9. Why do you think slavery is so often referred to as the "peculiar institution"?

10. What is the "color line"? How does Howard Zinn describe the way this color line was drawn in early America? Do you think the drawing of this line was intentional or unintentional?

11. What "clues" are provided in the documents of Chapter 2 in *Voices* and the narration in *A People's History* to the question Howard Zinn asks, "Is it possible for whites and blacks to live together without hatred" (p. 23, *People's History*)? Do you think living together was possible in colonial America? How and why? In contemporary America? How and why?

12. What new information did you acquire about African societies in this chapter? How does this new information shape your understanding of slavery and the way it developed in North and South America?

13. How does Howard Zinn describe the differences between slavery as it

existed in Africa versus its existence in America? Do you believe that these differences are significant? How and why?

14. How much did you know about resistance and rebellion of enslaved African Americans before reading these two chapters? Why do you think these "unimportant" voices are usually missing from our textbooks?

15. Despite the courageous efforts of thousands of the enslaved who resisted, rebelled, and tried to overthrow slavery, the "peculiar institution" thrived for over 240 years. What factors do you think were most responsible for its longevity? What factors do you think motivated the enslaved to resist, despite the terrible consequences of getting caught?

16. What are some specific examples from both chapters that illustrate the "complex web of historical threads" used to "ensnare blacks for slavery in America" (p. 38)?

17. Throughout the chapters, evidence exists of various divide-and-conquer strategies that whites used to create disunity among enslaved African Americans. Why was this so important to the empowered? Provide some examples of these divide-and-conquer strategies. What are some contemporary efforts of those in power to divide-and-conquer certain groups of Americans? How are their purposes for using these strategies similar to and dissimilar from those of those in positions of power in colonial America?

18. In *A People's History*, Howard Zinn indicates that Africans became victims of the largest forced migration in world history, not because they were uncivilized or weak, but because their white adversaries were so strong. What evidence of this white strength do you find reinforced in the documents in Chapter 2 of *Voices*?

Evaluation Tools

SUGGESTED ASSIGNMENTS

These assignments can be adapted to meet any classroom need—homework, short- or long-term research projects, individual or group work. The end product should be flexible, depending on teacher interest and student abilities—papers, journals, oral reports, visual aides, and the like.

1. Some of the voices of the enslaved you read were written by or about those who were enslaved in the northern colonies. However, we are often led to believe that slavery was restricted to the southern colonies. What evidence can you find in the reading to indicate that slavery was an issue for all the colonies, not just those in the south? Why do you think the belief that slavery and all its problems was confined to the southern colonies and later to the southern states continues to have credence in contemporary society?

2. Learn more about family relationships under the system of slavery. What do you believe are the short- and long-term repercussions of the deliberate steps that were taken to destroy the family structure of enslaved African Americans?

3. In 2002, a lawsuit was filed in the United States District Court in New York that claimed descendants of the enslaved had the right to seek reparations because such companies as the Lehman Brothers brokerage firm, Aetna Insurance, and R.J. Reynolds Tobacco made money off slavery. Learn as much about this case as possible—about the arguments made in court for and against reparations and the most recent disposition of the case. Compare the goals of this case for reparations with other attempts to gain reparations. Which do you feel are most viable, and why?

4. Peter Bestes's Petition (p. 55) mentions support for the return to Africa movement. What was this movement? Who supported it and why? Was it successful? How and why?

5. Beginning in the 1990s, many African Americans demanded that the federal government apologize for its support of and involvement in the system of slavery. Learn more about the arguments for and against such an action. What is your position? Do you feel an apology could "right the wrongs" of slavery? How and why?

6. During the New Deal, employees of the Federal Writers' Project conducted over 2,000 interviews with those who had been enslaved prior to and during the Civil War. Read a summary of these slave narratives and search through some of the actual narratives at this site: www.newdeal.feri.org/asn/. What questions the interviewers asked were of most interest to you? What additional questions might you have asked if you had been an interviewer? Which of these narratives added to your understanding of slavery? How and

why? What are some of the difficulties researchers face when accessing these stories under the conditions they were told between 1936–1938?

7. Learn more about Benjamin Banneker. What was his background? What were some of his greatest accomplishments? Why do you think he is he not mentioned in most of our textbooks?

8. Learn more about the original religions of the Africans. Since few, if any, were Christians prior to being forcibly kidnapped and taken to America, how and why did Christianity come to play such a prominent role in the lives of the enslaved African Americans? Why do you think that many African Americans began to convert to Islam beginning in the 1930s? What is the role of Islam within the African American population today?

9. Using a search engine of choice, find a web site that includes a variety of narratives by enslaved African Americans. What new information did you get about slavery from this web site? How does this new information complement what you learned from the documents in Chapter 2 in *Voices*?

10. Watch any feature-length movie or television program that deals with the topics discussed in Chapter 2 in both *Voices* and *A People's History*. Some possibilities include *Roots, Amistad,* and *Beloved.* How did the movie(s) reinforce or refute the voices that you learned about in these chapters? What parts of the movie do you feel to be historically accurate? Inaccurate?

SUGGESTED ESSAY QUESTIONS

1. Some historians have argued that you cannot study the civil-rights movement without learning about the 240 years that slavery was a legal and socially acceptable institution. Do you agree or disagree with this argument? Be sure to support your answer with examples from your reading.

2. Relying upon what you know about Thomas Jefferson's beliefs and practices in regard to slavery, compose a response that Jefferson might have written to Benjamin Banneker's letter.

3. Drawing upon the voices of enslaved African Americans and their masters found in both chapters, explain the role of fear in both white and slave societies. What do you think to be the short- and long-term repercussions of growing up in a society based on fear?

4. Describe several divide-and-conquer strategies that the men with power in colonial America used to maintain the status quo. Which do you think were most successful and why? Least successful?

5. How does the information in *Voices* (and in *A People's History*, if students are reading both) support any or all of the themes we discussed in commenting on *Voices*?

6. How did the stories of resistance add to your understanding of slavery in early America? Do you believe that these stories are relevant to your life today? Why, or why not? How?

✱ 7. What voices of resistance in chapters 2 in both *Voices* and *A People's History* were of most interest to you? How and why? Which did you find most compelling and why? Least compelling?

8. Howard Zinn poses an important question in this chapter: "Is it possible for whites and blacks to live together without hatred" (*People's History*, p. 23)? Using information from your reading, from other relevant sources, and from your own experience, write an essay that attempts to answer this question.

9. Howard Zinn refers to the "complex web of historical threads to ensnare blacks for slavery in America (*A People's History*, p. 38)." What were some of these historical threads?

SIMULATIONS AND OTHER CREATIVE APPROACHES

1. Stage a debate about the contentious political issue of whether or not the United States government should officially apologize for the institution of slavery. Be sure that each side draws upon historical and contemporary arguments, as well as on the research conducted by President Bill Clinton's commission on racial relations in regard to the contemporary problems of race in American society. If time permits, have students research the United Kingdom's Prime Minister Tony Blair's decision to formally apologize to the Irish for the potato famine and ways in which the United States might learn lessons from Blair's action.

2. Prepare students to conduct a mock trial in the Supreme Court based on lower court records and findings to date of the 2002 reparations lawsuit

filed in the United States District Court in New York against the Lehman Brothers brokerage firm, Aetna Insurance, and R.J. Reynolds. Students will have to draw upon the appellate court decisions to imagine how the Supreme Court would decide in this case.

3. Have students read a chapter in a traditional book for elementary students about slavery. Then ask them to work in groups to write a new chapter, adding information they have acquired from the voices of the enslaved African Americans and from Howard Zinn's narrative. The chapters should include relevant photographs, artwork, and maps. After the chapters are completed, have groups compare and contrast their chapters. Classmates should select one group's chapter for presentation to an elementary classroom.

4. Divide the class into several groups of students, each of which will work on a video collage of images about slavery. Students should find one-to-three-minute excerpts from various movies and documentaries about slavery and put them together into a maximum ten-minute computer-based presentation. Presentations can be PowerPoint or video. Each presentation must have a theme that links together all the images and that is prominently displayed on the opening slide. On the due date, groups will go to the computer lab, where each group will display and explain its video collage to classmates. Concluding discussion should include the ways in which the themes and content of the video collages compare and contrast.

5. Invite a number of historical characters to a tea party for a discussion that you imagine might have taken place in 1804. When making the list of whom to invite, be sure to include at least one prominent American policymaker, a slave trader, a slave owner, an abolitionist, a freed African American, and a journalist. During the course of the tea party, the participants will discuss the possible abolition of the slave trade. As the conversation becomes more heated, someone invites the slave who is serving tea for his opinion.

CHAPTER THREE

Servitude and Rebellion

Rebellion within the American colonies prior to the Revolutionary War is a topic seldom discussed in American history classes. Yet the fiery rhetoric of freedom and the brave actions of many colonists eventually defeated the military might of the most powerful nation in the Western world. Why, then, are we reluctant to introduce the stories of Americans who fought not only against the British Crown, but also against the aristocratic rule of the colonial elite? What is it that prevents us from presenting a balanced portrayal of early America in which the diverse voices of both the powerful and powerless are celebrated?

Perhaps part of the answer is that traditional history books and history classes pay little or no attention to either the contributions or the grievances of the indentured servants who journeyed to North America. Instead, these traditional treatments of history most often describe a harmonious melting pot of colonists who busily set about to create a classless, democratic new society. The reality is far less harmonious and democratic, but much more interesting and real. Indentured servants, who comprised almost fifty percent of all colonial immigrants, were among the hardest-working but poorest, most abused, and most disgruntled of all the colonists. The realities of their servitude fueled the fires of rebellion.

Document-Based Questions

RICHARD FRETHORNE

1. What is scurvy? What is the "bloody flux"? What role did disease play in the lives of the colonists? How does it compare and contrast with the role disease plays in our lives today?

2. Why do you think indentured servants were "not allowed to go and get" fowl? Why do you think they never saw any deer or venison?

3. Who is the "enemy" in Richard Frethorne's letter? What is his opinion of the "enemy"?

4. How do you think Frethorne's letters might have changed, as well as remained the same, if he was still writing to his family in the 1640s?

COMMISSIONERS' REPORT

1. What words do the commissioners use to describe Nathaniel Bacon? His followers? How do these words compare and contrast with the words that a contemporary government commission might use to describe a modern rebellion?

2. Why was Governor William Berkeley of "James Towne" "pretending to be loath to spill bloode"? Once the battle begins, how do the Commissioners describe the rebellion?

3. How do the commissioners describe Governor Berkeley? His men? How do you think Governor Berkeley will or will not revise colonial policies after Bacon's Rebellion?

PROCLAMATION OF THE NEW HAMPSHIRE LEGISLATURE

1. What were the actions of the men who were involved in the Mast Tree Riot?

2. What does the New Hampshire legislature propose to do in order that "the utmost justice may be done to his Majestic"? Do they succeed?

LETTER WRITTEN BY WILLIAM SHIRLEY

1. Howard Zinn's introduction to this letter explains that the riot described is in response to impressment. What is impressment?

2. How were militias raised in colonial America? What was the purpose of "the militia of the town? What did it accomplish?

3. Why does Governor William Shirley decide to stop "parleying with the mob"? How do our current governors at the state and federal level feel about such a word exchange?

MITTELBERGER'S JOURNEY TO PENNSYLVANIA

1. Keeping in mind the 124-year differences between the two letters, how does Gottlieb Mittelberger's account of indentured servitude compare and contrast with that of Frethorne?

2. How does Mittelberger's discussion of the ship's passage to and life in North America compare and contrast with that of the circumstances endured by slaves?

3. By 1754, when Mittelberger embarked upon his journey, he must have been aware of some of the hardships awaiting him. Why, then, do you think he and thousands of others came to America?

NEW YORK TENANT RIOTS

1. Why were local farmers living on land claimed by Van Rensselaer?

2. Was the treatment of the local farmers by Van Rensselaer's army legal?

3. From reading this account, what role do you think private property played in the hearts and minds of these colonists? Did everyone have access to private property? Why, or why not?

Main Points in *Voices*, Chapter 3, "Servitude and Rebellion"

After reading Chapter 3 in *Voices*, students should be encouraged to identify what they believe to be the main points therein. Following are five possible main points.

1. Indentured servants played a large role in shaping the structure of and struggles within colonial America.

2. From the early years of Euro-American colonization, the colonists were divided by social, economic, and political differences.

3. Either rebellion or the threat of rebellion was a constant factor in colonial North America.

4. The "wandering poor" have always been a component in North American society.

5. Although servant and slave rebellions were rare, the threat of such rebellion was constant, and masters were quite fearful.

Main Points in *Voices*, Chapter 3, "Servitude and Rebellion," and in *A People's History*, Chapter 3, "Persons of Mean and Vile Condition"

If your students are also reading *A People's History*, they should be encouraged to identify what they believe to be the main points in chapters 3 in both books. Following are five additional points to be stressed when *Voices* and *A People's History* are used together.

6. The governors of colonial Jamestown had two primary motives for suppressing Bacon's rebellion: to develop an Indian policy that would prevent tribal unity and would instead divide-and-conquer the Indian nations and peoples; and to teach poor whites that rebellion against the status quo had serious consequences.

7. More than half of all the colonists who immigrated to North America before the Revolutionary War came as servants.

8. While colonial North America was neither democratic nor egalitarian, more opportunities existed for economic, social, and political advancement than in Europe.

9. The fear of rebellion encouraged the wealthy white colonial elite to develop and implement policies designed to prevent unity among poor whites and blacks, among Indians and blacks, and among Indian nations and other Indian nations.

10. The "hope of leveling" was the motive behind many thoughts, plans, and actions undertaken by poor whites against the wealth and power of their colonial governors.

General-Discussion Questions for *Voices*

While the following questions are designed for classroom discussion about all the voices read in Chapter 3, they can also be rewritten and included as evaluation tools.

1. Why do you think students seldom learn about plans to rebel, actual rebellions, and the rebellious beliefs of the American colonists? Do you think it is important to hear these voices? Why, or why not?

2. How do these voices support Howard Zinn's contention that "the desperation of the poor was turned into profit by merchants and ship captains" (p. 63)?

3. What new information did you acquire about life in seventeenth-century colonial North America? How does this information compare and contrast with what you previously knew about life in the English colonies?

4. "Important" people in powerful positions within colonial society wrote three of these entries. What common words and phrases did they use to describe the rebels? What do these words and phrases tell you about social class in colonial North America?

5. What do the causes of and responses to the four rebellions have in common? How are they different?

6. What were the consequences of planning and/or carrying out a rebellion in colonial North America? Of running away from an indentured contract? If punishments were harsh, how can we explain the relatively large numbers of planned and actual rebellions as well as runaway servants?

7. How did the voices in this chapter reinforce any of the themes listed in "Main Points in *Voices*"?

8. Which of the voices in this chapter did you find most powerful? Least powerful? How and why?

General-Discussion Questions for *Voices* and *A People's History*

These general-discussion questions are additional questions posed for students who have read Chapter 3 in both books. For all questions, discussion must focus on ways in which the materials in both chapters help students formulate and articulate their answers.

9. What were the primary grievances of Bacon and his men? How do they compare and contrast with other planned and actual rebellions discussed in "Persons of Mean and Vile Condition"?

10. Howard Zinn describes Bacon's Rebellion as "antiaristocrat" and "anti-Indian" (p. 40). Provide examples from both books of both descriptions.

11. Howard Zinn claims, "It was a complex chain of oppression in Virginia" (p. 42). What was this "chain of oppression"? What evidence does he provide to enforce this contention?

12. What information do these two chapters provide in regard to English attitudes about crime and poverty in sixteenth- and seventeenth-century England? How did these attitudes contribute to the colonization of North America? How did they contribute to the ways the colonists dealt with crime and poverty?

13. How does Howard Zinn support his belief that "class lines hardened through the colonial period" (*A People's History*, p. 47)?

14. What is a feudal-type aristocracy? An almshouse? Squatting? Who were tenants? What does the use of these terms tell you about life in colonial North America?

15. What lessons about the "unimportant" people did the "wealthy elite" learn by the eve of the Revolutionary War? Do you agree or disagree with Howard Zinn's belief that the elite purposely turned poor whites against the Indians and blacks, as well as Indians and blacks against each other, "for the security of the elite" (*A People's History*, p. 54)? Why, or why not?

16. What role does fear play in the voices within these two chapters?

17. How does Howard Zinn describe the development of "a white middle class"

(*A People's History*, p. 56)? Do you agree with his statement that the middle class would provide a "solid buffer" for the elite? Why, or why not? Do you think this was a deliberate action by the elite? Why, or why not?

18. Why do you think enslaved African Americans and indentured white servants did not organize together to end their bondage?

19. White people justified the mistreatment of enslaved African Americans by arguing, in part, that they were racially inferior. How could white masters justify the mistreatment of white servants?

20. How did the development of a middle class help keep the wealthy in power?

Evaluation Tools

SUGGESTED ASSIGNMENTS

These assignments can be adapted to meet any classroom need—homework, short- or long-term research projects, individual or group work. The end product should be flexible, depending on teacher interest and student abilities—papers, journals, oral reports, visual aides, and the like.

1. In 1717, England began its Transportation policy. Learn as much as you can about Transportation. What were the goals and accomplishments of this British policy? How did Transportation influence colonization in North America? Were particular colonial regions impacted more than others? When and why did Transportation to North America end? What do you think about the use of such a policy to punish criminals?

2. Using at least three different sources, learn as much as possible about debtor's prison. How was it used in England? When the English colonists used debtor's prison in North America, was it the same system? When and why did debtor's prisons in North America end? Do you think people should be imprisoned for failing to pay their debts? Why, or why not? What happens to people who cannot pay their debts today?

3. Using a search engine of choice, locate and read Bacon's "Declaration of the People," written in July 1676. What were his grievances against the colonial government at Jamestown? Against the Indians? Do you think these were

legitimate grievances? Using sources from both chapters, defend your answers.

4. Many historians have claimed that in proportion to population, King Phillip's War was the bloodiest conflict in American history. Learn as much as possible about the participants of this war, the goals and grievances of both sides, and its long-term consequences.

5. What were the goals, actions, and consequences of Jacob Leister's farmer's revolt of 1689? How do they compare and contrast with the rebellions discussed in both chapters?

6. Using a search engine of choice, find other voices of indentured servants who lived in colonial North America. Do theirs echo or differ from the voices heard in these chapters? How and why?

7. For over ten years, the Association for the Preservation of Virginia Antiquities (APVA) has funded archeological research at the original site of the Jamestown colony. Spend some time at the Jamestown Rediscovery Project website at http://www.apva.org/jr.html. After browsing the site, how does this information, coupled with what you read in both chapters of the Howard Zinn books, give you a more balanced perspective on how the ordinary colonists of Jamestown struggled to adapt to their new environment?

8. Learn more about the Indian nations whose traditional lands existed on what became Jamestown shortly after contact. Using a search engine of choice, try to locate a first-hand voice that discusses the relationship between the native occupants of the land and the English colonists. How did the Indians greet the English colonists? How did the colonists treat them? How had relationships changed by the 1630s? What do you believe were the primary obstacles to peaceful coexistence?

SUGGESTED ESSAY QUESTIONS

1. Describe the various types of rebellions that were planned and carried out in colonial America. How did the goals of the rebels compare and contrast? Which were most successful in achieving their goals? Least successful? How and why?

2. Describe at least two rebellions that occurred in the late-twentieth and

early-twenty-first centuries. How do the goals of these rebellions compare and contrast with the goals of the colonial rebels?

3. Describe the life of a typical indentured servant before, during, and after immigration to North America. How did immigration change his/her life from that which was lead in Europe? How did his/her life compare and contrast with that of a slave?

4. Support or refute Howard Zinn's contention that "[t]he colonies . . . were societies of contending classes" (*A People's History*, p. 50).

5. Why is Chapter 3 in *A People's History* entitled, "Persons of Mean and Vile Condition"? How do the voices in "Servitude and Rebellion" reinforce that title?

6. Various comparisons between life in colonial America and serfdom in Europe are made in both chapters. Provide several examples of such comparisons and then support or refute the merits of this comparison.

7. What voices of resistance in chapters 3 in both *Voices* and *A People's History* were of most interest to you? How and why? Which did you find most compelling and why? Least compelling?

8. How do the voices and information in these two chapters improve your understanding of colonial history? Do you think it is important to learn about the voices of resistance, especially those of people who did not achieve their goals in the course of rebellion? Why, or why not?

SIMULATIONS AND OTHER CREATIVE APPROACHES

1. Make a drawing of class structure as you think it might have appeared in early America. Your drawing should illustrate the different conditions and amounts of power possessed by each group you identify.

2. Pick one person whom you read about or whose voice resonated with you. Based upon what you know about his life, write a short, reflective autobiography that he might have written toward the end of his life. It might include major accomplishments as well as regrets; stories to be passed on to grandchildren; historical experiences to be shared with a reporter or a historian.

3. Create a simulation of something that might have occurred in frontier Virginia prior to Bacon's Rebellion. Divide the class into four or five groups, each of which has six students who will work together to "overcome the small number of masters." Two students in each group will represent the Indian perspective, two the slave perspective, and two the poor white perspective. They will have twenty minutes to overcome any issues that might divide them and to determine what they have in common, so that they can design their response to their perceived dilemma. Each group then reports back to the class for an overall discussion of the following: the viability, or lack thereof, of each response; and how today's ordinary, powerless citizens might join together in a united response against perceived or actual injustice.

4. Stage a discussion forum during which Richard Frethorne and Gottlieb Mittelberger will discuss their experiences as indentured servants. The attending journalists (all the students in the class who will be sitting in the room) should have a series of politically astute questions ready for each of these men. After Frethorne and Mittelberger speak, the journalists will have the opportunity to ask questions of either speaker or of both. After the discussion, each student will write a short newspaper editorial summarizing his or her understanding of Frethorne's and Gottlieb's experiences and recommending either that indentured servitude continue or that it be abolished within the colonies.

CHAPTER FOUR

Preparing the Revolution

In most of our history courses, students learn about brave patriots who prepared for the Revolutionary War by uniting against a tyrannical king and oppressive English laws. In this well-known story, all Americans united in opposition to England and looked to their enlightened leaders to help them in their valiant struggle for freedom. While there certainly is some truth to this version of the Revolutionary War, a more balanced interpretation includes another perspective—that of the many ordinary colonists who had grown increasingly disillusioned and angry with their unresponsive colonial leaders and did not want to engage in a war for independence designed to benefit the colonial elite.

Some of those unimportant discontented colonists turned to rebellion against their colonial governors. In Chapter 4 of *A People's History*, Howard Zinn includes their perspective, weaving it carefully into the more traditional story and asking questions that must be answered before we can obtain a more accurate understanding of the years prior to the Revolution. The voices in this chapter give credence to the beliefs and behaviors of those imbued with the revolutionary spirit—a spirit full of anger directed at both the colonial elite and the British Crown.

Document-Based Questions

THOMAS HUTCHINSON

1. Do you think the Bostonians' reactions to the Stamp Act were treasonous? Why, or why not? Why do you think England responded by repealing the Stamp Act rather than arresting the rebellious colonists?

2. How does Thomas Hutchinson describe the main grievances of "the mob" against the Stamp Act? What are his feelings about "the mob"?

3. Why do you think the town was "under awe of this mob" with "no body

daring to oppose, or contradict" it? What does this tell you about the nature of colonial Bostonian society?

SAMUEL DROWNE'S TESTIMONY

1. Samuel Drowne stated that when the soldiers arrived, most of those gathered were "gentlemen." Later he stated that those who remained were sailors "and other persons meanly dressed." Do you think these descriptions indicate class-consciousness in colonial society? Why, or why not?

2. Does Drowne place blame on any group of participants in the Boston Massacre? How and why?

3. Do you think Drowne was a patriot or a loyalist? Support your answer with direct quotes.

GEORGE HEWES RECALLS THE BOSTON TEA PARTY

1. Why do you think the participants in the Boston Tea Party dressed as Indians?

2. How does Hewes describe his relationship with other participants in the Boston Tea Party? Do these descriptions, or any others in his recollection, sound like acts of rebellion? How and why?

3. Why is it important to Hewes and his fellow rebels to "render its [tea] entire destruction inevitable"?

NEW YORK MECHANICS DECLARATION

1. How does the New York Mechanics Declaration compare and contrast with the Declaration of Independence? What words and concepts are similar? Dissimilar?

2. What do you think the mechanics meant when they accused the King because he would "take pleasure in our destruction"? What evidence do they offer to support this belief? Do you agree with their assessment? Why, or why not?

3. Do you think the mechanics' arguments for independence are persuasive? Why, or why not?

THOMAS PAINE

1. Why does Thomas Paine argue against "reconciliation"? Are his arguments for independence persuasive? How and why? Are they more or less persuasive than those articulated by the New York Mechanics?

2. Some historians have called *Common Sense* one of the greatest early pieces of political propaganda. What is propaganda? In your opinion, is *Common Sense* propagandistic? How and why?

3. Do you agree with Paine that British rule "sooner or later must have an end" (p. 89)? Why, or why not?

Main Points in *Voices*, Chapter 4, "Preparing the Revolution"

After reading Chapter 4 in *Voices*, students should be encouraged to identify what they believe to be the main points therein. Following are four possible main points.

1. Pre-Revolutionary America witnessed the growth of anti-government beliefs aimed at both the colonial elite and the British Crown.

2. The formal arguments for colonial independence largely focused on England's tyrannical and oppressive laws and actions.

3. Prior to the eve of the American Revolution, colonial protesters had successfully forced the British Parliament to repeal taxes they believed to be unfair.

4. Only when the King refused to give in to colonial demands did the colonists turn to war.

Main Points in *Voices*, Chapter 4, "Preparing the Revolution," and in *A People's History*, Chapter 4, "Tyranny is Tyranny"

If your students are also reading *A People's History*, they should be encouraged to identify what they believe to be the main points in chapters 4 in both books. Following are four additional points to be stressed when *Voices* and *A People's History* are used together.

5. Tyranny and oppression were tools used by both the colonial and British elite against the ordinary American colonists.

6. By 1776, upper-class colonial politicians realized that they could mobilize the lower-class energy that had previously been directed against them and redirect such anger at the British Crown.

7. A totally united prewar effort did not materialize among the colonists; significant colonial resistance occurred both before and during the Revolutionary War.

8. Political, economic, and social divisiveness existed in colonial America—divisiveness that spilled over into the efforts to prepare for war with England.

General-Discussion Questions for *Voices*

While the following questions are designed for classroom discussion about all the voices read in Chapter 4, they can also be rewritten and included as evaluation tools.

1. Why do you think the English repealed the Stamp Act and removed their troops from Boston after the massacre? What message do you think these British actions sent to the colonists?

2. The Third Amendment of the Constitution declares, "No Soldier shall, in time of peace, be quartered in any house, without the consent of the Owner, nor in time of war, but in a manner to be prescribed by law." How do the voices in this chapter help to explain the impetus behind passage of the Third Amendment?

3. Why do you think John Adams, an avowed patriot, defended the British soldiers who were accused of firing into the crowd at the Boston Massacre?

4. What is "taxation without representation"? Do you think the colonists had a real grievance? How and why? How and why did colonial taxation before the French and Indian War differ from taxation after that war?

5. What is treason? Do you think the rebellious actions of the colonists explained in this chapter were treasonous? Why, or why not? If they were treasonous, why do you think the King did not arrest and try them for treason?

6. Some contemporary historians have described the colonial rebellions as acts of terror against the British Crown. What is terrorism? Do any of the voices in this chapter support or refute this assessment? What is your opinion? If American protesters today burned a merchant's home and papers, fired upon American soldiers, or destroyed almost one million dollars of a company's merchandise, would they be considered terrorists? Why, or why not?

7. Do you think the recollection of events that are recorded years later (such as George Hewes's recollection sixty-one years after the Boston Tea Party) should be considered an accurate account of a historical event? Why, or why not?

8. Do the words of Thomas Paine—especially those directed at "those who espouse the doctrine of reconciliation"—support or refute Howard Zinn's contention that the colonial elite turned the anger of ordinary colonists against England rather than risk having such anger aimed at them? How and why?

9. How did the voices in this chapter reinforce any of the four themes listed in "Main Points in *Voices*"?

10. Which of the voices in this chapter did you find most powerful? Least powerful? How and why?

General-Discussion Questions for *Voices* and *A People's History*

These general-discussion questions are additional questions posed for students who have read Chapter 4 in both books. For all questions, discussion must focus on ways the materials in both chapters help students formulate and articulate their answers.

11. What is tyranny? What is oppression? How do these two chapters help you better understand tyranny and oppression? What is the significance of the chapter title, "Tyranny is Tyranny"? How do the voices in "Preparing the Revolution" reinforce the meaning of the chapter title in *A People's History*?

12. In the first paragraph of "Tyranny is Tyranny," Howard Zinn makes a case

for the argument he posits in both chapters that by diverting anger that ordinary colonists had focused on the colonial elite to the British Empire, the "important people in the English colonies . . . could take over land, profits, and political power from favorites of the British Empire." Do you think he proves his case? How and why?

13. What was the Proclamation of 1763? Why did it anger many colonial Americans? What do you think motivated the Crown to pass such a law?

14. Given the voices of discontented colonists and the political and economic realities of the colonists after the French and Indian War, do you think war was inevitable? Why, or why not?

15. What is a town meeting? What role did it play in the politics of colonial America? Do you think town meeting politics influenced the course of the American Revolution? Do town meetings still exist? If so, what role do you think they play in local politics today?

16. What evidence do these chapters provide of class conflict? How does this information support or refute any of your earlier beliefs about American colonists?

17. Why do you think colonial governors, all of whom lived in eastern cities, were either slow to respond or unresponsive to the grievances of ordinary colonists, many of whom lived in the western regions of the growing colonies?

18. What evidence can you find in this chapter that the white urban population in some parts of colonial America was divided? Do you support or refute Howard Zinn's contention that the colonial leaders convinced the evolving middle class to unite with them against "the biggest problem," the "propertyless people" (*A People's History*, p. 65)? How and why?

19. What does Howard Zinn mean when he says that the "myth of the Revolution" was that "it was on behalf of a united people" (*A People's History*, p. 70)? Do you agree or disagree? How and why?

20. What were the Coercive Acts? Why did the colonists call them the Intolerable Acts? What do these two different terms tell you about the divisions between the colonists and the mother country?

Evaluation Tools

SUGGESTED ASSIGNMENTS

These assignments can be adapted to meet any classroom need—homework, short- or long-term research projects, individual or group work. The end product should be flexible, depending on teacher interest and student abilities—papers, journals, oral reports, visual aides, and the like.

1. The consequences of the French and Indian War are often cited as a primary cause of the Revolutionary War. Using a search engine of choice, locate and read at least two documents that support this belief. How do they demonstrate such support? Are their arguments convincing? Why, or why not?

2. Americans have repeatedly protested the payment of taxes. What were the primary anti-tax arguments posed by the colonists between 1763 and 1776? Learn more about at least two other anti-tax movements that occurred in the United States in the late twentieth century or early twenty-first century. What were the goals and consequences of each? How do the contemporary anti-tax movements compare and contrast with those of the colonists?

3. Appeasement has long been a controversial foreign-policy option. What is appeasement? Do you think Parliament's decision to repeal the Stamp Act and the Townshend Acts was intended to appease the colonists? Why, or why not? Provide at least two examples of more contemporary uses of appeasement within the global setting. How does its modern usage compare and contrast with its usage in colonial America?

4. Research the trial of the British soldiers who were involved in the Boston Massacre. What other accounts support or refute Samuel Drowne's interpretation? Read John Adam's defense of the soldiers. What do you think were his most convincing arguments? Least convincing? Do you agree or disagree with the court's opinion? How and why?

5. Boycotts were a common form of protest prior to the Revolutionary War. What is a boycott? Which colonial boycotts do you think were most successful? Least? How and why?

6. Americans continue to use boycotts to influence domestic and interna-

tional policies. Learn more about one late-twentieth and early-twenty-first century boycott. What were its goals and accomplishments? Would you have supported this boycott? Why, or why not? Do you think boycotts are an effective way to protest? How and why?

7. Pamphlets such as *Common Sense* provided the main source of political information in colonial America. Find and read the contents of another pamphlet that discusses colonial grievances with the British Crown. How does it compare and contrast with Paine's arguments? Which was more persuasive? Least? How and why?

8. In *A People's History*, Howard Zinn argues that there is a "long history of American politics" in which we have seen the "mobilization of lower-class energy by upper-class politicians, for their own purposes" (p. 61). Research and describe at least two such instances during other periods of American history. In your opinion, were the "upper-class politicians" successful or unsuccessful in achieving their goals? How and why? Were these actions comparable to those of the Founding Fathers? How and why?

9. Who were Ethan Allen's Green Mountain rebels? Who were the North Carolina Regulators? What were their goals and accomplishments? How were their grievances similar to other anti-government rebels in pre-Revolutionary America? Locate information about and study one contemporary anti-government group in America. How do the goals and actions of the contemporary group compare and contrast with those of the colonial groups?

SUGGESTED ESSAY QUESTIONS

1. In *A People's History*, Howard Zinn asks, "And how could people truly have equal rights, with stark differences in wealth" (p. 73)? How would you answer these questions? How do the voices in "Preparing for Revolution" inform your answer?

2. Support or refute this statement: "[T]he Declaration functioned to mobilize certain groups of Americans, ignoring others. Surely, inspirational language to create secure consensus is still used, in our time, to cover up serious conflicts of interest in that consensus, and to cover up, also, the omission of large parts of the human race" (*People's History*, p. 73).

3. *Common Sense* was one of the most widely read pamphlets in colonial

America. In your opinion, what was its appeal? Do you believe that it was propagandistic? Why, or why not?

4. Do you think the Revolutionary War was inevitable? Do you think reconciliation between the colonies and England may have been possible? How and why?

5. Using specifics from *Voices* (or *Voices* and *A People's History*), support or refute this statement: "[T]he Founding Fathers . . . created the most effective system of national control devised in modern times, and showed future generations of leaders the advantages of combining paternalism with command" (*People's History*, p. 59).

6. Many of the rebels discussed in these chapters developed an anti-government bias. What grievances did they share? Do you think their grievances were valid? How and why? How do their grievances compare and contrast with such anti-government grievances today?

7. What role did impressment, the quartering of British troops, and the publication of *Common Sense* play in gaining support for independence? Why do you think that these actions and voices did not convince all Americans to join the cause?

8. What voices of resistance in chapters 4 in both *Voices* and *A People's History* were of most interest to you? How and why? Which did you find most compelling and why? Least compelling?

9. What does the following phrase from the Declaration of Independence mean to you? "We hold these truths to be self-evident . . . . That to secure these rights, Governments are instituted among Men, deriving their just powers from the consent of the governed. That whenever any Form of Government becomes destructive of these ends, it is the Right of the People to alter or to abolish it, and to institute new Government." Do you think that the Founding Fathers supported open rebellion at any time the people no longer felt the government upheld their rights or represented their interests and needs? How and why?

10. Do you think the colonial rebellions against the colonial elite—those described in Chapters 3 and 4 in both *Voices* and *A People's History*—were justifiable? Why, or why not? Was the rebellion of the colonists against the English justifiable? Why, or why not? How do the two rebellions compare

and contrast? Can you think of any contemporary rebellion that is justified? Unjustified?

SIMULATIONS AND OTHER CREATIVE APPROACHES

1. Stage a debate in class over the following issue: "In 1776, the actions of the Founding Fathers were both treasonous and terrorist." Be certain that both sides define treason and terrorism—in terms that would be understood by late-eighteenth-century colonists. When the debate is over, class discussion should focus on how the terms treason and terrorism are defined today. Then students should discuss whether the actions of the Founding Fathers in 1776 would be considered acts of treason and terrorism in contemporary society.

2. Hold two town meetings. In the first, students will take the role of colonists who are deciding whether or not they should join the movement for independence. Prior to holding the meeting, students must select their town, learn something about its politics, determine the type of people (various classes, socio-economic background, and so forth) who might attend the meeting, and be familiar with New England attitudes about independence. In the second town meeting, students will take the role of contemporary citizens who are attending a town meeting and are discussing an important issue that has arisen in their community. Prior to holding the meeting, students must select an issue and investigate both sides of the community debate.

3. Write a letter to King George III in which you explain your position about a possible war for independence. In your letter, be sure to explain why the Coercive Acts are known as the Intolerable Acts in the colonies; what you believe the King's role to be in the divisions between England and its colonies; and what you think might be done to avoid war.

4. Write a poem or song that illustrates the emotional impact of the title of Chapter 4, "Tyranny is Tyranny."

5. Stage a debate about voting in American society. Topics for the debate should include: Voting is a privilege that is taken for granted in American society. Voting privileges have only recently been extended to all American citizens. Voting is both a right and a responsibility. Everyone's vote matters.

CHAPTER FIVE

Half a Revolution

"A rich man's war and a poor man's fight." This much-quoted phrase seems as relevant today as it did during the Revolutionary War. The documents in "Half a Revolution" illustrate this fight and the way in which it was carried out during and immediately after the Revolutionary War. Independence, it seems, did not bring an end to the fighting between various "factions." To Joseph Plumb Martin, the "poor soldiers" served their country well during the war, but afterward "they were turned adrift like old worn-out horses." Samuel Dewees recalled that the soldiers at York "were afraid to say or to do any thing" for fear of punishment, and Dewees avoided encountering officers lest they might "construe my conduct in some way or other into an offense." Henry Knox described the need of "men of reflection, and principle" to be protected "in their lawful pursuits" from "the violence of lawless men." And James Madison worried about ways to control "the majority" who may be led by "the mischiefs of faction."

These factions, and the way in which both the Articles of Confederation and the Constitution dealt with them, resulted in "half a revolution." Indeed, a revolution in its entirely would have required an end to class conflict by welcoming American Indians into North American society, outlawing slavery, and granting equal rights to American women—in other words, creating a new society characterized by economic, social, racial, and political equality.

Document-Based Questions

JOSEPH CLARKE'S LETTER

1. Why did the sight of Colonel John Worthington raise the "spirits" of the citizens of Springfield? Why were the ordinary people so upset by his actions?

2. Do you think the beliefs and actions of the colonists in Springfield, Massachusetts, were typical of colonists in other regions of the British colonies?

3. What words and phrases did Joseph Clarke use to describe the spirit and

atmosphere that accompanied rebellion? How do these descriptions compare and contrast with those you might use to describe a rebellion? Do you think Clarke was in favor of the rebellion or against it? How and why?

JOSEPH PLUMB MARTIN

1. Summarize Joseph Plumb Martin's grievances about his treatment at the hands of the Continental Army during the war. Do you think Martin's experiences during his enlistment in the Continental Army were similar to those of other soldiers who served during the Revolutionary War? How and why?

2. In explaining his experiences after the war, Martin claims, "The truth was, none cared for them; the country was served, and faithfully served, and that was all that was deemed necessary. It was, soldiers, look to yourselves; we want no more of you" (p. 96). How does he support this assertion throughout the letter?

3. Martin wrote his "Narrative" fifty-four years after his experiences in the Revolutionary War. For whom do you think he wrote this letter? Would it have had a different audience, and a different purpose, in 1830 than it would have if he had written it in 1783? How and why?

SAMUEL DEWEES

1. Why do you think the officers in charge ordered such a brutal punishment? Why did they force the soldiers to "look upon the bodies" after they were shot and killed?

2. Dewees remarked that the offenses for which the men were shot appeared to be "trivial." How might such extreme punishment for trivial offenses affect the relationship between the soldiers and officers? Do you think, as Howard Zinn posits, that this was yet another example of "class conflict inside the Revolutionary Army" (p. 100)? Why, or why not?

3. Do you think that Dewees really believed his statement that "[t]he execution of these men . . . was undoubtedly brought about by a love of liberty, the good of country, and the necessity of keeping proper subordination in the army, in order to ensure that good ultimately"? Provide support for your answer with quotes from his recollection.

HENRY KNOX

1. How did Henry Knox see the new federal constitution as working "inversely to the public good" (p. 105)?

2. According to Knox, the accusation by "desperate and unprincipled men" of increased taxation was "a deception." How does he support this belief? Do you agree or disagree with his assessment?

3. Why is "a body of 12 or 15,000 desperate and unprincipled men" such a threat to "every man of principle and property in New England"?

"PUBLIUS" (JAMES MADISON)

1. Why do you think James Madison used a pseudonym when writing this paper in 1787?

2. Why does Madison support a new constitution that creates a strong central government?

3. How does Madison describe "a faction"? How does he propose, "curing the mischiefs of faction" and "removing the causes of faction"? Do you agree with his remedies? How and why?

4. Do you agree or disagree with Madison that "a pure democracy . . . can admit of no cure for the mischiefs of faction"? How and why? How does he define a democracy? How does he define a republic? How are they similar and different? Which does he support and why?

Main Points in *Voices*, Chapter 5, "Half a Revolution"

After reading Chapter 5 in *Voices*, students should be encouraged to identify what they believe to be the main points therein. Following are five possible main points.

1. For at least a hundred years before the Revolutionary War, the colonies were divided by class conflict.

2. Internal class conflict was only temporarily obscured during the Revolutionary War; when the war was over, class conflict reemerged.

3. The Declaration of Independence provided the legal framework for, but not the full achievement of, a democratic nation.

4. The Founding Fathers deliberately created a Constitution that was designed to control the rebellious spirit of ordinary Americans and to maintain "law and order."

5. The Revolutionary War did not dramatically change the internal structure or content of American society for women, laborers, slaves, and other "unimportant" people.

Main Points in *Voices*, Chapter 5, "Half a Revolution," and in *A People's History*, Chapter 5, "A Kind of Revolution"

If your students are also reading *A People's History*, they should be encouraged to identify what they believe to be the main points in chapters 5 in both books. Following are five additional points to be stressed when *Voices* and *A People's History* are used together.

6. The Revolutionary War was a *war of independence* from colonial domination, a *civil war* between the various forces within American society, and a *world war* fought both in North America and on the European Continent.

7. Economic interests motivated the political clauses of the United States Constitution.

8. In order for the Founding Fathers to gain enough support for the war, they had "to woo the armed white population."

9. As early as the Revolutionary War, the American military was an avenue for the poor to achieve upward social and economic mobility.

10. The unequal political, social, economic, and ideological structure of American society remained intact after the Revolutionary War.

General-Discussion Questions for *Voices*

While the following questions are designed for classroom discussion about all the voices read in Chapter 5, they can also be rewritten and included as evaluation tools.

1. How do you think the "unimportant" English men and women felt about losing their North American colonies? The "important" English leaders?

2. Why do you think this chapter is entitled, "Half a Revolution"? What is half of a revolution? How is it different from a whole revolution? Do you think the Revolutionary War was half or a whole revolution? How and why?

3. What evidence of class conflict do you find in the entries in this chapter? Do they adequately support Howard Zinn's belief that the Revolutionary Army was rife with class conflict? How and why?

4. In Henry Knox's letter to George Washington, he stated that after the war, "Our political machine constituted of thirteen independent sovereignties, have been perpetually operating against each other, and against the federal head, ever since the peace." How do the other documents in this chapter support this contention? What were the main issues that pitted Americans against Americans? Colony against colony?

5. Henry Knox was clearly frustrated that "the powers of Congress" were "utterly inadequate to preserve the balance between the respective States." What powers did the Articles of Confederation give to Congress? To the states? Do you agree with Knox's belief that the new constitution pitted "State, against State" (p. 105)?

6. How is liberty described in these various entries? Is liberty the same as freedom? Do you think the ordinary, unimportant men and women of the new republic defined liberty and freedom the same as the propertied, important men and women? The same as the slaves? Do you think ordinary men and women today define liberty and freedom differently from those men and women in power? How and why?

7. How is tyranny described in these various entries? Do you think the ordinary, unimportant men and women of the new republic defined tyranny the same as the propertied, important men and women? The same as the slaves? Do you think ordinary men and women today would define tyranny differently from those men and women in power? How and why?

8. Did rich and poor have different reasons for supporting the Revolution? Explain.

9. How did the voices in this chapter reinforce any of the five themes listed in "Main Points in *Voices*"?

10. Which of the voices in this chapter did you find most powerful? Least powerful? How and why?

General-Discussion Questions for *Voices* and *A People's History*

These general-discussion questions are additional questions for students who have read Chapter 5 in both books. For all questions, discussion must focus on ways the materials in both chapters help students formulate and articulate their answers.

11. What is the significance of the titles of both chapters, "Half a Revolution" and "A Kind of Revolution" respectively? Do you think the examples used in both chapters support Howard Zinn's assertion in these titles? How and why?

12. Howard Zinn argues that prior to the Revolutionary War, many colonists did not support the war and thus, the Founding Fathers "would have to woo the armed white population" (*People's History*, p. 77). How does he support this contention? Do you agree or disagree with Howard Zinn on this point? How and why?

13. Was Alexander Hamilton correct when he wrote, "If we are saved, France and Spain must save us" (*People's History*, p.77)? What role did France play in helping the Americans win the war?

14. How does this chapter support the phrase, "It was a rich man's war and a poor man's fight"? Do you agree or disagree with this belief? How and why? Do you believe that this phrase is applicable to today's American army? How and why?

15. How were the class conflicts between rich and poor suppressed during the Revolutionary War? Why did they reemerge after the war's conclusion?

16. The threat of mutiny and actual mutinies occurred throughout the Revolutionary War. What were the grievances and actions of the mutineers? How were mutinies handled during the war? Do you think the threat of mutiny continues to be a problem with American combat troops? How and why?

17. Howard Zinn mentions that in Maryland after the war, ninety percent of the state's population could not vote. Do you think this was typical of the other states? How and why? When was the electorate broadened to include all men, regardless of property ownership? To include all American citizens?

18. How did the events before, during, and immediately after the Revolutionary War affect the major Indian Nations? Why did most Indians fight for Great Britain during the Revolution?

19. What did the enslaved and free African Americans stand to gain—or lose— from the Revolution? Why did Washington refuse to allow enslaved African Americans to fight the British in exchange for their freedom?

20. According to the historian Charles Beard, why did the wealthy want a strong federal government?

Evaluation Tools

SUGGESTED ASSIGNMENTS

These assignments can be adapted to meet any classroom need—homework, short- or long-term research projects, individual or group work. The end product should be flexible, depending on teacher interest and student abilities—papers, journals, oral reports, visual aides, and the like.

1. Watch any of the following movies: *The Patriot, The Madness of King George, 1776, Liberty* (PBS documentary, four parts). What do you think was historically accurate in the movie? Inaccurate? What new information about the Revolutionary War did you acquire? Would you recommend this movie to a friend? Why, or why not?

2. In pre-Revolutionary America, we often learn of various people who were tarred and feathered. What are the origins of this type of punishment? Who resorted to such behavior and what were their goals in using it? Was it an effective means of deterring behavior? Is this punishment in contemporary usage? How, when, and where?

3. After the Revolutionary War, many veterans shared grievances similar to those of Joseph Plumb Martin. Learn as much as possible about the expec-

tations of and benefits received by the veterans in the nineteenth and twentieth centuries. How did the allocation and actual receipt of benefits change after World War II? What benefits do you believe veterans should be entitled to after serving our nation?

4. In Samuel Dewees recollection, he mentions the threat of mutiny and actual mutinies that occurred during the Revolutionary War. What is a mutiny? Learn as much as you can about any mutinies that actually occurred during the course of the War. How many were officially recorded? What were the goals and accomplishments of the mutineers? Do you think the threat of mutiny continues to be a problem with American combat troops? How and why?

5. Samuel Dewees mentions the presence of Macaroney Jack's wife who was "with him in camp" (p. 100). Do you think her role, to keep him "very clean and neat in his appearance," was typical of the role women played in the Revolutionary War? How and why? Learn as much as you can about women's participation in the war. How do their roles compare and contrast with the roles of American women in war today?

6. One of the most best-known anti-government, anti-taxation movements that occurred in the early Republic era was the Whiskey Rebellion. What were the goals, actions, and consequences of the Whiskey Rebellion? How was this rebellion similar to those discussed in this chapter?

7. When Charles Beard published *An Economic Interpretation of the Constitution of the United States*, he revised what Americans had generally been taught about the Founding Fathers. After reading Howard Zinn's description of the book, find out more about Beard's view of the Constitution. When did he write it? Specifically, what did he find after conducting his research? How did the American public react? How do the documents in this chapter support or refute his primary findings?

8. No program of national conscription existed during the Revolutionary War. Instead, each colony/state had its own laws for creating a militia—some of which relied on conscription. What is conscription? When and why did the United States enact its first national conscription law? How did conscription laws change during World War I, World War II, Korea, and Vietnam? What are the current laws governing conscription? How might they change in the twenty-first century? How do you think the Founding Fathers might have felt about passage of a national conscription act?

9   A great deal of contention existed between Patriots and Loyalists before, during, and after the war. Who were the Loyalists? How were they treated by the Patriots? What happened to them after the colonists won the war? Locate at least one primary document written by a loyalist about his/her treatment during the war. Do you think this treatment was typical? How and why?

10. The Sedition Act of 1798 was the first attempt to legally limit our rights under the First Amendment. What did it do and how was it enforced? What other similar attempts occurred in the nineteenth and twentieth centuries? How are any of these efforts similar and dissimilar to the PATRIOT Act passed by Congress in October 2001?

SUGGESTED ESSAY QUESTIONS

1. Support or refute one of Howard Zinn's primary contentions in this chapter, such as his assertion that social class divisions dominated American society before, during, and after the Revolutionary War.

2. In Federalist No. 10, James Madison argues for the need to "break and control the violence of faction" (p. 108). Referring to all the entries in this chapter, do you think the various authors would agree that such factions existed? If so, how did they describe them? If not, why not?

3. Do you agree or disagree with Madison's statement, "But the most common and durable source of factions has been the various and unequal distribution of property" (p. 109). Provide examples from the documents in this chapter to support your answer. Madison continues that the "principal task of modern legislation" is the "regulation of these various and interfering interests." In Federalist No. 10, what specific regulation does Madison suggest?

4. What do you think are James Madison's most convincing arguments for creating a federalist system of central government? For supporting the creation of a republic rather than a "pure democracy"? Which are his least convincing arguments? Do you think that Henry Knox would support his arguments? Why, or why not?

5. Howard Zinn argues that prior to the Revolutionary War, many colonists did not support the war, and thus the Founding Fathers "would have to woo the armed white population" (*People's History*, p. 77). Using examples from the chapter (or both chapters), demonstrate how he supports this contention.

Do you agree or disagree with Howard Zinn on this point? How and why?

6. The American Revolution brought about the separation of church and state. Support or refute this statement. Do you believe that it is important today to adhere to the separation of church and state? Why, or why not?

7. What voices of resistance in chapters 5 in both *Voices* and *A People's History* were of most interest to you? How and why? Which did you find most compelling and why? Least compelling?

8. How do the voices and information in these two chapters improve your understanding of the Revolutionary War? Of the Constitution? Of the Founding Fathers? What information was especially useful? How and why?

9. According to Alexander Hamilton, one of the writers of the Constitution, the rich deserve more say in politics than the "mass of the people." Why did-n't Hamilton trust the "mass of the people"? Do you think Hamilton's attitude was shared by other Founding Fathers? Explain.

SIMULATIONS AND OTHER CREATIVE APPROACHES

1. Write a letter that you think George Washington might have written in response to the letter from Henry Knox. Write another letter from Washington to either Joseph Plumb Martin or Samuel Dewees in which the General responds to their particular wartime grievances.

2. Read the Declaration of Independence aloud and then have students role-play King George's reaction. Or have students stage an imagined trial in which the British Crown tries George Washington and Thomas Jefferson for acts of treason.

3. Stage an imagined debate among the Founding Fathers about a particularly contentious part of the Declaration of Independence.

4. Bring General George Washington and the five contributors in Chapter 5 in *Voices*—Joseph Clarke, Joseph Plumb Martin, Samuel Dewees, Henry Knox, and James Madison—together for a press conference. The attending journalists (all the students in the class who will be sitting in the room) should have a series of politically astute questions ready for each of these men. One student should be assigned the role of anchorman or anchorwoman to conduct the business of the press conference.

CHAPTER SIX

The Early Women's Movement

Students always shake their heads in total disbelief when they are reminded that women have had the right to vote for only just over eighty years. They are even more amazed when they read the fiery words and learn about the brave actions of women who dared to speak out against oppression in the early nineteenth century. They are shocked to learn that in 1872, Susan B. Anthony was arrested for "knowingly voting without having a lawful right to vote," and found guilty. Who would have thought that those committed to the early women's movement were but the first of several generations of brave women to fight against economic exploitation as well as physical, social, and racial inequality?

The road to the franchise was long and strewn with difficult and often danger-ous obstacles. But women persevered. They continued to use their voices to demonstrate that they would not be deterred from achieving their goals.

Document-Based Questions

MARIA STEWART

1. Maria Stewart states that "continual fear" has somewhat "lessened in us that natural force and energy which belong to man" (p. 116). What is her explanation of such a natural force and energy? Do you think that people who are oppressed in the world today have a similar natural force and energy? How and why?

2. What examples of "the prayers of self-righteousness and hypocrisy" (p. 116) could be found in pre-Civil War society?

3. How does Stewart's voice add to the belief that the economic foundations of the United States' success were built upon slave labor? Support or refute this belief.

ANGELINA E. GRIMKÉ WELD

1. Do you agree with Grimké Weld's assertion that those who do not support abolition "know not that they are undermining their own rights and their own happiness, temporal and eternal" (p. 117)? How and why? How does she use this speech to support her assertion?

2. What does Grimké Weld mean when she says that the "spirit of slavery" exists in the North and that Northerners must "cast out" that spirit (p. 117)? Do you think she provides adequate examples of precisely how that could be accomplished?

3. Grimké Weld claims that "there is no such thing as neutral ground. He that is not for us is against us" (p. 119). How would you compare and contrast this statement with the one President George W. Bush made to Congress on September 20, 2001, nine days after September 11: "Either you are with us, or you are with the terrorists"? Can there be neutral ground? Why, or why not?

HARRIET HANSON ROBINSON

1. Do you think that it was generally true in pre-Civil War America that "So little does one class of persons really know about the thoughts and aspirations of another" (p.121)? What examples does Robinson provide to support her statement? Do you think that the same is true in contemporary American society? How and why?

2. Why do you think that "the factory girl was the lowest among women" (p. 121)? What sorts of "degrading occupations" still exist for women in contemporary American society?

3. Why do you think that "one of the first strikes of the cotton-factory operatives that ever took place in this country" (pp. 122–123) occurred in Lowell, Massachusetts? What were their grievances in 1836? How would these grievances compare and contrast with grievances of working women today?

S. MARGARET FULLER OSSOLI

1. Do you agree or disagree with Margaret Ossoli's statement that "the free American so often feels himself free . . . only to pamper his appetites and

indolence through the misery of his fellow-beings" (p. 124)? Can anyone be free if that freedom is dependent on the enslavement of others? Why, or why not?

2. What primary arguments does Ossoli use to show how men tried to "keep women in their place" in the mid-nineteenth century? Is her rebuttal effective? Why, or why not?

3. Why do you think Ossoli's writing had, as Howard Zinn claims, "a profound impact on the women's rights movement in the United States" (p. 123)?

ELIZABETH CADY STANTON

1. Why do you think Stanton modeled her "Declaration of Sentiments and Resolutions" on the wording and structure of the Declaration of Independence? Do you think this strategy was effective? Why, or why not?

2. At the end of the Seneca Falls Convention, sixty-eight women and thirty-two men signed the "Declaration of Sentiments." Why would men join in this effort? Do you think the women needed their voices? Why, or why not?

3. Which grievances are most persuasive? Least? How do the voices of the other women in this chapter support these grievances?

SOJOURNER TRUTH

1. What is the primary impact of this famous speech? Why do you think that it is considered one of the most important speeches in the early women's rights movement?

2. Why do you think Sojourner Truth was invited to speak to feminists in Akron, Ohio, in 1851? Do you think that her speech would have been so well received had she delivered it in the South? Why, or why not?

LUCY STONE AND HENRY B. BLACKWELL

1. What were the "legal powers" that husbands had over their wives? Which do you find to be most "injurious"?

2. What do you think most men and women who were contemporaries of

Stone and Blackwell would think about this marriage protest? What segments of society do you think would be most receptive? Least receptive? How and why?

SUSAN B. ANTHONY

1. Why was the right to vote so important to Susan B. Anthony—so important that she was willing to be arrested many times?

2. What does Anthony mean when she writes, "Of all of my prosecutors . . . not one is my peer, but each and all are my political sovereigns" (p. 130–131)? How does she support her statement?

3. What would Anthony's "broad and liberal interpretation of the Constitution and its recent amendments" (p.131) entail? How did the court respond?

Main Points in *Voices*, Chapter 6, "The Early Women's Movement"

After reading Chapter 6 in *Voices*, students should be encouraged to identify what they believe to be the main points therein. Following are four possible main points.

1. For the first 150 years of this nation's history, women were denied a fundamental privilege of American citizenship, the right to vote.

2. Women involved in early-nineteenth-century social movements spoke out against and actively resisted many forms of political, social, economic, and racial oppression.

3. Even though women knew it to be dangerous to oppose the male-dominated status quo, many bravely persevered.

4. Men, as well as women, supported the early women's movement.

Main Points in *Voices*, Chapter 6, "The Early Women's Movement," and in *A People's History*, Chapter 6, "The Intimately Oppressed"

If your students are also reading *A People's History*, they should be encouraged to identify what they believe to be the main points in chapters 6 in both books. Following are five additional points to be stressed when *Voices* and *A People's History* are used together.

5. Early-nineteenth-century American women were trapped in two ways: those who stayed at home were trapped by the ideology of a "women's sphere," and those who were forced to work were enslaved by horrendous working conditions.

6. Despite the negative "bonds of womanhood," their common oppression helped women forge "bonds of solidarity."

7. Slave women faced a double oppression in pre-Civil War society.

8. The belief in "patriarchal sovereignty" was the justification for the subjugation of women.

9. "Women rebels have always faced special disabilities." (*People's History*, p. 108)

General-Discussion Questions for *Voices*, Chapter 6, "The Early Women's Movement"

While the following questions are designed for classroom discussion about all the voices read in Chapter 6, they can also be rewritten and included as evaluation tools.

1. Several of the women speak about the existence of fear in their society—fear of racial, political, and social oppression. What do you think it was that gave them the courage to resist in the face of such fear? What are some issues you might support or battles you might fight, regardless of your fear?

2. What is the right to petition? Many of the women in these readings claim

that using the petition would be beneficial to their cause. What is Grimké Weld's ultimate goal for using the petition? To what end would Elizabeth Cady Stanton use the petition? Do you think petitions will help the petitioners achieve their goals? Why, or why not?

3. What are the differences between the voices of the workingwomen and those of the middle and upper classes who are involved in the early women's movement? Do you think these differences will be resolved as the movement evolves? Why, or why not?

4. What common grievances do you hear in all eight of these voices? Are some more articulate than others? More evocative? How and why? What common methods of resistance do you hear in their voices?

5. Elizabeth Cady Stanton's "Declaration of Sentiments" emphasized that half of all people in the United States were disenfranchised (p. 127). Do you think that this is a completely accurate picture of disenfranchisement in American society in 1848? Who else was disenfranchised? What do you think might be a more accurate percentage of the disenfranchised prior to the Civil War?

6. How was United States citizenship defined in the nineteenth century? Do you think that Susan B. Anthony's address to the judge upon her sentencing in 1873 provides an accurate assessment of citizenship? How and why?

7. Why do you think men had so much power over women in early America? What justifications might men have offered for why women should not be given more rights? What reasons might some women have had for opposing more rights for women?

8. What similarities and dissimilarities do you see in the images of women's expected behavior in the media today and the way women were expected to behave in early America?

9. What resistance to gender equality remains in the twenty-first century?

10. In 1791, a girl stated that she looked at marriage much the same as she looked at death. What might have led her to say this? Do the readings in this chapter support this view? How and why?

11. How did the voices in this chapter reinforce any of the five themes listed in "Main Points in *Voices*"?

12. Which of the voices in this chapter did you find most powerful? Least powerful? How and why?

General-Discussion Questions for *Voices*, Chapter 6, "The Early Women's Movement," and *A People's History*, Chapter 6, "The Intimately Oppressed"

These general-discussion questions are additional questions for students who have read Chapter 6 in both books. For all questions, discussion must focus on ways the materials in both chapters help students formulate and articulate their answers.

13. How do the voices in "The Early Women's Movement" lend credibility to the narrative in "The Intimately Oppressed"? What does it mean to be "intimately oppressed"? Why is intimate oppression so "hard to uproot"? Do you think women today are still victims of intimate oppression? Explain.

14. What have you previously learned about colonial women resisters, such as Anne Hutchinson or Mary Dyer? About revolutionary-era women's resistance movements, such as boycotting, "coffee parties," and the Daughters of Liberty? What happens to your understanding of American history when women's voices are excluded? When they are included?

15. Why was demanding the right to vote considered to be "radical"—even among women—in the mid-nineteenth century? Do you think it was still considered radical at the time the Nineteenth Amendment was adopted in 1920? Why, or why not?

16. Why was there a "practical need for women in a frontier society" that "produced some measure of equality"? (*People's History*, p. 111) What were those measures? What were the special attributes of frontier life that would provide more equality for women than existed in urban life in preindustrial America?

17. What was the "cult of domesticity" (*People's History*, p. 104)? Do you agree that it was "a way of pacifying her [women] with a doctrine of 'separate but equal'"? Why, or why not?

18. What evidence does Howard Zinn provide to support his statement that

the conditions of bondage faced by workingwomen and upper-class women "created a common consciousness of their situation and forged bonds of solidarity among them" (*People's History*, p. 117)? If they indeed shared such common bonds, what stood in the way of a unified effort to break their bondage?

19. Given what you know about America in 1776, what do you think the Founding Fathers meant when they wrote in the Declaration of Independence that all men are created equal?

20. Do you think most American women supported the women's movement in the pre-Civil War years? Why, or why not? What might have united them? What might have divided them?

21. Howard Zinn suggests that the growing capitalist economy in the United States required that women play particular roles. What was the relationship between the economy and the "proper" attitudes and behaviors expected of women?

22. What were the similarities and dissimilarities between the conditions of enslaved African Americans and white women?

Evaluation Tools

SUGGESTED ASSIGNMENTS

These assignments can be adapted to meet any classroom need—homework, short- or long-term research projects, individual or group work. The end product should be flexible, depending on teacher interest and student abilities—papers, journals, oral reports, visual aides, and the like.

1. The abolition movement was widespread on the eve of the Civil War. What were the primary goals of the abolitionists? Who were the abolitionists? What roles did they play in pre-Civil War American society? How and why were white and African American women involved in the movement? Learn as much about the life and background of one female abolitionist. Do you think she was typical or atypical of other abolitionists? How and why?

2. Excerpts from the *Lowell Offering* are available online at

www.berwickacademy.org/millgirls/offering.htm. After reading several of these entries, how do the voices of these women compare and contrast with the recollections of Harriet Hanson Robinson? Locate at least two other primary sources that describe the experiences of young women in the pre-Civil War work force. What do they contribute to your understanding of early nineteenth-century women activists?

3. What is a "factory town" (*People's History*, p. 122)? Was Lowell a factory town? How and why? Find out as much as possible about another nineteenth-century factory town. Where was it located? What was produced? What were working and living conditions like? Did the occupants ever protest? How and why? When did it cease to exist? What brought about its closure? Are any factory towns still in existence today? If so, where, and how are they similar and dissimilar to the factory towns of the nineteenth century?

4. Those who study the early women's rights movement draw tremendous inspiration from the words of the women themselves. An especially rich source is the correspondence between Susan B. Anthony and Elizabeth Cady Stanton. Much of this, as well as hundreds of primary written and visual materials, have been included in *Not for Ourselves Alone: The Story of Elizabeth Cady Stanton and Susan B. Anthony*, a PBS documentary of their lives and struggle. View the movie. What new information did you gain about the women's movement? What did you learn about Susan and Elizabeth's personal struggles for equality? Would you recommend this movie to a friend? Why, or why not?

5. The World Anti-Slavery Convention of 1840, held in London, voted to exclude women from the convention floor but allowed them to attend meetings in a curtained enclosure. Research this convention and learn more about the reasons for such exclusion, as well as the protest activities of the women who came to London for the meeting. What were the long- and short-term consequences of their exclusion from this convention?

6. The Seneca Falls Convention was treated with scorn from all corners of American society. The press and religious leaders loudly denounced the happenings at Seneca Falls. Using a search engine of your choice, learn as much as possible about the reaction to the Convention and the "Declaration of Sentiments." What did the newspapers report? Why do

you think they were so opposed to the meeting? What insight does this opposition give you into the nineteenth-century efforts to "keep women in their place"?

7. Extending the franchise to all American citizens has been a long process—a process that was initially organized by brave women in the early nineteenth century. Who else did not have the right to vote in the nineteenth century? How was the franchise extended, and to whom, in the early-to-mid-twentieth century? When was the vote legally extended to every American citizen? When was it truly available to every American citizen?

8. Controversy has arisen over the exact wording of Sojourner Truth's speech. Since no one recorded her exact words, and Frances Gage did not write her account of the speech until twelve years later, no one can be certain. Two accounts exist, that of the 1851 newspaper record, and that of Gage. And here Howard Zinn has offered a third, modernized version, based on Gage's account. A website devoted to Sojourner Truth discusses these accounts at http://www.kyphilom.com/www/truth.html. After reviewing this site as well as at least one other, what do you think was the message Sojourner Truth sought, not just in her famous 1851 speech, but also throughout her life?

9. Historian Laurel Thatcher Ulrich won a Pulitzer Prize for *A Midwife's Tale*, her story of Martha Moore Ballard, one of the women Howard Zinn mentions in "The Intimately Oppressed" (p. 112). Find out more about Martha's life and Ulrich's research by watching the PBS film *A Midwife's Tale* and accessing the rich details of the PBS website that accompanies the film at http://www.pbs.org/wgbh/amex/midwife/. Who was Martha Ballard? How would you describe her life? Do you think she felt oppressed? How and why? Do you think she would have supported the views of the women you read in these chapters? Why, or why not?

SUGGESTED ESSAY QUESTIONS

1. Use the voices and information available in *Voices* (or in both *Voices* and *A People's History*) to support or refute Howard Zinn's contention that "Societies based on private property and competition, in which monogamous families became practical units for work and socialization, found it especially useful to establish this special status of women, something akin

to a house slave in the matter of intimacy and oppression" (*People's History*, p. 103).

2. Explain the similarities and differences in the goals and grievances of the women you learned about in these chapters. Which of these voices provided the best blueprints for achieving such goals? The least effective blueprints? How, and why?

3. What issues united and divided the early women's movement? Which issues do you think might have helped you to support the movement if you had lived at this time?

4. Explain how the voices in Chapter 6 reinforce the revolutionary statement Susan B. Anthony invoked at her trial in 1873, "Resistance to tyranny is obedience to God." Do you agree with this statement? Why, or why not?

5. Using the voices in these chapters, support Howard Zinn's statement in "The Intimately Oppressed" that "Women rebels have always faced special disabilities" (p. 108). What special disabilities does he discuss? Which do the women discuss in their own words? Do women continue to face special disabilities in their contemporary efforts for equal rights? Explain.

6. Why do you think that so many women became involved in the abolitionist movement and in antislavery societies? What did the women's rights movement have in common with abolition movements? Ultimately, which movement was most successful in the nineteenth century? Why?

7. Explain the major types of resistance to women's rights in the early nineteenth century. Why do you think there was so much resistance? What resistance to equality for women remains in the twenty-first century?

8. As Howard Zinn points out, Nancy Cott's book, *The Bonds of Womanhood*, has many meanings. What were some of the "bonds of womanhood" in the early nineteenth century?

9. What voices of resistance in Chapter 6 in both *Voices* and *A People's History* were of most interest to you? How and why? Which did you find most compelling and why? Least compelling?

10. How do the voices and information in these two chapters improve your understanding of the early women's movement? What information was especially useful? How and why?

SIMULATIONS AND OTHER CREATIVE APPROACHES

1. Write a new Declaration of Independence or "Declaration of Sentiments" that expresses the contemporary grievances of American women.

2. Imagine the life of English women who arrived in the North American colonies in 1619—women who had been sold, supposedly "with their own consent." Write a letter home to your family in England describing, among many other things, your voyage to North America, your experiences upon arrival, and what you think the future holds for you in the New World.

3. Design a statue or other visual memorial to any of the women you have read about in this (these) chapter(s).

4. Stage a discussion in which the following quote from Laurel Thatcher Ulrich is debated: "Well behaved women seldom make history."

5. Write a letter to Susan B. Anthony and Elizabeth Cady Stanton telling them about the status of American women in the twenty-first century. Be sure to tell them, among other things, what women have achieved, what rights are still elusive, and what you might do to help women gain full equality in contemporary society.

CHAPTER SEVEN

Indian Removal

"Manifest Destiny": The phrase is evocative of so many things that Euro-Americans call progress: populating the west with hard-working settlers, expanding profitable agriculture and industry, sharing the attributes of democracy and Christianity, and removing the Indians. For the American Indian people, however, such "progress" brought cultural, political, economic, and spiritual genocide.

Yet despite the movement of Euro-Americans who believed that they had the God-given right to spread their "yearly multiplying millions" across continental North America, many Indian people resisted such encroachment. They united in peaceful and wartime opposition to the flood of westward expansion; they entered into trade agreements that encouraged strong economic ties with white Americans; they met with federal agents to plead for their survival; and they spoke in front of the Supreme Court in unsuccessful attempts to prove the unconstitutionality of state and federal actions. None of these efforts stopped the tide of Indian Removal, and no actions of the settlers could fully silence or stem the power and eloquence of Indian resistance.

Document-Based Questions

TECUMSEH'S SPEECH TO THE OSAGES

1. Why does Tecumseh need to convince the Osage people that the "white men" are dangerous and not to be trusted?

2. Do you think that Tecumseh's grievances against the "white men" are an accurate reflection of nineteenth-century Euro-Americans attitudes about Indian people? Which of his grievances do you feel to be most egregious? How and why?

3. What does this speech tell you about Tecumseh? What kind of man was he? Do you think Tecumseh's speech successfully united the Indian nations? How and why?

CHEROKEE NATION, 1829

1. What did the author of the Congressional message mean when he said, "The strength of the red man has become weakness" (p. 136)?

2. The authors claim that "In addition to that first of all rights, the right of inheritance and peaceable possession, we have the faith and pledge of the U[nited] States, repeated over and over again, in treaties made at various times. By these treaties our rights as a separate people are distinctly acknowledged, and guarantees given that they shall be secured and protected" (p. 138). What is meant by "the right of inheritance and peaceable possession"? How is this claim related to the issue of tribal sovereignty? What is a treaty? How do the Cherokee interpretations of the treaties differ from those of the United States?

3. The authors reference the 1790 Intercourse Act (www.tngenweb.org/ tnland/intruders/17900722.html) that placed nearly all interaction between Indians and non-Indians under federal—not state—control, established the boundaries of Indian country, protected Indian lands against non-Indian aggression, subjected trading with Indians to federal regulation, and stipulated that injuries against Indians by non-Indians was a federal crime. The conduct of Indians among themselves while in Indian country was left entirely to the tribes. How do the grievances in this entry violate the spirit and law of the Intercourse Act?

LEWIS ROSS ET AL.

1. What are the authors' primary arguments against removal? Which do you think is their strongest argument?

2. What do the authors' believe will become of the Cherokee nation if they are forced to remove themselves from their ancestral lands?

3. Why do you think their arguments did not end the removal of the Cherokees?

BLACK HAWK'S SURRENDER SPEECH

1. Black Hawk's message is one of defiance, dismay, and dignity. What specific examples illustrate each of these characteristics?

2. How does Black Hawk describe white men? How are these descriptions similar to those of other Indian descriptions of white men in this chapter?

3. What cultural differences between American Indians and the "white man" are evident in this entry? Do you think matters could have been handled differently to bridge the gap between such differences? How and why?

JOHN G. BURNETT

1. What is your reaction to this account of the Trail of Tears? How do you think Private Burnett's description of this tragic event would compare and contrast with that written by a member of the Cherokee Nation? How might Burnett's account have compared and contrasted with that of another soldier who was not so well acquainted with the Cherokee people?

2. The Trail of Tears was the official result of the Indian Removal Act in which land "exchanges" were to occur. What is the difference between a land exchange and forced removal? Does this account sound like a land exchange? Why, or why not?

3. If Burnett's account of the Trail of Tears had been published in 1838 rather than recorded for his family in 1890, do you think that it would have prompted a public outcry? Why, or why not?

CHIEF JOSEPH OF THE NEZ PERCÉ

1. What is significant about Chief Joseph's statement, "If the white man wants to live in peace with the Indian he can live in peace" (p. 147)? Do you think most Indian nations would have been willing to coexist with the white settlers? Was conflict inevitable?

2. What is Chief Joseph's complaint about reservations?

3. What does Chief Joseph want? Do you think his requests were reasonable, given the situation in North America in the late 1870s? How do you think federal government officials responded to his requests?

BLACK ELK

1. Accounts of Wounded Knee are usually referred to as either the Wounded

Knee Massacre or the Battle of Wounded Knee. What is the difference between a battle and a massacre? From Black Elk's account, what proof do you find of a massacre? Why do you think the federal government referred to it only as a battle?

2. Why was Wounded Knee the end of Black Elk's dream?

3. How are Black Elk's reactions to defeat similar to those of Black Hawk and Chief Joseph?

Main Points in *Voices*, Chapter 7, "Indian Removal"

After reading Chapter 7 in *Voices*, students should be encouraged to identify what they believe to be the main points therein. Following are five possible main points.

1. Despite many eloquent speeches and organized attempts to resist westward expansion into Indian Territory, determined Indian resistance was no match for the congressional actions and the armed forces of the United States government.

2. The Era of Jacksonian Democracy was marked by the brutal treatment of American Indians.

3. During the early 1800s, congressional laws and the Supreme Court decisions eroded the sovereign status of Indian nations.

4. After losing battles on land and in court, Indian leaders demonstrated defiance and dismay at their betrayal by the white man, and dignity in the face of their losses.

5. Indian people were not just victims of genocidal policies; they were also survivors in the face of almost insurmountable odds.

Main Points in *Voices*, Chapter 7, "Indian Removal," and in *A People's History*, Chapter 7, "As Long as Grass Grows or Water Runs"

If your students are also reading *A People's History*, they should be encouraged to identify what they believe to be the main points in Chapters 7 in both books. Following are five additional points to be stressed when *Voices* and *A People's History* are used together.

6. Indian Removal was believed to be necessary for Euro-American progress in the West.

7. Because Indian people were perceived as obstacles to Euro-American settlement, federal Indian policy was built on paternalism and brute force.

8. When negotiating most treaties with Indian Nations, the federal government used pressure and deception.

9. The desire to assimilate and to "civilize" the Indians were only secondary goals of federal Indian-policy makers; their primary goal was to acquire land for Euro-American agriculture, mining, railroads, and settlement.

10. While history most often portrays American Indians as victims, it must also portray them as survivors—heroic people who, despite the genocidal policies of the United States government, have survived and revived their traditional cultures, languages, religions, and political structures.

General-Discussion Questions for *Voices*

While the following questions are designed for classroom discussion about all the voices read in Chapter 7, they can also be rewritten and included as evaluation tools.

1. The Commerce Clause of the United States Constitution (Article 1, Section 8) declares that "[t]he Congress shall have Power . . . [t]o regulate Commerce with foreign Nations and among the several States, and with the Indian Tribes." Thus, the Constitution specified that there were three governmental entities within the United States with forms of sovereignty— Indian tribes, state governments, and the federal government. In short, Indian governments were sovereign. What is sovereignty? If Indian nations were sovereign at the time of Euro-American contact and their sovereignty was recognized in the United States Constitution, how has their sovereignty been compromised?

2. The official subtitle for the Indian Removal Act of 1830 was "An Act to provide for an exchange of lands with the Indians residing in any of the states or territories, and for their removal west of the river Mississippi" (www.mtholyoke.edu/acad/intrel/removal.htm). What is a land exchange? Does the use of the word exchange mask the true intent and results of the law? How and why?

3. In his fifth annual message to Congress in December 1833, President Andrew Jackson made the following report about Indian Removal efforts: "That those tribes can not exist surrounded by our settlements and in continual contact with our citizens is certain. They have neither the intelligence, the industry, the moral habits, nor the desire of improvement which are essential to any favorable change in their condition. Established in the midst of another and a superior race, and without appreciating the causes of their inferiority or seeking to control them, they must necessarily yield to the force of circumstances and ere long disappear" (www.synaptic.bc.ca/ejournal/JacksonFifthAnnualMessage.htm). What is President Jackson's message? How do his conclusions mirror federal policies in regard to westward expansion and its effect on Indian people?

4. What common grievances do the Indian voices of resistance share in regard to federal Indian policies and the effects of Euro-American frontier settlement?

5. These voices of resistance are articulate and their goals are clear. Why, then, do you think that none of those in power rose to the defense of the Indian people? Do you think that were other voices like those of John G. Burnett who protested Indian Removal policies? Why were these voices ignored?

6. The Indian voices of resistance echo a common theme—that sovereignty is a fundamental right. What does this mean? What specific portions of these speeches demonstrate this belief?

7. In Chief Joseph's recollections of his trip to Washington, D.C., in 1879, he emphasized that he was "tired of talk that comes to nothing" (p.147). What evidence of such talk can you find in all the entries in this chapter? Why do you think that many Indian people were willing to engage in such talk during the early years of negotiations? Do you think the representatives of the United States government who engaged in such talk intended to keep their promises? How and why?

8. What are the similarities of the reactions to defeat described by Black Elk, Black Hawk, and Chief Joseph? How are their recollections evidence of the horrendous victimization and of the courageous survival of their people?

9. In Chief Black Hawk's 1832 surrender speech, he says, "The white men do not scalp the head; but they do worse—they poison the heart" (pp. 141–142). What did he mean? What examples can you find in today's society of people's hearts being "poisoned"? How, why, and by whom?

10. If the United States government consistently broke its treaties with American Indian nations, why do you think they negotiated treaties in the first place?

11. How did the voices in this chapter reinforce any of the five themes listed in "Main Points in *Voices*"?

12. Which of the voices in this chapter did you find most powerful? Least powerful? How and why?

General-Discussion Questions for *Voices* and *A People's History*

These general-discussion questions are additional questions for students who have read Chapter 7 in both books. For all questions, discussion must focus on ways the materials in both chapters help students formulate and articulate their answers.

13. What were the various methods United States policy makers used to take land from the Indians? How did the policy makers justify these actions?

14. According to Article II of the International Convention on the Prevention and Punishment of Genocide, genocide involves actions "committed with the intent to destroy, in whole or in part, a national, ethnical, racial or religious group as such: (a) Killing members of the group; (b) Causing serious bodily or mental harm to members of the group; (c) Deliberately inflicting on the group conditions of life calculated to bring about its physical destruction in whole or in part; (d) Imposing measures intended to prevent births within the group; (e) Forcibly transferring children of the group to another group." (See www.preventgenocide.org/law/convention/index.htm#text for

the full text of the Convention.) Given this definition, do you think that the Indian Removal Act was genocidal in its intent and/or in its consequences?

15. Why do you think most of the largest and most powerful Indian nations fought with the British and against the Americans during the Revolutionary War? How were they rewarded at the War's conclusion?

16. How did American leaders define civilized? Is there anything you read in either chapter that leads you to believe that the Indian people were not civilized? Why did so many Euro-Americans believe the Indians were not civilized? How would your definition of civilized differ from that of nineteenth-century policy makers and the American public?

17. Before reading these chapters, what was your impression of Andrew Jackson as a soldier and as president? How and why has your impression changed? How did John Burnett's memories of fighting with Jackson influence your opinion? Why do you think much of the information on Indian removal contained in these two chapters has been ignored in more traditional interpretations of Jackson?

18. Do you think most of the 371 treaties enacted between 1776 and 1871 were "made under pressure and by deception" (*People's History*, p.134)? Explain.

19. During the first half of the nineteenth century, the United States government fought three wars with the Seminole Nation. One of them lasted eight years, cost $20 million dollars, and took 1,500 lives. Why did the government find the Seminoles especially threatening? Why do you think this story is omitted from our textbooks?

20. How did the federal government negotiate the Treaty of New Echota? Why is this deception often called an example of the government's use of a divide-and-conquer strategy against the American Indians?

21. In the 2000 Census, 4.1 million Americans identified themselves as American Indian or Alaska Native, and another 1.6 million identified themselves as being American Indian or Alaskan Native and at least one other race. Yet our textbooks usually end their discussion of American Indians with the Wounded Knee Massacre in 1890. How does teaching about Indians as victims influence the way in which we think about Indians in the twenty-first century?

Evaluation Tools

SUGGESTED ASSIGNMENTS

These assignments can be adapted to meet any classroom need—homework, short- or long-term research projects, individual or group work. The end product should be flexible, depending on teacher interest and student abilities—papers, journals, oral reports, visual aides, and the like.

1. Andrew Jackson, the president who ushered in "The Era of Jacksonian Democracy," was also the president who authorized Indian Removal. Examine the exact wording of the Removal Act of 1830, as well as several of Jackson's annual presidential messages. (See www.synaptic.bc.ca/ ejournal/jackson.htm.) What were Jackson's attitudes about Indian people? About westward expansion? How did he define *progress*? Do you think his policies were genocidal in their intent? Provide exact quotes from the documents to support your answer.

2. Tecumseh, Black Hawk, Chief Joseph, and Black Elk were just four of many articulate Indian leaders who resisted white encroachment during the era of Manifest Destiny. Pick one of these famous men to study in more detail. Who were his people? Where was his ancestral land? How did Indian Removal policies affect his nation? What interactions did he and his people have with whites as they moved into his territory?

3. Understanding the geography of Indian Removal is essential to understanding nineteenth-century westward expansion. Examine various maps that illustrate removal patterns, especially the Trail of Tears, Indian land losses, confinement on reservations, and various wars the federal government declared on Indian Nations. What do these maps tell you about Indian endeavors to remain on their ancestral lands? What do they tell you about federal Indian policies? Pick one map that you found to be especially effective in demonstrating the overall effects of Manifest Destiny on American Indians. How and why was it more illustrative than the other maps you reviewed?

4. In *Cherokee Nation* v. *Georgia* (http://www.mtholyoke.edu/acad/intrel/ cherokee.htm) the Supreme Court found, among other things, that "[t]he

acts of our government plainly recognize the Cherokee nation as a state, and the courts are bound by those acts. A question of much more difficulty remains. Do the Cherokee constitute a foreign state in the sense of the constitution?" After reading the decision in its entirety, what constitutional rights guaranteed to white Americans of the time were denied the Cherokee nation by the state of Georgia? What did the court decide? After reading the court's decision and rereading the arguments presented to the court by John Ross, do you think the Justices made the correct decision? Why, or why not? What was President Jackson's response to the ruling? How do you think the court's decision will change the course of federal Indian policy throughout the nineteenth and twentieth centuries?

5. Learn as much as possible about resistance to the passage and implementation of the Indian Removal Act. Can you find other nonsupportive military voices like those of John G. Burnett? What were their primary objections to removal? What did they propose instead? Why do you think these voices were ignored?

6. The Wounded Knee Massacre was largely a response to the 1876 Battle at Little Big Horn. What were the goals and consequences of both battles? In order to better understand the American public's reaction to both battles, locate at least two newspaper accounts of each battle. Why is the 1877 battle commonly called Custer's Last Stand? How did the response to the first battle help to reinforce the public's attitude about the Wounded Knee Massacre? What did you find to be most interesting in these primary accounts? Most surprising? How and why?

7. Research the impact of American Indians on today's world, especially in terms of architecture, foods, social organization, medicines, or religion. For assistance, see Jack Weatherford, *Indian Givers: How the Indians of the Americas Transformed the World* (New York: Fawcett Columbine, 1988), and Bruce Johansen, *Forgotten Founders: How the American Indian Helped Shape Democracy* (Boston: Harvard, 1982).

8. Learn as much as possible about the contents and rulings of the Marshall trilogy—the three Supreme Court cases that shaped the nature of federal Indian policy and Indian law from in the era of Manifest Destiny (*Johnson v. McIntosh, Cherokee Nation v. Georgia, Worcestor v. Georgia*). What were the particularly paternalistic aspects of the rulings? How did they erode

tribal sovereignty? Do you think they continue to affect federal Indian policy in the twenty-first century? Why, or why not?

SUGGESTED ESSAY QUESTIONS

1. Using evidence from *Voices* (or from both books), support one of Howard Zinn's primary contentions in this chapter, that Indian people were obstacles to Euro-American settlement and thus "could be dealt with by sheer force, except that sometimes the language of paternalism preceded the burning of villages" (*People's History*, p.125).

2. The 1829 Cherokee statement to Congress stated, in part, "We have already said, that when the white man came to the shores of America, our ancestors were found in peaceable possession of this very land. They bequeathed it to us as their children, and we have sacredly kept it as containing the remains of our beloved men. This right of inheritance we have *never ceded*, nor ever *forfeited*. Permit us to ask, what better right can a people have to a country, than the right of *inheritance* and *immemorial peaceable possessions*" (*Voices*, p. 137)? How does this statement, as well as some of the other voices in this chapter (or in both books), support the historical and contemporary belief among Indian nations that sovereignty is an inherent right?

3. Do you think there is any contemporary truth to John Burnett's statement in his memories of the Trail of Tears: "Truth is, the facts are being concealed from the young people of today. School children of today do not know that we are living on lands that were taken from a helpless race at the bayonet point to satisfy the white man's greed" (*Voices*, p. 145). Do you think elementary and secondary schools have an obligation to teach this "truth"? Why, or why not?

4. Do you think conflict between white settlers and Indians could have been prevented, or was it inevitable? Explain.

5. Using as many examples as possible from *Voices* (or both books), demonstrate how Indian people were both victims and survivors of nineteenth-century federal Indian policies.

6. Many historians claim that from European contact forward, Euro-Americans deliberately used divide-and-conquer strategies to eliminate the

perceived threat posed by American Indians. What are divide-and-conquer strategies? Support this discussion with information from *Voices* (or both books).

7. Discuss the resisters you met in *Voices* (or in both books)—the Indians who resisted removal and other genocidal federal policies, as well as those Euro-Americans who spoke out against such policies. What were the goals of each group? The consequences of their efforts? Were their voices ignored?

8. The Indian voices in these chapters were eloquent and their battles were fiercely fought. Nonetheless, they were no match for congressional laws and the United States Army. Use as many examples of possible to explain why.

9. What voices of resistance in *Voices* (or in *Voices* and *A People's History*) were of most interest to you? How and why? Which did you find most compelling and why? Least compelling?

10. How do the voices and information in these two chapters improve your understanding of nineteenth-century federal Indian policies that resulted in genocide? What information was especially supportive of this understanding? How and why?

SIMULATIONS AND OTHER CREATIVE APPROACHES

1. Write and illustrate a short book for elementary students about the American Indians who originally lived in your community when Europeans first arrived in the Americas. Explain their history from first contact to the present with words, traditional stories, illustrations, and maps.

2. Create a large map of Indian Removal that can be shared with other students and then posted in your classroom. Be sure to include removal patterns of Indian Nations from across the country, as well as any artistic additions that will make the map a compelling illustration of the effects of removal.

3. Locate the discussion of Indian relations with Southerners and Indian Removal in either your assigned textbook or another textbook of choice. Rewrite that portion of the chapter to include multiple voices from the

Indian perspective, as well as important arguments before the Supreme Court in regard to Cherokee claims in Georgia. Be sure to include illustrations and maps.

4. Write an interior monologue from the perspective of a member of the Cherokee Nation in which he/she ponders the way contact with white society changed the Cherokee people.

5. Stage an imagined debate on the floor of the United States Senate in 1830 about passage or defeat of the proposed Indian Removal Act.

CHAPTER EIGHT

The War on Mexico

In *Occupied America*, Rodolfo Acuna argues that Anglo-Americans invaded Mexico for the sole purpose of forging an economically profitable North American empire. In justifying their use of conquest and violence to bring about progress, bitterness arose between two people—a bitterness that actually "gave birth to a legacy of hate." Like Howard Zinn, Acuna demonstrates how President James K. Polk manufactured the war with Mexico.

The war with Mexico may have been one of America's most unpopular wars from start to finish. Soldiers spoke out against the war, and many deserted; abolitionists abhorred the possibility that a victory might add more slave territory to the Union; others refused to pay their taxes for an unjust cause. For many reasons, resisters spoke out, acted upon their beliefs, and protested the actions of an expansionist president and a large segment of the American public that supported the philosophy of Manifest Destiny.

Document-Based Questions

ETHAN ALLEN HITCHCOCK

1. What are the "annexation resolutions of our Congress" to which Ethan Hitchcock refers?

2. Using a map of Texas, examine the difference in territory of the Mexican claim that the "original limit" of the Texas boundary was at the Neuces River, versus the American claim that the boundary was at the Rio Grande River. Whose claim does Hitchcock support and why?

3. Specifically, what "changes in character" and in "the real status and the principles for which are forefathers fought" is Hitchcock referring to? Do you agree with him that the Founding Fathers would have disagreed with Polk's expansionist philosophy? How and why?

MIGUEL BARRAGAN

1. What sort of insults to both the Mexican government and the Mexican people does Miguel Barragan describe?

2. Barragan describes Mexico as "the civilized world." How might the American colonists have responded to this description? Could both sides be civilized? Uncivilized? How and why?

3. How can both the Mexican government and the United States government fight a war for "God and Liberty"? How can "justice and power" be on both sides?

JUAN SOTO

1. What are the primary arguments for trying to convince Irish, French, and German Catholics to join Mexico in the fight against the United States?

2. Since the Mexican government lost the war, how do you think the victorious Americans treated the members of the San Patricio Battalion?

FREDERICK DOUGLASS

1. Why did Frederick Douglass consider the war with Mexico to be "a war against the free States"?

2. Twice in this speech there was "applause and hissing." Who might have been applauding and why? Who might have been hissing and why?

3. What were the "compromises and guaranties" in the Constitution that favored the slave system?

NORTH STAR EDITORIAL

1. The author states: "No politician of any considerable distinction or eminence, seems willing to hazard his popularity with his party, or stem the fierce current of executive influence, by an open and unqualified disapprobation of the war." What does the writer mean? Do you think this characteristic was common among nineteenth-century politicians? Among today's politicians? How and why?

2. How does this editorial highlight the racial, class, and religious issues that the author feels fueled the war with Mexico? Do you think he makes a convincing argument? Why, or why not?

3. Why do the abolitionists and "the friends of peace" have no faith in the political parties and their stand on the war? What problems does the author attribute to the Democrats and Whigs?

HENRY DAVID THOREAU

1. Why does Henry Thoreau believe that "All men recognize the right of revolution; that is, the right to refuse allegiance to, and to resist, the government, when its tyranny or its inefficiency are great and unendurable"? From what document does Thoreau derive this belief? Do you think people still believe in this "right of revolution"? Why, or why not?

2. Thoreau writes that what is legal is not necessarily right. Do you agree or disagree? Provide specific examples from his essay.

3. Do you agree with Thoreau that, "government is best which governs not at all"? What do you think he meant when he wrote, "It is not desirable to cultivate a respect for the law, so much as for the right"? Do you agree or disagree with this statement? How and why?

Main Points in *Voices*, Chapter 8, "The War on Mexico"

After reading Chapter 8 in *Voices*, students should be encouraged to identify what they believe to be the main points therein. Following are five possible main points.

1. From the beginning of his presidency, Polk was determined to acquire California as part of his plan for expanding the continental boundaries of the United States.

2. The incident leading to the "war on Mexico" was largely manufactured by the powerful advocates of Manifest Destiny.

3. Attitudes against the war on Mexico were widespread, particularly among abolitionists.

4. After the Mexican government prohibited immigration into Texas, large numbers of American settlers illegally immigrated into Mexican territory.

5. Once settled, Texan colonists failed to abide by the national laws and customs of Mexico.

Main Points in *Voices*, Chapter 8, "The War on Mexico," and in *A People's History*, Chapter 8, "We Take Nothing by Conquest, Thank God"

If your students are also reading *A People's History*, they should be encouraged to identify what they believe to be the main points in Chapters 8 in both books. Following are five additional points to be stressed when *Voices* and *A People's History* are used together.

6. Despite the years between battles and the different issues that bring us into conflict, the language of those who favor war often shows strong continuity.

7. The war with Mexico was fought by ordinary Americans and Mexicans but was driven by the interests of elites from both countries.

8. The early foundations of the United States tradition of civil disobedience have their roots in the war with Mexico.

9. The war with Mexico was fueled by racist conceptions of Mexicans as inferior and a less "civilized" people.

10. President Polk provoked war with Mexico in order to gain California and other lands for the United States.

General-Discussion Questions for *Voices*

While the following questions are designed for classroom discussion about all the voices read in Chapter 8, they can also be rewritten and included as evaluation tools.

1. What do you think the typical soldier felt he was fighting for in the war with Mexico? What factors were influential in some soldiers' decision to desert?

2. Why do you think ordinary citizens—workers or farmers, with no slaves and no plans to move into Mexican territory—might join demonstrations supporting the war?

3. What is civil disobedience? Can you provide various historical and contemporary examples of civil disobedience? Does civil disobedience constitute a legal or illegal action in the United States?

4. Why were many abolitionists against the war with Mexico?

5. Why was Texas such an attractive colonial opportunity for Americans?

6. All these voices of resistance share a few common grievances. What are they? What do you think bound together the antiwar resistance of American and Mexican soldiers, African-Americans, abolitionists, and an author?

7. How do Thoreau's suggestions for opposing the war compare and contrast with those of Frederick Douglass?

8. In what ways could it be said that the war with Mexico was based on racist attitudes? Could it also be argued that it was a war between classes? Why, or why not?

9. How did the voices in this chapter reinforce any of the five themes listed in "Main Points in *Voices*"?

10. Which of the voices in this chapter did you find most powerful? Least powerful? How and why?

General-Discussion Questions for *Voices* and *A People's History*

These general-discussion questions are additional questions for students who have read Chapter 8 in both books. For all questions, discussion must focus on ways the materials in both chapters help students formulate and articulate their answers.

11. By referring to Chapter 8 in *A People's History* as well as to a world map, explain why you think President Polk wanted to integrate California into the United States.

12. What would you do if you were alive in 1846 and felt the war with Mexico

was immoral? Whose antiwar actions presented in both chapters might you be willing to follow? Which would you reject?

13. In *A People's History*, Howard Zinn writes, "Accompanying all this aggressiveness was the idea that the United States would be giving the blessings of liberty and democracy to more people" (p. 154). Do you think this was a valid reason for going to war? What other acts of "aggressiveness" have been undertaken by the United States government in the name of liberty and democracy? Do you think this is a valid reason for going to war today? How and why?

14. What were the short- and long-term consequences of the war with Mexico for the American people? For the Mexican people?

15. What is the significance of the phrase—and the title of Chapter 8 in *A People's History*—"We take nothing by conquest, thank God"?

16. Why do you think that Congress not only "rushed to approve the war message," but also continued to support President Polk throughout the war?

17. Howard Zinn asks, "Were the newspapers reporting a feeling in the public, or creating a feeling in the public?" What do you think? Support your answer with specifics from the reading.

18. Howard Zinn reports that "Mexico was a despotism, a land of Indians and mestizos . . . controlled by criollos—whites of Spanish blood" (*People's History*, p. 159). Does this information make you think any differently about the war with Mexico? Why, or why not? Do you think this information helped fuel the war in 1846? How and why?

19. The war with Mexico was fought by the first all-volunteer army in United States history. Why did men volunteer? Why did men refuse to fight? Why did men desert? What were the recruits promised upon honorable discharge? What did most receive after the war?

Evaluation Tools

SUGGESTED ASSIGNMENTS

These assignments can be adapted to meet any classroom need—homework, short-

or long-term research projects, individual or group work. The end product should be flexible, depending on teacher interest and student abilities—papers, journals, oral reports, visual aides, and the like.

1. Learn as much as possible about anti-Mexican immigration efforts that have occurred in the last twenty years. What are the main reasons Anglo-Americans give for excluding documented and undocumented Mexican immigrants? What are the implications of this merger? What are your reactions to these reasons? How and why did the Immigration and Naturalization Service (INS) get incorporated into the Office of Homeland Security? Given the origins and nature of the war with Mexico, how might today's Mexicans respond to the efforts to exclude Mexicans from United States territory?

2. After reading Henry David Thoreau's entire essay titled "Civil Disobedience," write a letter to Thoreau in which you take one of the following approaches: Write Thoreau as his contemporary; tell him what you think about his ideas and how they might or might not be applied in 1846. Or write Thoreau as a citizen in the twenty-first century; tell him how you think his ideas about civil disobedience might or might not be applied to issues in your time.

3. Examine the war with Mexico from a Mexican perspective. Begin your research by reading an account of the war in a Mexican secondary-education textbook. Then learn as much as possible from other sources about Mexican perspectives and thoughts on the goals, conflicts, and consequences of the war. Compare and contrast these perspectives with an account of the war in your textbook. How do the two accounts compare and contrast? Write a new account for your textbook in which both the United States and Mexican perspectives are included.

4. Find out more about Lincoln's "spot resolutions." What was Lincoln's motivation for the resolutions? What do they tell you about Lincoln's support for the war with Mexico? What was the presidential and congressional response to the resolutions?

5. Read more about William Lloyd Garrison and his newspaper *The Liberator*. What events helped to shape Garrison's life as a political activist? Read at least four issues of *The Liberator* that were written during the war with

Mexico. What similarities do they share with the antiwar voices you heard in *Voices* (or both books)? How did Garrison's antiwar pleas compare and contrast with those of Frederick Douglass?

6. Learn more about the San Patricio Battalion. Who were the men who joined? What were their reasons for joining? How were they treated by the Mexican army? What was their fate after the war? How were they treated by the Americans? By the Mexicans?

7. Research the similarities and differences of both independence movements conducted by Americans who immigrated to Texas and California. Do you think one was more legitimate than the other? How did the Treaty of Guadalupe Hidalgo help the Americans living in the newly acquired territories of the United States? How did it affect the Mexicans living in those territories?

SUGGESTED ESSAY QUESTIONS

1. Howard Zinn calls the Mexican-American War "Polk's War" and "the war on Mexico," and he indicates that the war was a pretense for taking California and the territory between. Agree or disagree with this position, using material from *Voices* (and *A People's History*).

2. Although most Americans supported the War with Mexico, a great deal of antiwar sentiment arose during this period. What were the sentiments and objectives of antiwar activists? Which of their objections do you find especially persuasive? Which are not persuasive? How and why?

3. Describe the similarities that existed between the War with Mexico and the wars against the Indians.

4. Using examples from *Voices* (or from both books), defend or refute the contention that the war with Mexico was based on both class and racial prejudice.

5. Howard Zinn claims that the war with Mexico was "a war of the American elite against the Mexican elite." Using evidence from *Voices* (or from both books), support or refute this contention.

6. Why was this war so unpopular with American soldiers? Who deserted, and why?

7. What voices of resistance in Chapters 8 in both *Voices* and *A People's History* were of most interest to you? How and why? Which did you find most compelling and why? Least compelling?

8. How do the voices and information in these two chapters improve or change your understanding of the war with Mexico? What information was especially useful? How and why?

SIMULATIONS AND OTHER CREATIVE APPROACHES

1. Design a monument or memorial exhibit to commemorate the war with Mexico. Decide which perspective your memorial will represent—one from the United States or one from Mexico. Be prepared to explain how the symbols you use demonstrate the perspective you choose.

2. Conduct a community discussion to which the following have been invited: Stephen Douglass, Henry David Thoreau, Colonel Ethan Allen Hitchcock, President Miguel Barragán, and President James Polk. The distinguished guests in the audience (class members) must ask one question of any of the speakers.

3. Write a brief children's book on the war with Mexico. Be sure to include both perspectives about the war—the American and the Mexican.

4. Make a thorough investigation of the way in which civil disobedience is discussed in your history textbook—especially in regard to the chapter(s) on the war with Mexico and/or civil rights. Using information from your reading in Zinn's books, revise the textbook portions to present a full and balanced discussion of civil disobedience. If there is no discussion of civil disobedience in your textbook, write an entry and explain where, how, and why it can be integrated into the textbook.

CHAPTER NINE

Slavery and Defiance

In the PBS documentary *Africans in America*, historian Margaret Washington says, "In some ways, when you enslave a person, you enslave yourself." If everyone in pre-Civil War society was victimized by slavery, it should come as no surprise that some Americans, both black and white, resisted the "peculiar institution." Yet these stories of resistance are largely omitted from traditional classroom discussions about slavery in pre-Civil War America.

When resistance is examined in many classroom settings, all too often it is from the perspective of the white abolitionists—those who supported Frederick Douglass and made the Underground Railroad a reality. The voices and actions of ordinary free and enslaved African Americans who defied the system—who risked their lives for freedom—are rarely included in traditional classroom analyses of slavery. "How can their voices be silenced?" students ask. "Why have I never heard of Nat Turner before this class?" These are good questions. Students usually determine that the fear engendered in many Americans tells them that if we learn about and celebrate defiance of the law, and if we question the actions of our historical leaders who made the laws, we are being unpatriotic. Yet, in the spirit of revolutionary America, what could be more patriotic than fighting for freedom?

Document-Based Questions

DAVID WALKER'S *APPEAL*

1. What parts of this appeal do you think were especially inflammatory to Southern slaveholders? Explain.

2. Do you think Walker makes an effective argument in regard to the hypocrisy in the language and promises of the Declaration of Independence? Explain.

3. If you had lived in 1830 when this appeal was published, how would you

have answered Walker's question, "Now, Americans! I ask you candidly, was your sufferings under Great Britain, one hundredth part as cruel and tyrannical as you have rendered ours under you?"

HARRIET A. JACOBS AND JAMES NORCOM

1. What was Nat Turner's "insurrection"? How and why did it affect Harriet Jacobs's life and the lives of other slaves throughout the south?

2. What was the goal of the Reverend Pike's message to his enslaved congregation? What is your response to this message?

3. Why were Jacobs and her friends "amused at brother Pike's gospel teaching"? What are the moral and ethical implications of a minister's endorsement of slavery?

4. How would you respond to James Norcom's statement that Jacobs "absconded from the plantation of my son without any known cause or provocation"? Do you think it is possible that slaveholders truly believed that there were not reasons for the enslaved to run away? Explain.

JAMES R. BRADLEY

1. How does James Bradley feel about being owned by someone who was called "a wonderfully kind master"? How do you think the southern states were able to convince people in the so-called free states that the enslaved were "happy and contented"?

2. Do you agree with Bradley that "there was never a slave who did not long for liberty"? Explain.

3. What does Bradley's letter tell you about the relationship between white and black people in pre-Civil War society?

REVEREND THEODORE PARKER

1. What are Reverend Parker's main objections to the Fugitive Slave Act? How does he think its passage has changed the manner in which the Constitution was interpreted?

2. What did the Reverend Parker mean when he claimed that the Bostonians were "subjects of Virginia"? How does this support the idea of a "slave power" in the South that determines the law for the rest of the nation? Do you think slave power existed? Explain.

3. What does Parker describe as "*deeds* done for liberty"? Do you agree with his statement that when "liberty is the end . . . sometimes peace is not the means towards it"? Explain. What kinds of "deeds for liberty" might be used in today's society? Do you think the Founding Fathers would approve of such deeds?

TWO LETTERS FROM SLAVES

1. By legally defining the enslaved as property, how were slave owners able to justify enslavement?

2. What common complaints do these formerly enslaved men share in regard to their masters? Do you think Henry Bibb would agree with Jermain Wesley Loguen that he pities his former master "from the bottom of my heart"? How do their feelings about their former masters compare and contrast?

3. Do you think that slave masters truly believed that they raised their slaves "as we did our own children"? Explain.

FREDERICK DOUGLASS

1. What are Douglass's objections to celebrating the Fourth of July? What did he mean when he said, "Your high independence only reveals the immeasurable distance between us"?

2. How do you think the Rochester Ladies Anti-Slavery Society responded to Douglass's speech? What do you think would especially resonate with them? To what parts of the speech do you think they may have objected? Explain.

3. Do you agree or disagree with Douglass's statement that "[t]here is not a nation on the earth guilty of practices more shocking and bloody than are the people of the United States, at this very hour"? Explain. What other injustices were going on in the United States in 1852 that could further justify Douglass's statement?

JOHN BROWN'S LAST SPEECH

1. Why do you think large numbers of black and white people did not join in John Brown's struggle?

2. In 1859, most Americans thought that John Brown was a treasonous murderer. Why do you believe such famous Americans as Henry David Thoreau, Ralph Waldo Emerson, and Frederick Douglass thought John Brown was a hero?

3. How does John Brown try to justify his actions? Do you think he is convincing? Why, or why not? What did his death accomplish?

OSBORNE P. ANDERSON

1. What is the purpose of Osborne Anderson's statement about John Brown's raid on Harper's Ferry? Do you think he accomplished his purpose?

2. What do you think accounted for Anderson's observation that "the free blacks [of the] South are much less reliable than the slaves, and infinitely more fearful"?

3. Did Anderson's prediction come true—that the "future historian will record" that John Brown's mistakes at Harper's Ferry "were productive of great good"? How have historians dealt with Harper's Ferry and John Brown?

MARTIN DELANY'S ADVICE

1. Delany describes the passive resistance he would have used had he been a slave. What is passive resistance? How does he describe it? How do other voices in this chapter describe their use of passive resistance? How did slaveholders interpret acts of passive resistance?

2. What advice does Delany offer the freedmen and women? What is it that he most fears that freedmen and freedwomen will do?

3. Who does Delany most mistrust? How and why?

HENRY MCNEAL TURNER

1. For what "crime" is Turner being tried? What rights does Turner demand before the Georgia legislature? Do you think his arguments are convincing? How and why do you think his fellow legislators decided as they did?

2. Three years after the end of the Civil War, the Georgia legislature had been "reconstructed"—yet it found Turner guilty of the "crime" of being black and forced Turner to conclude that freedmen and freedwomen were "strangers in the land of our birth." What does this attitude tell you about the success and failure of reconstruction in Georgia?

3. To what constitutional rights were the freedmen and freedwomen entitled? Why was the state of Georgia able to ignore these rights?

Main Points in *Voices*, Chapter 9, "Slavery and Defiance"

After reading Chapter 9 in *Voices*, students should be encouraged to identify what they believe to be the main points therein. Following are five possible main points.

1. Enslaved African Americans resisted slavery from the moment it was institutionalized into colonial law until it was constitutionally prohibited by the Thirteenth Amendment.

2. The political, economic, and religious nature of southern society, all reinforced the belief that slavery was a benevolent institution as well as one that was endorsed by God.

3. The federal government not only failed to challenge the system of institutionalized slavery created by each Southern state; it also legitimized the system through passage and enforcement of the Fugitive Slave Act.

4. The abolitionist movement consisted of whites and free blacks, all of whom challenged and sometimes defied the laws upholding slavery.

5. While the Thirteenth, Fourteenth, and Fifteenth Amendments promised previously enslaved African Americans their freedom and equality, that promise was negated by the end of Reconstruction.

Main Points in *Voices*, Chapter 9, "Slavery and Defiance," and in *A People's History*, Chapter 9, "Slavery Without Submission, Emancipation Without Freedom"

If your students are also reading *A People's History,* they should be encouraged to identify what they believe to be the main points in Chapter 9 in both books. Following are four additional points to be stressed when *Voices* and *A People's History* are used together.

6. The events before, during, and after the Civil War continue to shape race relations in the United States today.

7. The Emancipation Proclamation declared slaves in the Confederate states still fighting against the Union to be free but failed to free slaves living behind Union lines.

8. The end of institutionalized slavery led to a reconstruction of national politics and economics that was both safe and profitable for the Northern and Southern elite who supported the war.

9. Lincoln signed the Emancipation Proclamation only when many of his supporters began to act against slavery.

General-Discussion Questions for *Voices*

While the following questions are designed for classroom discussion about all the voices read in Chapter 9, they can also be rewritten and included as evaluation tools.

1. What common experiences are recorded in the voices of the enslaved? Do you think all slaves had similar experiences? Explain.

2. Why do you think there were few voices of resistance to slavery among poor southern whites—most of whom had no slaves? Why do you think more poor southern whites did not unite with blacks to attack the plantation system?

3. How were some slaves able to buy their own freedom and/or the freedom of their family members?

4. What does liberty mean to the people whose voices you heard? Do you think liberty meant the same thing to white Americans as it did to the enslaved African Americans? To poor white Americans versus wealthy white Americans? What does liberty mean to? Would you be willing to fight for your liberty? Under what circumstances?

5. What was the Freedman's Bureau? How did it help the newly emancipated African Americans? Did it achieve as much as its creators hoped it would? Explain.

6. Many historians of this period have concluded that the agricultural and industrial foundations of the United States were built largely on the backs of enslaved African Americans. How do the voices in this chapter support or refute this allegation? What is your opinion? Explain.

7. How did the voices in this chapter reinforce any of the five themes listed in "Main Points in *Voices*"?

8. Which of the voices in this chapter did you find most powerful? Least powerful? How and why?

General-Discussion Questions for *Voices* and *A People's History*

These general-discussion questions are additional questions for students who have read chapters 9 in both books. For all questions, discussion must focus on ways the materials in both chapters help students formulate and articulate their answers.

9. How do you think slavery influenced the lives of white people in Southern slave-holding regions?

10. How do you think slavery influenced the lives of white people in the Northern states? What incentives did whites in the North have for joining the abolitionist cause?

11. How and why have some historians tried to downplay or dismiss the effects of slavery?

12. How do Howard Zinn's descriptions of Abraham Lincoln compare and contrast with your previous knowledge about Lincoln?

13. Do you think that Lincoln was being honest when he claimed that, as president, he was legally powerless to abolish slavery? Explain.

14. Why do you think that Congress needed to enact the Thirteenth, Fourteenth, and Fifteenth Amendments? Why wasn't the Thirteenth Amendment sufficient to grant the slaves their freedom and all the rights of citizenship? Did the legal end to slavery and the legal granting of rights to the freedmen and freedwomen bring about their freedom? Why, or why not?

15. Who were the Radical Republicans? What was their political agenda? Were they successful? Explain.

16. What were some of the accomplishments of African Americans and their allies during the era of Reconstruction? Do you think these accomplishments will continue after the end of Reconstruction? Explain.

17. What was the compromise in the so-called Compromise of 1877? Who was involved in the compromise? Who was left out? Who benefited from the compromise?

18. How would you describe the "New South" that emerged after the end of Reconstruction? Do you really think it was new? Explain.

19. Do you agree or disagree with Howard Zinn's assertion that the end of slavery led to a reconstruction of national politics and economics? What were the limits of this reconstruction? Explain.

Evaluation Tools

SUGGESTED ASSIGNMENTS

These assignments can be adapted to meet any classroom need—homework, short- or long-term research projects, individual or group work. The end product should be flexible, depending on teacher interest and student abilities—papers, journals, oral reports, visual aides, and the like.

1. In William Styron's controversial, Pulitzer Prize-winning novel, *The Confessions of Nat Turner* (New York: Random House, 1967), the white

author—an ancestor of Southern slave owners—uses the final confession of Nat Turner as the focus of a biography of the famous African American revolutionary. Using a search engine of choice, learn as much as possible about this book and about Nat Turner. Who was Nat Turner, and what was his rebellion? What are the primary messages of Styron's book? How and why did Turner's rebellion change the lives of white and black people living in the Southern states? After reading some of the reviews of the book when it was published in 1967, why do you think it was so controversial? Why do you think it won a Pulitzer Prize?

2. Research the role that free blacks played in the abolitionist movement. What role did whites play in the movement? What evidence can you find of white and black abolitionists working together? What common bonds of resistance united them? Divided them?

3. Read the full text of the Fugitive Slave Act. What were its major provisions? What were the arguments posed in Congress for and against passage of the act? What states opposed it and why? How did the act benefit slave owners? How was the act resisted? How and why did the Wisconsin Supreme Court challenge the act in 1857? When the Supreme Court heard the case in 1859, how did it decide?

4. Historians who have researched the Ku Klux Klan have pointed to several stages in its evolutionary development. Research the goals and activities of the first Klan that arose after the Civil War, the second Klan that arose during World War I, the third that arose during the civil-rights movement, and the contemporary Klan. How do the goals and activities of each period compare and contrast across time? In particular, how is the contemporary Klan different from those of the past? Do you think the KKK is a terrorist organization? Explain.

5. In his recent book, *The Slave Power* (Baton Rouge: Louisiana State University Press, 2000), historian Leonard L. Richards uses a rich array of primary and secondary resources to document his thesis that the Republicans correctly believed they were losing control over Congress because of the overwhelming influence of a southern Democrat "slave power." Learn more about the so-called slave power. Do you think there is enough evidence to support Richard's thesis? Explain.

6. In 1846, Dred Scott sued for freedom for himself, his wife, and his daugh-

ter. His was but one of over 200 similar cases filed at the St. Louis, Missouri courthouse in the early-to-mid-nineteenth century. In 1857, the Supreme Court handed down its famous decision in *Scott* vs. *Sanford.* What were the facts and the findings of this case? Why were so many cases filed in the St. Louis courthouse? What happened to Scott and his family after the case was decided.

7. In the last two decades, many historians have written about the emergence of a "Lost Cause Argument" that arose in the South after the Civil War. In their book, The Myth of the Lost Cause and Civil War History (Bloomington: Indiana University Press, 2000), historians Gary Gallagher and Alan T. Nolan refute the argument and claim instead that it was more myth than fact. Learn as much as possible about the argument—what its supporters claim to have been the real cause of the war; about the role slavery played in the war; about the reasons the South lost the war; about the symbolism of the Confederate flag; about the role of liberty in the war. Why do you think Gallagher and Nolan call all these a myth? Which side do you support, and why?

8. The slave trade was abolished in the United States in 1808. However, despite the legal end of slave importation, slaves were still bought and sold in North America. Learn as much as possible about the slave trade before and after its abolition. What was the impetus for legally ending the trade? Who supported its abolition and why? How were slaves traded after 1808? Did ending the slave trade change the nature of slavery in North America? How and why?

SUGGESTED ESSAY QUESTIONS

1. Howard Zinn writes, "It would take either a full-scale slave rebellion or a full-scale war" to end slavery (*People's History*, p. 171). Using examples from your reading in Howard Zinn's books, agree or disagree with this statement. Do you think that slavery could have been ended without war? Explain.

2. It has often been argued that slavery was a regional problem, confined largely to the southern states. Using examples from Chapters 2 and 9 in your reading, write an editorial that would appear in a northern abolitionist newspaper in 1860 that either supports or refutes this contention.

3. How does the legacy of slavery continue to affect our society today?

4. Support or refute one of Howard Zinn's primary contentions in this chapter—that the United States government "would never accept an end to slavery by rebellion. It would end slavery only under conditions controlled by whites."

5. What is the message behind the title of Chapter 9 in *A People's History*, "Slavery Without Submission, Emancipation Without Freedom"? Do you agree that the slaves neither submitted to the institution of slavery during its existence nor were they emancipated by its legal termination? Explain.

6. Historian Richard McMurray has argued in his essay, "The War We Never Finished" (*Civil War Times Illustrated*, November/December 1989), that the Civil War was a complex struggle between four groups: Confederates, Unionists, abolitionists, and egalitarians. He argues that by 1877, the first three were victorious and that only the egalitarians truly lost the war. What do you think he means? Learn more about this argument and then think about what you have read in Howard Zinn's books that might support or refute McMurray's position. Do you agree or disagree with McMurray? Explain.

7. What were some of the ways that enslaved African Americans fought for freedom before, during, and after the Civil War? What were some of the ways that whites and blacks worked together to ensure such freedom? What were the ways that whites tried to block that freedom?

8. How and why did the Compromise of 1877 continue to influence the lives of African American men and women through the end of the civil-rights movement? Do you think it still affects race relations in America today? Explain.

9. How did the "New South" of the late nineteenth century compare and contrast with the "Old South" in pre-Civil War America?

10. What voices of resistance in Chapter 9 in both *Voices* and *A People's History* were of most interest to you? How and why? Which did you find most compelling and why? Least compelling?

11. How do the voices and information in this chapter (or these two chapters) improve your understanding of the Revolutionary War? What information was especially useful? How and why?

SIMULATIONS AND OTHER CREATIVE APPROACHES

1. Stage a debate around the topic, "Historical and contemporary nonviolent actions of the Ku Klux Klan (rallies, marches, cross burnings, recruiting in schools, on-campus clubs) should be protected by the First Amendment." Be sure to examine the role fear plays in communities where the KKK may be exercising its First Amendment rights.

2. Have students create a wall map that demonstrates the existence of slavery in the United States before the Civil War. Once the map is completed, have them discuss the following questions: What does the map tell us about the regional spread of slavery in the United States at the time of the war? Does the map add any evidence to the argument that slavery was a national, not a regional, problem? Why, or why not? Where do you think slavery would have spread next if the South had won the war? Using the answers to this discussion, as well as any other questions and answers that the students raise during the course of this assignment, have a small group of student volunteers take the map and the information it generated to an elementary classroom and conduct a similar discussion.

3. Conduct a series of conversations that would be held in several communities in the early 1850s after passage of the Fugitive Slave Act. Divide students into five communities, each of which would have the following representatives that will discuss the ramifications of the Act on their lives, as well as why they do or do not support its provisions: a wealthy white southern plantation owner, a middle class northern white abolitionist, an enslaved African American male, a free northern African American woman, a northern worker who wants to immigrate to the west, and a poor white southern farmer. Students should script and then hold their conversations.

4. Assign a creative writing project that consists of the following two components: a letter written by a white northern abolitionist to the Supreme Court after its decision in the Dred Scott case; and a letter written by Dred Scott to the Supreme Court after the decision.

CHAPTER TEN

Civil War and Class Conflict

"Class conflict?" many students ask, "What does the Civil War have to do with class conflict?" Indeed, among the thousands of books that dissect the Civil War from almost every angle, most fail to examine what was happening *within* the divided nations during the four years the two sides waged war upon one another. Traditional texts unravel the causes and consequences of the war, the military battles, and the multiple tragedies of the conflict without looking at what Howard Zinn calls "The other Civil War"—the class conflict fought by the poor who lived in the industrializing North and by those who lived in the impoverished rural South.

By including the voices of class resistance, a more complete story emerges about the lives of ordinary Americans in the period 1861–1865. More importantly, their voices highlight the continuous thread of class conflict that arose in colonial America, became a permanent part of the political, economic, and social fabric of post-Revolutionary America, played a powerful role in the shaping of nineteenth and twentieth century America, and continues to influence the lives of Americans in the twenty-first century.

Document-Based Questions

AN EYEWITNESS ACCOUNT OF THE FLOUR RIOT

1. The event recorded here occurred twenty-four years before the Civil War. What warning signs would the reader have about how class tensions in New York City might eventually erupt into greater violence?

2. According to the eyewitness, what are the major grievances of "the mob in Dey Street"? Who were "the infatuated multitude" participating in the riot?

3. Why you think the eyewitness presents an unsympathetic portrayal of the rioters? What are your sympathies? Do you think the rioters had a "just" cause? Were their actions justifiable? Explain.

HINTON ROWAN HELPER

1. Why do you think Hinton Rowan Helper's book, *The Impending Crisis of the South*, was banned by some southern states?

2. How does this statement illustrate Helper's critique of class conflict in the pre-Civil War South: "The lords of the lash are not only absolute masters of the blacks, who are bought and sold, and driven about like so many cattle, but they are also the oracles and arbiters of all non-slaveholding whites, whose freedom is merely nominal, and whose unparalleled illiteracy and degradation is purposely and fiendishly perpetuated"?

3. How could it benefit slave owners to claim that "the free States are quite sterile and unproductive, and that they are mainly dependent on us for breadstuffs and other provisions" and that "our Northern brethren . . . are dependent on us for the necessaries of life"? Was this true? Explain.

"MECHANIC"

1. How do the words of this unknown writer echo those of Helper?

2. What were the promises made by the Confederacy to the ordinary people before the war? How does the author believe they are being ignored?

3. Do you think the author provides enough evidence to support his statement that "the poor soldiers . . . are fighting the rich man's fight"?

JOEL TYLER HEADLEY

1. What were the grievances of the draft resisters? Do you think they were legitimate? Why, or why not?

2. Joel Headley variously describes the draft resisters as "gangs," a "wild, savage, and heterogeneous-looking mass," and a "heterogeneously weaponed army." How do his words shape his story? How do you think he might define the word "gang"? How does his description of gangs compare and contrast with the contemporary understanding of urban gangs?

3. At one point in his account, Headley notes that the rioters sent "terror into the hearts" of families who were in a building that was set on fire. In the 1860s, how, when, and by whom might a riot be considered an act of terrorism?

FOUR DOCUMENTS BY DISAFFECTED SOUTHERNERS

1. What are the common wartime grievances in these four documents? Do they differ between women and men?

2. Do you think the actions of the bread rioters in Savannah are more acceptable during times of war than they would be in during times of peacetime poverty? How and why?

3. Who are the "truly worthy deserving poor" written about in the News editorial about the bread rioters? Who do you think the author might describe as the unworthy, undeserving poor? How is this distinction an example of class division in Southern society?

4. How is the "To Go, or Not To Go" document similar to the "To Be, or Not To Be" soliloquy in William Shakespeare's play *Hamlet*? Why do you think the author made this comparison? Is it effective? How would you answer his question, "Would patriotism pay my debts, when dead"? What do you think he decides to do—or not to do?

5. How are the "wants" of the women in Miller County similar to the needs of the women of Savannah?

6. What grievances does the author in the *Columbus Sun* editorial harbor toward "men of wealth"?

J. A. DACUS

1. What does J. A. Dacus believe to be the "potent cause of the Great Strikes"?

2. What was the International Association of Workingmen? Why did it "cause so much anxiety to the governments of Europe"?

3. Knowing that you would have to face government reprisals—arrest, injury, or even death—would you have supported the railroad strike? Why, or why not?

Main Points in *Voices*, Chapter 10,
"Civil War and Class Conflict"

After reading Chapter 10 in *Voices*, students should be encouraged to identify what they believe to be the main points therein. Following are four possible main points.

1. Between 1861 and 1865, the United States experienced not only a Civil War between the northern and southern states, but also class conflict between the rich and the poor on both sides of the conflict.

2. Many poor in America saw the Civil War as a rich man's battle but a poor man's fight.

3. Temporary unity during the Civil War was artificially created by politicians who enforced the shaky truce with military might.

4. When the Civil War was over, the class and racial divisions that had long been a part of the American landscape reemerged in new forms.

Main Points in *Voices*, Chapter 10, "Civil War and
Class Conflict," and in *A People's History*, Chapter 10,
"The Other Civil War"

If your students are also reading *A People's History*, they should be encouraged to identify what they believe to be the main points in Chapter 10 in both books. Following are four additional points to be stressed when *Voices* and *A People's History* are used together.

5. Prior to the Civil War, many Americans were disenfranchised and disillusioned with a system in which they believed they had little social, political, or economic stake.

6. During this era, big business sought to achieve economic stability by decreasing competition, organizing business interests, and moving toward monopoly.

7. Before, during, and after the Civil War, the working men and women of America resisted exploitation by organizing and carrying out strikes.

8. Congressional and federal court actions during this period supported the growth of largely unregulated capitalistic development at the expense of working men and women.

General-Discussion Questions for *Voices*

While the following questions are designed for classroom discussion about all the voices read in Chapter 10, they can also be rewritten and included as evaluation tools.

1. What are the similarities among these voices? How might those in the upper class have responded to these voices?

2. How could there be, as Helper states, "white victims of slavery"? Who were these victims?

3. What is an oligarchy? Can you find other sources in this chapter or elsewhere that may support Helper's belief that a "slave-driving oligarchy" ruled the South? What role did such an oligarchy play in bringing the South into the Civil War? What role did it play in southern class conflict?

4. Do you think that such incidents as the Flour Riot of 1837 were typical within large cities in pre-Civil War America? Explain.

5. During the Civil War, men on both sides of the conflict were able to buy their way out of the draft. What are the implications of this practice? How do you think this contributed to class divisions throughout the war?

6. What evidence of class and racial conflict do you hear in these voices?

7. What "growing costs of the war" were ordinary people forced to shoulder? Do you think you might lift your voice in or commit your actions to the cause of resistance if you were forced to assume such wartime costs? How and why?

8. Several of these entries saw speculators as practitioners of "extortion." How do they define speculation? Do you believe speculators were extortionists? How and why?

9. What social conflicts remained after the end of the Civil War?

10. How are the problems of the railroad workers in 1877 similar to the grievances expressed by those who resisted during the Civil War?

11. How did the voices in this chapter reinforce any of the five themes listed in "Main Points in *Voices*"?

12. Which of the voices in this chapter did you find most powerful? Least powerful? How and why?

General-Discussion Questions for *Voices* and *A People's History*

These general-discussion questions are additional questions for students who have read Chapter 10 in both books. For all questions, discussion must focus on ways the materials in both chapters help students formulate and articulate their answers.

13. What is the significance of the title in Chapter 10 of *A People's History*, "The Other Civil War"? How do the entries in Chapter 10 of *Voices* reinforce the significance of the title?

14. How do the grievances expressed by the farmers in the Anti-Renters movement echo those expressed by the resisters you read about in Chapter 10 in *Voices*?

15. "Mechanic" decries the fact that equality is denied ordinary Southerners in the Confederacy through "disenfranchisement." Dorr's Rebellion in Rhode Island was also a response to disenfranchisement. How were people throughout the Union and the Confederacy disenfranchised? How could lawmakers justify such laws?

16. Do you think the violent actions of any resisters you read about in these chapters were justifiable given their circumstances? How and why? Do you think it is ever justifiable to use violence to change unjust laws? If so, in what circumstances?

17. How did the federal and state governments help corporations during the period described in Chapter 10?

18. What common grievances did workers share throughout the period described in Chapter 10? Do workers continue to have any of these grievances today?

19. On page 226 of *A People's History*, historian David Montgomery is quoted as noting that class conflicts in nineteenth-century America "were as fierce

as any known to the industrial world." What evidence can you find in the readings to support this claim?

20. How does Howard Zinn account for the huge increase in strikes and labor organizing during the Civil War?

21. What was the role of women in labor reform? What were their accomplishments? What impediments did they face that were both similar to and different from those faced by men in the labor movement?

22. How was the emergence of the two-party system an "ingenious mode of control," as Howard Zinn asserts?

23. How did big business during this era attempt to achieve economic stability? Was it successful? Explain.

24. How did the economic crisis of 1857 contribute to class conflict? To the outbreak of the Civil War?

25. How was the Civil War "one of the first instances in the world of modern warfare"?

26. How and why did Marxism become more attractive to some of the working men and women in the period before, during, and immediately after the Civil War?

Evaluation Tools

SUGGESTED ASSIGNMENTS

These assignments can be adapted to meet any classroom need—homework, short- or long-term research projects, individual or group work. The end product should be flexible, depending on teacher interest and student abilities—papers, journals, oral reports, visual aides, and the like.

1. While watching the movie *The Gangs of New York*, pay particularly close attention to its portrayal of the New York Draft Riots of 1863. Then using information from Chapter 10 as well as other sources at your disposal, answer the following: How does the film's interpretation of the riots compare and contrast with what you have read? Why did some Irish people get

so caught up in the riots? Who were the primary victims of the riots? How was this both a class and a race riot? Why do you think most traditional textbooks do not discuss the Draft Riots?

2. Find out more about Hinton Rowan Helper and his book, *The Impending Crisis in the South* (Reprint Services Corp., 1857). What was his background? Was he a Southerner or Northerner? Republican or Democrat? What was his purpose in writing the book? How was it received in the North? Did he receive *any* acclaim in the South for his book? How accurate was his research? How accurate were his predictions?

3. Learn more about urban riots that occurred before, during, and immediately after the Civil War. In what cities were they most prevalent? How were the riots similar and dissimilar? In what ways are these riots that took place over 140 years ago similar to and different from urban riots in the late twentieth and early twenty-first centuries?

4. Discover more about the labor movement that arose during and immediately after the Civil War. How and why did it arise? What were the goals and achievements of labor activists? Failures? How powerful were the unions? Why do you think the government was so threatened by the growth of unions? How did the government work to defeat the power of the unions? Did much public sympathy exist for labor strikes? How and why?

5. Examine a traditional history book's treatment of labor struggles in 1877. How does it compare and contrast with the descriptions in *A People's History* and the documents in *Voices*?

6. Explore the origins and evolution of the patroonship system in the Hudson River Valley. How did the system exacerbate class tensions? What were the immediate causes of the Anti-Renter movement? What were its short- and long-term consequences? What was the cause of its demise? Do you think such movements still exist in the United States? Explain.

7. Research the origin and growth of the Molly Maguires. Who were its members? What were their goals and accomplishments? Why were they such a threat to mine owners? What led to their demise? How were they similar to and different from other labor movements during the time?

8. Find out more about the Supreme Court case *Luther* v. *Borden*. How does this decision establish what Howard Zinn claims was the "essentially con-

servative nature of the Supreme Court"? What portions of the actual decision reinforce this conservative nature? What are some other ways in which Congress and the courts during this period support and promote the capitalist development of the nation—usually at the expense of the working man and woman?

9. Examine the role and prevalence of disease in the rapidly urbanizing areas of the United States prior to and during the Civil War. What diseases were most common? Most deadly? Why were they so difficult to contain? What did the medical community know about the diseases? How was the spread and treatment of disease another example of class conflict?

SUGGESTED ESSAY QUESTIONS

1. Support or refute Howard Zinn's primary contention in this/these chapter(s) that the class conflict that had been brewing in the United States since its inception did not disappear during the Civil War.

2. Some historians have argued that the Civil War was the rich man's battle but the poor man's fight. How does what you read in this/these chapter(s) support that argument? What is your position? Explain.

3. In his account, Headley notes that the rioters sent "terror into the hearts" of families who were in a building that was set on fire. In Dacus's account of the 1877 railroad strike, he mentions unions that "caused a thrill of astonishment and terror to fall upon the urban populations of the country." In the late nineteenth century, how, when, and by whom might a riot or strike be considered an act of terrorism? Would these same considerations apply in the twenty-first century? Explain.

4. How did learning about the voices of resistance before, during, and after the Civil War give you a more complete and balanced understanding of the years between 1861 and 1877?

5. In the years before the Civil War, the famous orator Daniel Webster wrote, "The great object of government is the protection of property at home, and respect and renown abroad." How do you think the ordinary authors of the documents in Chapter 10 of *Voices* might have responded to this statement? How does this "great object" of the mid-nineteenth century compare and contrast with the "great object" of the United States government today?

6. In your opinion, why did the federal government take the owners' side during labor disputes?

7. Howard Zinn quotes the historian David Montgomery as writing that in reality, the class conflicts of nineteenth-century United States "were as fierce as any known to the industrial world." Support or refute this statement.

8. What voices of resistance in Chapter 10 in both *Voices* and *A People's History* were of most interest to you? How and why? Which did you find most compelling and why? Least compelling?

9. Using examples from both chapters, support or refute this statement: "on the eve of the Civil War it was money and profit, not the movement against slavery, that was uppermost in the priorities of the men who ran the country" (*People's History*, p. 220).

10. How do the voices and information in these two chapters improve your understanding of how American was affected by the Civil War? What information was especially useful? How and why?

11. Explain how the voices and events in these two chapters illustrate Howard Zinn's statement, "Jackson was the first President to master the liberal rhetoric—to speak for the common man." Do you agree or disagree with his statement? Do you think this political innovation benefited the working men and women of America? Explain.

SIMULATIONS AND OTHER CREATIVE APPROACHES

1. Stage a town-hall meeting that takes place in New York shortly after the Flour Riot of 1837. Invite a panel of four eyewitnesses to attend and to discuss their role in the riot and their perception of liberty: one of the persons in the mob who was arrested; one of the shop owners whose property was destroyed; a police officer at the scene of the crime; and the mayor of New York City. Allow each to explain their perspective to the audience in three to five minutes. When the panelists are finished, the audience can make comments and ask questions.

2. Design a creative cover and dust jacket for a book you have been hired to write on the topics included in "The Other Civil War." What will be the title of your new book? On the jacket, you need to write a brief description

of your book's contents. Remember, you want to sell this book—you need to make the book's cover inviting and the narrative intriguing so that the reader will want to buy and read your book!

3. Write a new Declaration of Independence for the centennial celebration of 1876. Write it from the perspective of an African American, a working man or woman in the industrial North, a recently arrived immigrant, or a poor white farmer in the rural South.

4. Write a letter home to your family in Ireland that describes your voyage to America in 1845, your reception upon arrival, and your life in the city during the ten years you have been in the United States.

CHAPTER ELEVEN

Strikers and Populists in the Gilded Age

In 1872, two neighboring families in Hartford, Connecticut, shared dinner. As they argued over the quality of popular fiction, the two men concluded that they could write a better novel than any currently popular one. Although neither had ever written a novel, together Mark Twain and Charles Dudley Warner co-wrote *The Gilded Age: A Tale of Today*, in which they satirized the business and politics of their day. The novel eventually gave a name to the Gilded Age—the historical period between 1860 and 1890 characterized by the sharp contrasts in society, in which America's surface gleamed with gold while camouflaging the cheap base metal underneath.

Such symbolism was hardly lost on the ordinary people who lived through the Gilded Age and who experienced tremendous hardships and losses. Whether they lived in the rapidly industrializing cities where they had few services and even fewer amenities, or in small rural communities where they were victimized by grueling poverty, their hardships were similar. And while they got poorer, the rich were getting richer. The inequities that flourished in this seemingly gilded environment fueled a new generation of struggles.

Document-Based Questions

HENRY GEORGE

1. What is the message in Henry George's statement, "The vice, the crime, the ignorance, the meanness born of poverty, poison, so to speak, the very air which rich and poor alike must breathe"? Do you agree or disagree?

2. Do you agree or disagree with George's central point, that "the great majority of those who suffer from poverty are poor not from their own particular faults, but because of conditions imposed by society at large"? Do you think the same could be said about the poor today? Explain.

3. What did George mean when he wrote that "there is no natural reason why we should not all be rich"? Do you agree or disagree? Explain.

AUGUST SPIES

1. Do you think August Spies presented a powerful self-defense? How could it have been more powerful? Why do you think the court sentenced Spies to death?

2. From what Spies says, do you think he was convicted on circumstantial evidence? How and why? What do you think might have been the most persuasive testimonies leading to his conviction?

3. What is the "subterranean fire" that Spies declares the court cannot put out? Do you think he was correct?

ANONYMOUS, "RED-HANDED MURDERER"

1. Were the actions of the African American resisters legal? If so, how was the government's response justified?

2. Why were those in power so enraged about the fact that white laborers helped and harbored the black laborers? Is this the first time in American history that whites and blacks united in order to bring about change?

3. What is your reaction to this report?

REVEREND ERNEST LYON, ET AL.

1. How could African Americans be disenfranchised just over twenty years after passage of the Thirteenth, Fourteenth, and Fifteenth Amendments? How were they victimized by Ku Klux Klan (KKK) terror just eighteen years after the Civil Rights Act of 1875 was passed?

2. Why do you believe so few white persons rose to the defense of African Americans and denounced the activities of the KKK?

3. Why does the author criticize members of the Democratic Party?

MARY ELIZABETH LEASE

1. What is a monopoly? How does Lease explain that monopoly has become "a master" over "the common people of this country [who] are slaves"?

2. How would abolishing the national banks and home foreclosure or receiving the power to make loans directly from the government empower rural "slaves"?

3. Why does the author believe that the Farmers' Alliance movement is not "a passing episode in politics"? What proof does she offer to back up her belief?

THE OMAHA PLATFORM OF THE PEOPLE'S PARTY

1. Why are the people "demoralized"?

2. What is the "vast conspiracy against mankind [that] has been organized on two continents"?

3. Do you think the platform provides a realistic plan to "restore the government of the republic to the hands of 'the plain people' with whose class it originated"? Explain.

REVEREND J. L. MOORE

1. What arguments does Reverend Moore use to show the similarities among white and black labor interests? Why do you think more whites did not join in such an alliance?

2. How is Moore's entry similar to the anonymous report of the riot in Louisiana and to the Reverend Ernest Lyon's statement about KKK violence?

3. How did Congress fail to provide "protection at the ballot box" for African Americans?

IDA B. WELLS-BARNETT

1. How does Wells-Barnett account for the acceptance and maintenance of lynching practices in the United States?

2. What does she mean when she writes, "Masks have long since been thrown aside and the lynching of the present day take place in broad daylight"? Do you think one type of terror is worse than the other? Explain.

3. What is the "crime of outrage" that Wells-Barnett exposes? How do you think the white public responded to this article—and especially this particular accusation—which was published by a black woman in 1893?

STATEMENT FROM THE PULLMAN STRIKERS

1. How did unions during this period provide their members with hope?

2. What are the worker's grievances? How do they support their contention that "Pullman, both the man and the town, is an ulcer on the body politic"?

3. Why would Pullman decrease wages "from 30 to 70 percent"? Do you agree with the strikers that "preposterous profits have been made"? Is this analogous to twenty-first-century grievances in some sectors of the American working community? Explain.

EDWARD BELLAMY

1. How does the society Edward Bellamy envisioned for the year 2000 compare and contrast with society as you know it in the early twenty-first century?

2. Can you envision a time as described by Dr. Leete, in which officials would no longer be "under a constant temptation to misuse their power for the private profit of themselves or others"? Explain.

3. Do you feel Bellamy has created the hope for a utopian society? Do you like the society he describes? Would you want to live in such a society?

Main Points in *Voices*, Chapter 11, "Strikers and Populists in the Gilded Age"

After reading Chapter 11 in *Voices*, students should be encouraged to identify what they believe to be the main points therein. Following are four possible main points.

1. By the late nineteenth century, many working-class Americans believed that instead of protecting their life and liberty, the government deliberately sought to deprive them of their rights in order to protect the vested interests of the wealthy.

2. Although the Populist movement of the late nineteenth century was short-lived, its political influence lasted well into the twentieth century.

3. Working-class people—white and black, rural and urban—suffered at the hands of corporate industrial and agricultural interests during the Gilded Age.

4. Federal, state, and local governments devised many divide-and-conquer policies that discouraged workers from uniting.

Main Points in *Voices*, Chapter 11, "Strikers and Populists in the Gilded Age," and in *A People's History*, Chapter 11, "Robber Barons and Rebels"

If your students are also reading *A People's History*, they should be encouraged to identify what they believe to be the main points in Chapter 11 in both books. Following are five additional points to be stressed when *Voices* and *A People's History* are used together.

5. Technological innovations of the late nineteenth century dramatically changed the urban and rural workplace.

6. The massive immigration of different ethnic groups during this period contributed to "the fragmentation of the working-class" (*People's History*, p. 265).

7. The Horatio Alger "rags to riches" story was largely an American myth.

8. Throughout the Gilded Age, industries comprised of "shrewd, efficient businessmen" (*People's History*, p. 257) built empires, destroyed competition, maintained high prices, kept wages low, and used government subsidies—all the while becoming the first beneficiaries of the "welfare state."

9. During the Gilded Age, government, business, churches, and schools worked to control the ideas and actions of working-class Americans.

General-Discussion Questions for *Voices*

While the following questions are designed for classroom discussion about all the voices read in Chapter 11, they can also be rewritten and included as evaluation tools.

1. How do the voices in this chapter challenge the myth of individual blame for poverty?

2. What is wage slavery? How do some of the entries in this chapter reinforce the idea of wage slavery? Do you see a difference in these entries between white and black wage slavery?

3. What is anarchism? Why were corporate and governmental powers so worried about the growth of anarchist thought toward the turn of the century?

4. How and why was it dangerous to belong to a union during the Gilded Age?

5. What is lynching? Why do you think it was most popular between the 1880s and the 1920s? Do you think lynching still occurs today?

6. Do you think late-nineteenth and early-twentieth-century activities of the Ku Klux Klan were acts of terrorism? Did the federal, state, or local governments classify them as such? Why, or why not?

7. What similarities are shared among the voices of urban whites and urban and rural blacks in this chapter? How are they different from each other?

8. What were the reasons that rural men and women joined the Farmers' Alliance?

9. Howard Zinn mentions a "betrayal of the former slaves by the national administration in 1877." What was this betrayal? How did it lead to violence, especially lynching violence, in the next five decades?

10. What is the "mob spirit" Ida B. Wells-Barnett discusses in her essay? How it is described by and used against other voices in this chapter? Is this spirit still alive in America? Explain.

General-Discussion Questions for *Voices* and *A People's History*

These general-discussion questions are additional questions for students who have read Chapter 11 in both books. For all questions, discussion must focus on ways the materials in both chapters help students formulate and articulate their answers.

11. What is the significance of the Chapter 11 title in *A People's History*, "Robber Barons and Rebels"?

12. These chapters illustrate many ways in which the government benefited the wealthy. If Howard Zinn is correct, what explains this behavior? Does the government continue to benefit the wealthy today? Explain.

13. Why was it important during the industrializing period for working-class children to learn "obedience to authority" (*People's History*, p. 263) in school? What behaviors are taught in schools today?

14. How did large numbers of new immigrants arriving from southern and eastern Europe alter urban life and work patterns in the United States?

15. What are some of the demands that working people and unions made of corporate owners?

16. What tactics did workers and unions use to try to better their working conditions and living wages?

17. Why did Eugene Debs become a socialist?

18. Debs wrote, "Money constitutes no proper basis of civilization." What did he mean? What is the "basis of civilization" today? In your opinion, what should be the "basis of civilization"?

19. Do you think it was possible that either the Republican or Democratic parties could have become parties of true reform for farmers and workers of this period? Why, or why not?

20. What role did the railroad corporations and corporate owners play in the development of the late-nineteenth-century United States? What price did working-class Americans pay for their success?

21. What is a welfare state? Do you agree with Howard Zinn that corporations were the first beneficiaries of the welfare state?

22. What reforms took place during the Gilded Age? What was the impetus behind such reforms?

23. How was the Supreme Court "doing its bit for the ruling elite" (*People's History*, p. 260) during this period? How did the other two branches of government help?

24. What problems did immigrants face upon arrival in the United States during the Gilded Age? Which groups were most and least successful and why?

Evaluation Tools

SUGGESTED ASSIGNMENTS

These assignments can be adapted to meet any classroom need—homework, short- or long-term research projects, individual or group work. The end product should be flexible, depending on teacher interest and student abilities—papers, journals, oral reports, visual aides, and the like.

1. In the late nineteenth century, Horatio Alger published over 118 novels in book form and another 280 novels in magazine format. All the young heroes in all the books have remarkably similar characteristics. Read one of Alger's books or passages from several. What central theme in these books gave rise to what many have called the Horatio Alger myth? Why do you think this myth became so popular in the early twentieth century? Do you believe that all Americans in the late nineteenth century had an equal chance to become wealthy? Do you believe people today have such an opportunity? Use socioeconomic facts and statistics from the late nineteenth and late twentieth centuries to support your answer.

2. Using a wide variety of primary documents, learn more about the antilynching movement. What efforts did such people as Ida B. Wells-Barnett make on behalf of the antilynching movement? What do you think were the most and least persuasive arguments for a federal antilynching law? Why do you think there was so much resistance to a federal law against lynching? Who led the fight against such a measure?

3. Using the Internet, primary documents, and secondary resources, find out more about the company town of Pullman. What did George Pullman

envision for the town when it was built? What rules and regulations governed the town? In what way did Pullman feel these to be beneficial? How did the workers come to see them as oppressive? What led to the 1894 strike against Pullman? Do you think the workers had the right to strike? How and why did the federal government break the strike? Do you think this an appropriate use of federal troops? Explain your answers.

4. In 1892, Francis Bellamy—a well-known Baptist minister and Edward Bellamy's cousin—was asked to design the National Educational Association's (NEA) National Columbus Public Schools Celebration. He created a program that focused on a flag-raising ceremony and a flag salute. After reading the "Official Programme" in the September 8, 1892, issue of *The Youth's Companion* and the original flag salute, trace the origins and use of that first salute. Then examine the ways in which it has changed over the past hundred years. Learn more about the Supreme Court case on the flag salute that was decided in 2004. How do you think Francis Bellamy— a man of the Gilded Age—might have responded to the ongoing debate about the flag salute in contemporary society?

5. Third parties played a big role in the politics of the latter part of the nineteenth century. Learn as much as possible about these new parties and their political platforms. Why did they attract a following? Then research the growth of third parties from the turn of the twentieth century forward. When were they most influential, and why? What are the largest third parties of the twenty-first century? What are their political goals and accomplishments? Are there any that you might support? Explain. Do you think casting your vote for a third-party presidential candidate in a tight race is "wasting your vote"? Defend your answer.

6. Conduct biographical research on one of the robber barons of this era. Once you learn as much as possible about his upbringing, involvement in corporate America, and the manner in which he accumulated and maintained his wealth, learn how his endeavors influenced workers in his industrial sphere. Search for primary documents that describe how his workers responded to the rules and regulations of his industry. After learning as much as possible about the robber baron, describe how his particular biography does or does not fit the description of "Robber Barons and Rebels" in Chapter 11 of *A People's History*.

7. Read the presidential inaugural addresses given between 1877 and 1901. What similarities do they contain in terms of support for or against corporate control? What similar promises, if any, do they make to working-class Americans? Which do you find most and least compelling? Explain. Which are most and least reflective of Gilded Age values? Explain.

8. Beginning in the 1870s, corporate lawyers argued that corporations were not "artificial persons" but were instead "natural persons," with the same rights as persons. With such status, they hoped, corporations would gain a great deal of leverage against legal restraint. In 1886, in *Santa Clara County* v. *Southern Pacific Railroad Company*, the Supreme Court gave corporations all the rights of "natural persons." Research this case, being certain to learn about its origins, the controversy over the decision, and the consequences of this decision for the next hundred years. Do you think corporations ought to have personhood? Explain.

9. Learn more about the Haymarket Square Riot. Using primary documents written from the perspective of the workers, the police, the government, and the corporations, write a journalistic report for your local newspaper to commemorate the 120-year anniversary of the riot in 2006. Be sure to explain all sides of the conflict, as well as the short- and long-term consequences on the national labor movement as a whole and the movement in Chicago.

10 Learn more about unions in the United States today. How are their philosophies, goals, and actions similar to and different from their counterparts that operated more than a hundred years ago? What historical factors do you think account for decreases in union membership and in union power? Which unions continue to be strong in the twenty-first century and why? Which are weaker and why?

11 Learn more about the Pinkertons. How and why did they originate during the Gilded Age? What was their purpose? Who used them and why? How did their use of private security differ from the government's use of militias? Are they still in existence today? How and why are they used? What conficts between private and public security exist in the twenty-first century?

12. Learn more about Alexander Berkman and his plot to kill Henry Clay Frick. Who was Berkman? How and why did he become an anarchist? What led him to believe that killing Frick would help other workers? What

were the consequences of his failed attempt to kill Frick? What did Berkman contribute to the growing anarchist movement? Why do you think the movement was never able to gain a huge number of supporters in the United States?

SUGGESTED ESSAY QUESTIONS

1. Henry George argues that a "crime of poverty" existed in America during the Gilded Age. What was this crime? Provide examples from George, the other authors in Chapter 11 in *Voices*, and Howard Zinn in *A People's History* to support this statement. Might the description still be applicable to American society today? Explain.

2. In her speech of 1890, Mary Elizabeth Lease declared, "This is a nation of inconsistencies." Support or refute her declaration, using evidence from the readings to back up your position.

3. It has been argued by many historians that lynchings and Ku Klux Klan activities were tolerated at best and actively encouraged at worst by those in power in order to reinforce the status quo. What does this claim mean? How do the voices in your reading reinforce this belief?

4. When the Pullman strikers delivered their message to the American Railway Union in 1894, they began their speech by declaring, "We struck at Pullman because we were without hope." Describe how the hopes and dreams of others whose voices we heard in the readings echo this sentiment. Do you think that at the end of the nineteenth century there was more reason for hope? Explain.

5. In "Robber Barons and Rebels," Howard Zinn writes that the United States government was behaving almost exactly as Karl Marx had predicted by "pretending neutrality to maintain order, but serving the interests of the rich" (*People's History*, p. 258). Use examples from both chapters to support this contention. Do you agree or disagree with Zinn? Explain.

6. Describe the demands that working people and unions made of corporate owners during the Gilded Age. What tactics did workers and unions use to try to better their working conditions and wages during this era? How did the corporations and government respond to their demands and tactics? What did the workers achieve?

7. Most textbooks refer to this period as the Gilded Age. Using examples from your reading, defend the use of this phrase to describe the era. Then create another phrase for the era and defend its use with examples from the readings.

8. Using examples from the reading, support or refute Howard Zinn's contention that late-nineteenth- and early-twentieth-century corporations were the "first beneficiaries of the 'welfare state.'" Do you think twenty-first-century corporations continue to benefit in a similar manner? Explain.

9. Describe how the three branches of the federal government helped the ruling elite at the expense of the working-class during the Gilded Age.

10. Using examples from the reading, defend or refute Joel Spring's statement in *Education and the Rise of the Corporate State*, "The development of a factory-like system in the nineteenth-century schoolroom was not accidental."

11. Using examples from the reading, defend or refute Howard Zinn's assertion that the massive immigration of different ethnic groups during this period contributed to "the fragmentation of the working-class."

12. Describe what was happening in rural America during the last three decades of the nineteenth century. Who were the robber barons and rebels of rural America?

SIMULATIONS AND OTHER CREATIVE APPROACHES

1. Imagine that you are an eighteen-year-old male or female laborer working in a textile mill during the Gilded Age. You have heard rumors of a strike, and you have been considering joining a union. If you lose your job or if you are arrested, your family will suffer. Write a weeklong diary in which you describe your working conditions, your options for change, your feelings about corporate management, and your concerns about your possible choices. Then describe the final choices you make, being sure to make your reasons clear.

2. Make a drawing of the United States' "pyramid of wealth" that shows the "skillful terracing" designed to "create separate levels of oppression" as Howard Zinn describes at the beginning of "Robber Barons and Rebels."

3. Write a short story about a poor working-class teenage immigrant in

America today in which you describe her or his hopes and dreams for the
future, as well as her or his fears about impediments to such dreams. Then
compare and contrast these hopes, dreams, experiences, and accomplishments with those experienced by the young people in Horatio Alger's rags-
to-riches stories.

4. Write a letter to your local city council in which you ask the council to
   consider passing a resolution demanding an end to granting local corporations the rights to corporate personhood. In your letter, be sure to describe
   the history and abuses of corporate personhood. Draw your model resolution upon the efforts of a few of the over a hundred communities around
   the nation that by the year 2000 had denounced corporate personhood in
   their municipal and county legislative bodies.

5. Stage a town meeting in which you have invited Mark Twain to speak.
   Members of the community (all the students in the class) have come prepared with questions about Twain's beliefs related to political, social, and
   economic conflict in the late nineteenth century. Stage the question and
   answers.

CHAPTER TWELVE

The Expansion of the Empire

From the first days of English settlement, the boundaries of the New World were shaped by expansionist policies that pushed out the Indians, drove out the French and the Spanish, and eventually overwhelmed the Mexicans. When we examine foreign policy from this perspective, it is clear that the late nineteenth century represented, not a revolutionary departure from past policies, but an evolutionary shift. How else can we explain the three international wars and the untold number of wars between the colonists and the Indians that preceded the American Revolution among "the 103 military interventions in other countries between 1798 and 1895"?

Despite the widespread support for "progress" surrounding the quest for empire, many Americans spoke out against the shortsighted goals of expansionist, interventionist, and imperialistic policymakers. Without these voices, students may inaccurately believe that expanding the empire was a universally accepted and supported goal of all Americans. Our goal, then, is to divest our students of this mythical belief and to introduce them to the eloquent voices of resistance to empire.

Document-Based Questions

CALIXTO GARCIA

1. What are General Garcia's complaints? Do you think they are legitimate? How do you think the United States government justified its actions in regard to General Garcia?

2. What is your impression of Garcia and his followers? How and why were the descriptions of uncivilized, savage, and barbarian applied to them?

3. Why would the victorious United States government reappoint the same Spanish authorities who had been in Cuba prior to the revolution?

LEWIS H. DOUGLASS

1. Why did some African Americans oppose the presidency and policies of William McKinley?

2. To what and to whom is Lewis H. Douglass referring when he writes about "that section of the country from which this administration accepts dictation and to the tastes of which the President, undoubtedly, caters"? How do the voices in other chapters of this book reinforce this assertion?

3. To what governmental hypocrisy does Douglass refer in this document? Do you agree? Explain.

THE ATLANTA, GEORGIA, A.M.E. CHURCH

1. Do you agree with the author that blacks should not enter the army because they have no social, economic, or political stake in the United States?

2. Why would "a Cuban from Havana" be "compelled to ride" in a Jim Crow car? What was his reaction to segregation?

3. Why does the author view the flag as a "miserable dirty rag"?

I. D. BARNETT, ET AL.

1. I.D. Barnett notes that his people have suffered, "since your accession to office." Given what you know about the Jim Crow South, was life more difficult under McKinley than under previous presidents? Explain.

2. What is the author's grievance with the administration in terms of Cuba?

3. How is the hypocrisy to which I.D. Barnett alludes similar to that addressed by Lewis Douglass?

SAMUEL CLEMENS (MARK TWAIN)

1. What is a satirist? Why is this essay an example of political satire?

2. Who are the heroes of Samuel Clemens's essay? Why do you think the President and American newspapers were silent on the massacre of the Moros?

3. What forms of racism do you find described in Clemens's essay?

SMEDLEY D. BUTLER

1. Why does Smedley Butler think that war is a "racket"? Why do you think he didn't recognize this fact until he retired from the military?

2. What are the costs of the wars that are made by millionaires and billionaires?

3. This book was written thirty-seven years after the Spanish-American War. What might have prompted Butler to write this book on the eve of World War II?

Main Points in *Voices*, Chapter 12, "The Expansion of Empire"

After reading Chapter 12 in *Voices*, students should be encouraged to identify what they believe to be the main points therein. Following are four possible main points.

1. Colonial expansion into the Pacific Ocean was the logical extension of manifest destiny.

2. Two of the primary goals of foreign policy at the turn of the century were to locate new markets for our surplus products and to gain access to raw materials and labor.

3. Although many American people supported United States imperialist ideology, a vocal and substantial minority of Americans belonging to every socioeconomic group opposed such policies.

4. Racist beliefs fueled many of the imperialist policies applied to Cuba and the Philippines.

Main Points in *Voices*, Chapter 12, "The Expansion of Empire" and in *A People's History*, Chapter 12, "The Empire and the People"

If your students are also reading *A People's History*, they should be encouraged to identify what they believe to be the main points in Chapters 12 in both books. Following are five additional points to be stressed when *Voices* and *A People's History* are used together.

5. In the face of new foreign policies that enabled Americans to become an overseas colonial and commercial power in the Caribbean, in Latin America, in the Pacific Islands, and in Asia, not all Americans agreed with imperialism, and many were quite vocal in their opposition.

6. The promoters of imperialism believed that America was an exemplary model of economic, political, and spiritual development that should be extended to other peoples and nations that were not able to solve their own problems.

7. At the end of the Spanish American War, the United States had become a global colonial power.

8. The domestic and international costs of American imperialism at the turn of the Century were high.

9. The long-range repercussions of imperialist policies of this era are still being felt

General-Discussion Questions for *Voices*

While the following questions are designed for classroom discussion about all the voices read in Chapter 12, they can also be rewritten and included as evaluation tools.

1. Why did the United States want to intervene in Cuba? How did the United States government justify remaining in Cuba after the war?

2. Why do you think Secretary of State John Hay referred to the Spanish American war as "a splendid little war"?

3. Why did many Americans support the imperialistic actions discussed in this chapter?

4. How does Samuel Clemens's line, "The splendid news appeared with splendid display-heads in every newspaper in this city," reflect his opinion of President Theodore Roosevelt?

5. Why do you think President George W. Bush cited the invasion and occupation of the Philippines as a model for the Iraq occupation in 2003? What are the parallels between the two invasions?

6. How do the voices in this chapter support Smedley D. Butler's belief that "war is a racket"? What is a racket? Do you believe war is a racket? Explain.

7. What is a "war millionaire"? Do you think the rich have a great deal to gain by going to war? Why do ordinary people bear the brunt of war? Explain.

8. What is an "entangling alliance"?

9. Which of the voices you learned about in this chapter most or least resonated with you? How and why?

General-Discussion Questions for *Voices* and *A People's History*

These general-discussion questions are additional questions for students who have read Chapter 12 in both books. For all questions, discussion must focus on ways the materials in both chapters help students formulate and articulate their answers.

10. Why do you think there was so much opposition to the war with the Philippines but very little to the war with Cuba?

11. Why do you think that Theodore Roosevelt wrote in 1897, "I should welcome almost any war, for I think this country needs one"? Do you think we needed a war at the turn of the century? Why, or why not?

12. What was the Monroe Doctrine? How does it pave the way for the imperialistic foreign policies of the late nineteenth century?

13. What do you think the writer of the *Washington Post* editorial meant when he wrote that at the eve of the Spanish-American war, "The taste of Empire is in the mouth of the people" (*People's History*, p. 299)? Do you agree or disagree with his statement?

14. How does this chapter influence your understanding of Theodore Roosevelt as both a leader and a man?

15. What is the open-door-policy that Howard Zinn claims "became the dominant theme of American foreign policy in the twentieth century" (*People's History*, p. 301) ?

16. What "special interests" benefited from the wars with Cuba and the Philippines?

17. Why do you think there was so much "excitement" over the sinking of the *Maine*?

18. Why do you think that United States historians "have generally ignored the role of the Cuban rebels in the war" (*People's History*, p. 309)? Why do you think there is little mention in traditional textbooks about the resistance of the Filipinos to the American occupation of the Philippines?

19. What was the Teller Amendment, and why was the United States able to circumvent its provisions after the war was over? Why do you think the Cubans eventually capitulated by agreeing to the Platt Amendment?

Evaluation Tools

SUGGESTED ASSIGNMENTS

These assignments can be adapted to meet any classroom need—homework, short- or long-term research projects, individual or group work. The end product should be flexible, depending on teacher interest and student abilities—papers, journals, oral reports, visual aides, and the like.

1. A great deal of mythology surrounds the newspaper circulation wars waged by William Randolph Heart and Joseph Pulitzer before, during, and after the war with Cuba. Find out as much as possible about both newspaper empires in the late nineteenth century and the power of both owners. Read articles in both newspapers leading up to war. Do you think the press was irresponsible in its coverage of the conflict in Cuba? Was it at least partially responsible for bringing the United States into war? Explain. Could this happen in the United States today?

2. Find out more about the Anti-Imperialist League. When was it founded? What were its goals and actions? How was it able to attract such well-known members of the upper class? Where and how was it most influential? Are there any organizational equivalents in the twenty-first century? If so, who do you think would be attracted to such organizations? How are their goals similar to and different from those organizations operating at the turn of the century? Explain.

3. In I.D. Barnett's open letter to President William McKinley, written in

1899, he decries the fact that his messages to Congress contain "incomprehensible silence on the subject of our wrongs." Examine President McKinley's annual and other messages to Congress at the turn of the century. What are the primary topics of his discussions on domestic policy? On foreign policy? Are his primary interests any different from those of President Grover Cleveland, who preceded him in office, and President Theodore Roosevelt, who followed? How and why? Explain.

4. In his 1906 essay, Samuel Clemens (Mark Twain) describes his response to the "Moro Massacre." The majority inhabitants of Moro Province—the independent Muslim Filipinos—refused to give in to United States leadership. Comparing the "uncivilized" Moros to American Indians, the United States military ordered them to submit or to be exterminated. By 1906, the Moros were defeated: 600 were killed in one battle, women and children included. Learn more about this conflict with the Moros. Find other primary accounts of the massacre. How do you think this incident has contributed to contemporary feelings about the United States in the Muslim-dominated part of the Philippines?

5. Read more of Mark Twain's political essays written at the turn of the century. How do they illustrate an anti-imperialist stance? Then find various pro-imperialist essays from the time period. Compare and contrast their contents. Which do you find most or least persuasive? Explain.

6. After examining the sample from "103 interventions in the affairs of other countries between 1798 and 1895," select one of these interventions for further research. How and why did the United States intervene? What were the results of such intervention? Did the American public generally support the government's actions? Who spoke out against it? What have been the long-term repercussions of our intervention?

7. Find out more about the Haitian revolution and creation of the first black republic in 1803. What were the causes and consequences of the revolution on the Haitian people? What role did ordinary people play in the success of the revolution? What lessons did United States foreign policymakers learn from the revolution? What is the twenty-first-century relationship between the Haitian and the United States governments? Do you think this contemporary relationship has been shaped by the 1803 revolution? Explain.

8. Learn more about the origins of May Day celebrations in the United States and overseas. What was the original purpose of May Day? How was it celebrated? Is May Day still celebrated in the United States? Is it celebrated abroad? How and why?

9. Learn more about the annexation of Hawaii. Begin by examining the 1893 proposal to annex Hawaii at www.alohaquest.com/archive/treaty_annexation _1893.htm; then the 1897 formal letter of protest at www.hawaiian-kingdom.org/protest_1898.shtml; and finally the congressional joint resolution at www.hawaiiankingdom.org/us-joint-resolution-1898.shtml. Using a search engine of choice, find other primary documents that both oppose and support the annexation of Hawaii. What does reading these primary documents add to your understanding about the annexation of Hawaii? Then learn more about recent attempts by some Native Hawaiians to become independent and regain their sovereignty.

10. Read George Washington's Farewell Address. What, in President Washington's words, are the consequences of involving ourselves in the affairs of other nations? Have other presidents followed his advice? How realistic was it at the turn of the twentieth century to avoid "entangling alliances"? How realistic is it in the twenty-first century?

SUGGESTED ESSAY QUESTIONS

1. Scholars have written many books and articles about the racism that propelled the United States into war with Cuba and the Philippines, and kept both peoples under the colonial yoke of the United States years after their "liberation." Using evidence from the readings, defend or refute the assertion of racism.

2. Using examples from the readings, explain how the imperialistic actions of the United States government in regard to the wars with Cuba and the Philippines continue to influence our relations with those countries today.

3. Using examples from the readings, support or refute the idea that war is profitable. Who profits most from war? Who profits least?

4. Drawing from examples in the readings, explain who supported expansionist foreign policies at the turn of the twentieth century. What was the basis of that support? Who resisted such policies and why? Do you see any

parallels between early-twentieth-century expansionist foreign policies and those of the early twenty-first century? Explain.

5. Using examples from the readings, explain why United States labor unions supported the Cuban rebels in their fight against Spain, but opposed American expansionism. Why do you think there were "mixed reactions of labor" to the war in the Philippines? How were the two wars similar and different? Would you have supported either or both of the wars? Explain.

6. Do you agree or disagree with the assertion that colonial expansion into the Pacific Ocean was the logical extension of Manifest Destiny? Support your answer with examples from the readings.

7. Provide specific examples to support the contention that foreign policy at the turn of the century was fueled by the need to find new markets for America's surplus products.

8. Describe the domestic and international costs of American imperialism at the turn of the century.

9. At the end of the Spanish American War, the United States had become a global colonial power. Using ample examples from the readings, explain how and why this happened.

10. In *Voices*, Howard Zinn states, "From the end of the Revolutionary War on, the history of the United States is one of continuous expansion" (p. 239). Using examples from the readings, support this statement.

SIMULATIONS AND OTHER CREATIVE APPROACHES

1. Create a wall-sized map entitled, "American Imperialism: 1800–1910." Locate all the territories that the United States added to its borders and its colonial possessions during this time. Near the map's legend, write five "bottom line" themes that would describe characteristics of United States expansionist policies during this period. Present your map and themes to your classmates.

2. Imagine that you are a reporter for an independent newspaper in February 1898 and you have been asked to write a well-balanced, non-jingoistic investigative article on the sinking of the battleship *Maine*. Write your article and read it to the class. Ask your classmates to compare and contrast what you

wrote with the way the events in regard to the sinking were actually portrayed in the Hearst and Pulitzer papers.

3. Write two letters that reflect what you believe might have been President McKinley's response to Lewis H. Douglass and I.D. Barnett's pleas to oppose the growth of empire.

4. Stage a discussion between George Washington, William McKinley, and George W. Bush about the wisdom of becoming involved in "entangling alliances."

CHAPTER THIRTEEN

Socialists and Wobblies

Today's generation of young adults have a difficult time imagining the early twentieth century. Indeed, it is hard to imagine a time when there were 100,000 registered Socialists, 1,200 of whom held elected offices; when there were 4,000 labor strikes in a single year; when an avowed Socialist ran for president and received 900,000 votes; when women put their lives on the line for the right to vote. These were heady times, full of spirited resistance to a system that had ignored working Americans for far too long.

Almost a hundred years later, the actions and deeds of those who dared to question the establishment are vivid reminders of our power as ordinary Americans. It is an important message—the power of our dissenting voices and of our commitment to a more egalitarian society for our students to hear.

Document-Based Questions

MOTHER JONES

1. What is a "motley gathering"? Do you think Mother Jones would have described her audience in the same manner as did the reporter?

2. Do you think this speech aroused the audience from its "lethargy"? How and why? Might it have moved you to action if you had been a worker in the audience? Explain.

3. Why do you think that, although she "violated injunction after injunction," Mother Jones was not re-arrested? What made Mother Jones an especially dangerous radical in the eyes of the corporate owners?

UPTON SINCLAIR

1. Do you agree with Sinclair's "two carefully worded propositions," describ-

ing what a Socialist believes? Do you think he has appropriately described what an anarchist believes? How might you change his descriptions?

2. Why do you think Dr. Schliemann's "formula of modern proletariat thought" did not attract enough of the American proletariat to enact the restructuring of the country's political, social, and economic structure at the turn of the century?

3. How would you answer the question Sinclair posed, "Do you think that it would be too much to say that two hours of the working time of every efficient member of a community goes to feed the red fiend of war"? Could this same formula be applied in the early twenty-first century?

W.E.B. DU BOIS

1. What is the "peculiar sensation, this double-consciousness" that W. E. B. Du Bois describes? How and why do African Americans in today's world continue to cope with this sensation?

2. How did Du Bois describe the African Americans' "vain search for freedom"? How did this search contribute to the "new vision" that replaced the "dream of political power"? What was the vision?

3. What are Du Bois's dreams for a better future? Which do you believe were accomplished in his lifetime? Which remain to be accomplished?

EMMA GOLDMAN

1. How does Emma Goldman describe patriotism? Do you think most Americans would similarly describe patriotism in the early twenty-first century?

2. Do you think Goldman makes a convincing argument for her belief that patriotism is a "menace to liberty"? What are her strongest and weakest points?

3. Goldman repeatedly mentions the growth of solidarity in her address. What evidence do you find in her address, as well as within the other voices in this chapter, of such solidarity?

"PROCLAMATION OF THE STRIKING TEXTILE WORKERS"

1. Why do you think this proclamation resonated with workers from around the world? Do you think it might have had greater support from abroad than from within the United States? How and why?

2. The proclamation is deliberately modeled on the language and format of the Declaration of Independence. Do you think this structure and style is effective? Do you think the two tyrannies—the tyranny of the Crown and the tyranny of the mill owners—are comparable? How and why?

3. Why do you think the city government and local police upheld the rights of the mill owners rather than the strikers?

ARTURO GIOVANITTI

1. What is the "ethical side" of striking that Arturo Giovanitti describes? Do you think these are just the words of "dreamers" or "fanatics"—a question he poses to the District Attorney?

2. President Abraham Lincoln stated that the Union could not exist "half free and half slave." Why does Giovanitti—who wrote fifty years later—feel that America was still "half free and half slave"?

3. Why do you think the jury acquitted Giovanitti?

WOODY GUTHRIE

1. To whom is this song addressed? Who is the "you" who "would kill our children," and whose "soldiers" were waiting while the miners slept?

2. Guthrie mentions "wire fence corners" twice. What is he describing? Why is this important to understanding the song—or is it?

JULIA MAY COURTNEY

1. Julia May Courtney predicted that, "every workingman in Colorado and in America will not forget" the cry, "Remember Ludlow." Is this true? If not, why?

2. Do you think the statement, "[F]or the first time in the history of the labor

war in America the people are with the strikers" was correct? Do you think the people did support them? Why, or why not? Why would they support these strikers and not others?

3. Do you think there is another side to the Ludlow Massacre, other than that presented by Courtney and Guthrie? How would that side justify its actions?

JOE HILL

1. Why do you think Joe Hill cabled Haywood from his jail cell and told him, "Don't waste time mourning. Organize!"? Do you think Haywood and other organizers honored Hill's request?

2. Why do you think Joe Hill remains a hero for those involved in the contemporary struggles related to labor?

3. What "fading flower" do you think Joe Hill would wish to see "come to life and bloom again"?

Main Points in *Voices*, Chapter 13, "Socialists and Wobblies"

After reading Chapter 13 in *Voices*, students should be encouraged to identify what they believe to be the main points therein. Following are five possible main points.

1. Early twentieth-century radicalism in the United States was fueled by overseas wars, miserable working conditions, the growing gap between the rich and the poor, and unremitting poverty.

2. Socialism reached the height of its popularity in America during the early twentieth century.

3. Despite almost three hundred years of victimization, many African Americans approached the turn of the twentieth century with dreams for a better future.

4. To some workers in the United States labor movement, true freedom for the working-class depended on the abolition of "wage slavery."

5. Union membership and activity grew at an unprecedented rate during the early twentieth century.

Main Points in *Voices*, Chapter 13, "Socialists and Wobblies," and in *A People's History*, Chapter 13, "The Socialist Challenge"

If your students are also reading *A People's History*, they should be encouraged to identify what they believe to be the main points in Chapter 13 in both books. Following are five additional points to be stressed when *Voices* and *A People's History* are used together.

6. War and imperialistic impulses postponed, but did not suppress, the class conflict brewing in America at the turn of the century.

7. While the Wobblies (the IWW) never had a huge membership at any given time, their energy, commitment, inspiration to others, and ability to mobilize made them far more influential in the country than their numbers might suggest.

8. Progressive Era reforms were intended to "stabilize the capitalist system by repairing its worse defects, blunt the edge of the Socialist movement, and restore some measure of class peace" (*People's History*, p. 354).

9. During this period, socialism moved out of the small circles of city immigrants and "became American."

10. Women of the early twentieth century were members of a pioneering generation who set the agenda for social reform for the next several decades.

General-Discussion Questions for *Voices*

While the following questions are designed for classroom discussion about all the voices read in Chapter 13, they can also be rewritten and included as evaluation tools.

1. How is the "wage slavery" described by Mother Jones similar to that described by many of the voices in Chapter 11?

2. Were conditions better or worse for the working poor in the early twentieth century than they had been in the Gilded Age?

3. Who were the United Mine Workers? How strong was their union in West Virginia? What specific labor battles did they fight?

4. Why do you think some people were willing to become strike breakers?

5. How is corporate hiring of strike breakers yet another example of the divide-and-conquer strategy used by those in power?

6. How do you think the white reading public reacted to the publication of *The Souls of Black Folk*?

7. Why are many of the authors in this chapter so disdainful of "reformers"?

8. Do you think it is more possible today for "a man to be both a Negro and an American" then it was at the turn of the twentieth century?

9. How do you think the authors of these entries would describe a truly free society?

10. Do textile workers, or any other organized groups of workers, ever "rise in armed revolt against their oppressors" as the mill workers in Lawrence predicted?

11. Do you think striking is justified? If so, under what conditions? If not, why not? Should doctors, police, or fire fighters be allowed to strike? Why, or why not?

12. How do you think federal, state, and local governments justified their responses to strikes?

General-Discussion Questions for *Voices* and *A People's History*

These general-discussion questions are additional questions for students who have read Chapter 13 in both books. For all questions, discussion must focus on ways the materials in both chapters help students formulate and articulate their answers.

13. Emma Goldman wrote about the Spanish-American War that, "the lives, blood, and money of the American people were used to protect the interests of the American capitalists." How do the voices in chapters 12 and 13 echo her sentiments?

14. What do you think attracted people like Jack London, Upton Sinclair, and Helen Keller to socialism?

15. Who were the "muckrakers" of the early twentieth century? Who are the muckrakers of the twenty-first century?

16. What led to the panic and financial collapse of 1907? How did the crisis contribute to the social, political, and economic unrest of the early twentieth century?

17. Why do you think that a memorial parade in which 100,000 people marched was held for the victims of the Triangle Shirtwaist Factory, while there was little media coverage and far less interest in the victims of the Ludlow Massacre, which occurred two years later?

18. How do you feel about the fact that in the early twenty-first century, forty-four families made $1 million a year—a sum equal to the total income of 100,000 families who each made $500 a year?

19. Why were African Americans kept out of the trade-union movement for so long? How might their membership have strengthened the unions?

20. What made the IWW different from other unions?

21. What does Howard Zinn mean when he writes that "there was almost a religious fervor" (*People's History*, p. 340) to the Socialist movement?

22. What role did African Americans play in the founding and leadership of the National Association for the Advancement of Colored People? What were the early goals of the naacp, and who were some of its early leaders?

23. What is a trust buster? According to Howard Zinn, was Theodore Roosevelt really a trust buster?

Evaluation Tools

SUGGESTED ASSIGNMENTS

These assignments can be adapted to meet any classroom need—homework, short- or long-term research projects, individual or group work. The end prod-

uct should be flexible, depending on teacher interest and student abilities—
papers, journals, oral reports, visual aides, and the like.

1. Find out more about the United Mine Workers. What were the goals and
    activities of their union in West Virginia? What specific labor battles did
    they fight? What were their accomplishments? How are the labor griev-
    ances of miners different from and the same as the labor grievances of other
    workers throughout the United States in the early twentieth century?
    Compare and contrast the labor conditions of these miners with those of
    the twenty-first century.

2. Read *The Communist Manifesto* by Karl Marx and Friederich Engels.
    What are their specific grievances against capitalism and capitalists? How
    do they propose that socialism will cure these evils? Does this more in-
    depth discussion of socialism help you to better understand why it was
    so attractive to many workers in the early twentieth century? How and
    why?

3. Read *The Jungle* by Upton Sinclair. Why do you think this classic novel is a
    century old but still resonates with many American readers? What do you
    believe to be the three primary themes that Sinclair wants you to under-
    stand about Jurgis's story? Do you agree or disagree with them? Explain.
    When you are finished, read "The Chain Never Stops" by Eric Schlosser, pub-
    lished in *Mother Jones* magazine. (See http://www.motherjones.com/
    news/feature/2001/07/meatpacking.html) How does this article about work-
    ers in the meatpacking industry at the end of the twentieth century compare
    and contrast with the experiences faced by Jurgis and his family almost a hun-
    dred years earlier?

4. Go to the website for *Mother Jones* magazine at http://www.mojones.com/.
    Read the most recent issue and then determine why the journal is named
    after Mother Jones. What is your overall impression of the articles? Who
    do you think would subscribe to this journal? Would you subscribe? Why,
    or why not?

5. Learn as much as possible about the Ludlow Massacre. What were the ini-
    tial grievances of the workers at Ludlow? Locate several newspaper articles
    that reported the event. Were they supportive of the strikers, strikebreak-
    ers, and/or the federal government's response? How and why? Do you think

Woodie Guthrie's lyrics accurately portrayed the event? Why do you think it was thirty-three years before the Ludlow Massacre was memorialized by Guthrie's song? Why would he write this song in 1946?

6. Find a recording of "Ludlow Massacre." Then locate recordings and lyrics of other songs written between the late 1940s and the 1960s about union organization that occurred during the early twentieth century. What do they have in common? Which do you think most accurately portrayed the events? How successful were these recordings? Why do you think folk singers and writers of the mid-twentieth century were attracted to this early-twentieth century movement?

7. Find out more about the labor organizer Joe Hill. What was his background, and how did it influence his decision to join the IWW? Locate some of his songs. Read the lyrics and listen to any recordings. How do his songs reflect his experiences as a labor organizer? What was the nature of the crime for which he was indicted and found guilty? Learn as much about the trial as possible. Do you think he received a fair trial? Do you think Hill became a martyr to the labor movement? How and why?

8. In 1925, Alfred Hayes wrote the lyrics for what later became the famous song—set to music by Earl Robinson—"Joe Hill." Over the next several decades, Paul Robeson performed, popularized, and recorded this song repeatedly. In the 1960s, such well-known folk performers as Pete Seeger and Joan Baez further popularized the song. Read the lyrics for all six verses, then listen to several different renditions of the song. Which do you think is most powerful and why? Do you think Hayes's purpose in writing the song was to make a labor-union hero out of Hill? Did the song accomplish this? Explain. Do you think this song would resonate with American workers in the early twenty-first century? Explain.

9. Pick one of the early twentieth-century muckrakers for a biographical sketch. Ida Tarbell, Lincoln Steffens, Jacob Riis, Upton Sinclair are all possibilities. Learn more about their backgrounds and what led them to print what they witnessed. How did their muckraking efforts lead to reform? What opposition did they face?

10. Howard Zinn describes the existence of sweatshops at the turn of the century. Learn as much as possible about sweatshops in one urban area between 1900 and 1920. How did they operate? Who was involved with sweatshop

labor? Were sweatshop workers involved in unions? Who benefited from sweatshop labor? What were working conditions like for sweatshop laborers? Then learn about contemporary sweatshops that operate in American today. Compare and contrast sweatshop conditions in the United States at the turn of the twentieth century with conditions at the turn of the twenty-first century.

11. Learn more about the Wobblies—the IWW. How did it arise and gain momentum in the United States? What were its goals and accomplishments? Where, regionally were its efforts most or least successful? Explain. To whom did the Wobblies appeal?

12. Find out more about Emma Goldman. How did her background contribute to her decision to become a political activist devoted to overthrowing capitalism? Why did the government consider her to be a dangerous woman? Do you think she was dangerous? Explain. Would the government today think she was dangerous? How and why?

SUGGESTED ESSAY QUESTIONS

1. In Mother Jones's speech, she states that "a contented workman is no good." Using examples from your reading, explain how this statement illustrates the ongoing struggle between corporation owners and labor.

2. Provide examples from the reading to support Du Bois's statement that "the problem of the Twentieth century is the problem of the color line." Has the problem been solved in the twenty-first century? Explain.

3. Many of the voices in this chapter discuss their quest for freedom. How are their concepts of freedom similar? Which have more realistic expectations for achieving freedom? Which have more unrealistic expectations? Explain. How do their definitions of freedom compare and contrast with your own?

4. In her 1908 speech, Emma Goldman predicted that as America became the "most powerful nation on earth," it would "eventually plant her iron foot on the necks of all other nations." What did she mean? Using examples from the reading, explain how her prediction did or did not come true.

5. The striking mill workers in Lawrence wrote in 1912 that "as useful members of society and as wealth producers we have the right to lead decent

and honorable lives." How and why would others whom you have read about during this period have supported this statement? How do you think they would describe such a "decent and honorable" life? Do you think that everyone has such a right? Why, or why not? What role, if any, should the government play in helping people to lead such a life?

6. Almost a hundred years ago, Margaret Sanger wrote, "No woman can call herself free who does not own and control her own body." How do you suppose this sentiment was accepted at the turn of the century? How is this very same sentiment used in the twenty-first-century context?

7. Howard Zinn argues that the Progressive period did not usher in real reform because "fundamental conditions did not change . . . for the vast majority of tenant farmers, factory workers, slum dwellers, miners, farm laborers, working men and women, black and white" (*People's History*, p. 349–350). Support or refute this statement with ample examples from your reading.

8. Using examples from the reading, how and why were African Americans excluded from involvement in the socialist and union movements in the early twentieth century? How were they included?

9. Using examples from the readings, explain how and why Socialism was so attractive to some workers in the early twentieth century. Why do you think Socialism failed to attract a larger following among the working and middle classes? Why do you think that almost a hundred years later, Socialism and Socialists have less influence than they had at this time?

10. Many of the people whose voices you have read in this/these chapter(s) were considered dangerous to the public good in the early twentieth century. Which do you think were believed to be most dangerous, and why? Do you think they posed a real danger to the nation? Do you think the real or perceived danger they posed justified placing any limits on civil liberties?

SIMULATIONS AND OTHER CREATIVE APPROACHES

1. Write a one-person play about a union organizer, antiwar activist, or feminist who was involved in a social movement at the turn of the century. Some of your dialog should originate with the actual speeches and essays of the activist. Perform this play for an audience of your choice.

2. Imagine you are a contemporary muckraker who has been hired to write an article for the next issue of *Mother Jones*—a magazine founded in 1976 as an independent, nonprofit publication committed to social justice. Select a contemporary labor issue to investigate and be sure your research includes a comparison with labor conditions that existed at the turn of the twentieth century. Then write your article. To learn more about *Mother Jones*, refer to its online journal at http://www.mojones.com/index.html.

3. Conduct a survey among young adults in which you will ask two questions: How would you define patriotism? What thoughts or actions would you consider unpatriotic? Make a list of all the characteristics the answers have in common and another list for singular characteristics. Using these various definitions, create the following: your own definition of patriotism in the twenty-first century and a list of actions considered to be unpatriotic in contemporary society. Then write a short children's book in which you compare and contrast these definitions and perceptions of patriotism in the early twenty-first century with ideas about patriotism in the early twentieth century.

4. Write a poem or compose a song that memorializes one of the persons involved in or events that were part of the resistance movements at the turn of the twentieth century.

5. Stage a town meeting as you imagine it would have been held in an industrial town in the early twentieth century. Invite at least three persons whom you learned about in your reading. Each will give a 3–5 minute speech about his or her commitment to and involvement in Socialism and the beliefs about how Socialism can help United States workers. Invite three other persons from corporate management who will refute their claims. Community members (the remaining students in the class) will ask questions of the speakers.

CHAPTER FOURTEEN

Protesting the First World War

by Colby Smart

Evocative primary source documents are especially important to our discussions of World War I. While any analysis of the war "to make the world safe for democracy" demonstrates the downward spiral into militaristic violence that ushered in a century of unparallel destruction, most traditional discussions are devoid of antiwar voices and actions. Yet without this perspective, students leave the subject of World War I thinking that the vast majority of Americans willingly fought in the war and/or unquestioningly supported the war effort. As historians, we know that such was not the case.

In Chapter 14, students are exposed to first-hand accounts of how Americans opposed the war and the trend toward militarism. These voices not only illustrate the widespread nature of the antiwar movement, they also highlight the federal government's calculated reaction to the movement and the way in which the war influenced art and literature among the generation who survived the war. Our students will learn of the dynamic nature that comprised the antiwar appeal to the imperialistic foundation of the war, and they will come away with an understanding of how the views of these antiwar activists were, in many cases, systematically suppressed. Finally, these documents of resistance better equip our students with the tools they will need to become, critical, responsive and thorough practitioners of historical thought.

Document Based Questions

HELEN KELLER

1. Explain what Keller meant when she said that "the future of America rests on the backs of 80,000,000 working men and women and their children."

2. Cite Keller's explanation of the motive Congress had in preparing for war.

3. Instead of preparing for war, Keller states, "the kind of preparedness the workers want is reorganization and reconstruction of their whole life, such as has never been attempted by statesmen or governments." Explain what Keller meant.

JOHN REED

1. In what ways were wealthy industrialists placing pressure on working Americans to conform and enlist?

2. "I know what war means. I have been with the armies of all the belligerents except one, and I have seen men die, and go mad, and lie in hospitals suffering hell." Compare and contrast this quote from Reed with the dominant view of the "nobility" of war.

3. What hypocrisies does John Reed point out concerning the ways atrocities are viewed by the United States government? Give two examples.

"WHY THE IWW IS NOT PATRIOTIC TO THE UNITED STATES"

1. Why is the IWW not patriotic to the United States? Do you believe this excerpt illustrates Howard Zinn's statement that the IWW was opposed to the "class character of the war"? How and why?

2. Using details from the reading in Chapters 14, support or refute the statement of the IWW that "[t]his war is a business man's war"?

EMMA GOLDMAN

1. What point about political violence was Emma Goldman trying to make in her analogy of a physician and his medicine?

2. In what ways does Goldman believe that the violent tactics of the establishment encouraged a backlash of political violence?

3. How does Goldman present the ways in which the antiwar movement posed a threat to established government and economic interests in the world?

EUGENE DEBS

1. Why did Eugene Debs admit to being a "disloyalist"? What did he mean by this admission?

2. Which segment of American society do you think would be most receptive to the ideas expressed in these two speeches? Explain.

3. In his "Statement to the Court," Debs makes the case that Socialism must replace the existing social order of capitalism. What are the main reasons Debs outlines to make his case? In contrast, what argument could be made against Debs's Socialist views?

RANDOLPH BOURNE

1. Assess the validity of this statement: In time of war "[t]he citizen throws off his contempt and indifference to Government, identifies himself with its purposes, revives all his military memories and symbols, and the State once more walks, an august presence, through the imaginations of men."

2. Does Randolph Bourne place blame on citizens for conforming to and accepting the state as a king or savior in times of war? Why, or why not? What evidence from the document lends support to your argument?

3. Bourne states that "agreements which are to affect the lives of whole peoples must be made between peoples and not by Governments, or at least by their representatives." What is Bourne alluding to in this statement?

E. E. CUMMINGS

1. From your perspective, is it important for societies to allow people, who disagree with war and violence, to make a conscious choice to avoid it without consequence? Why, or why not?

2. What support for becoming a conscientious objector do you find in this poem?

JOHN DOS PASSOS

1. John Dos Passos continues to repeat the line, "how can I get back to my out-

fit," throughout the first part of the document. Why? Why does he stop making this statement toward the end?

2. Why is the main character named John Doe in this story?

3. What opinions does Dos Passos express about the tragedy of war? What is he trying to say at the end of the passage about the pomp and circumstance surrounding a soldier's death?

DALTON TRUMBO

1. Why does the main character insist on being seen by so many people? Is it to teach people about the tragedies of war, or is it to fill them with shame for letting something like this happen to a fellow human being?

2. Why, in your opinion, was this "brain" left alive? For what purposes was it taken and shown to people?

3. In *Johnny Got His Gun*, Dalton Trumbo is making a serious condemnation. Who and/or what is he condemning?

Main Points in *Voices*, Chapter 14, "Protesting the First World War"

1. After reading Chapter 14 in *Voices*, students should be encouraged to identify what they believe to be the main points therein. Following are five possible main points:

2. The antiwar movement was in part a manifestation of a rift that existed in American society between organized labor and industrialists.

3. The voices of protest in the antiwar movement cut across racial, ethnic, and gender boundaries.

4. World War I influenced art and literature both during the war and after the end of hostilities.

5. Official United States policy suppressed dissent during the war, suggesting that to be a patriot, one must always support the government's policies.

6. Individual liberties are often restricted during times of war.

Main Point in *Voices*, Chapter 14, "Protesting the First World War" and in *A People's History*, Chapter 14, "War Is the Health of the State"

7. If your students are also reading *A People's History*, they should be encouraged to identify what they believe to be the main points in Chapter 14 in both books." Following are five additional points to be stressed when *Voices* and *A People's History* are used together.

8. World War I was in large part a war for imperialistic gain.

9. The war effort was not universally endorsed.

10. Civil liberties were limited during the war in order to suppress antiwar activism.

11. Working people of both the Allied and Central Powers bore the true cost of war with their lives.

12. At the end of the war, a generation of people ushered in new forms of art and literature that reflected the terrible toll the war placed on humanity.

General-Discussion Questions for *Voices*

While the following questions are designed for classroom discussion about all the voices read in Chapter 14, they can also be rewritten and included as evaluation and simulation tools.

1. What similarities existed in the messages about class conflict in the documents by Helen Keller, John Reed, and Eugene Debs?

2. How do the various voices in this chapter illustrate the point that fear was used to promote consensus for war? What role did fear play in attempts to build support for other twentieth-century wars? Do you think similar efforts to use fear were apparent in the effort to create support in 2003 for the invasion of Iraq? Explain.

3. How do the voices in this chapter demonstrate that young men from working-class families on both sides of the conflict actually fought the war? Do you think World War I was yet another example of "the rich man's war and the poor man's fight"?

4. These voices provide many examples of how the antiwar movement was suppressed. Which examples do you feel were most convincingly expressive?

5. Do you think the Espionage and Sedition Acts were unconstitutional? Explain. Was this the first time in United States history that such laws were passed? Was it the last time?

6. From your own understanding of United States history, do you think it is possible for the world to live, as Eugene Debs said, in "the harmonious cooperation of every nation with every other nation on earth"? Do you think it is more or less possible in the twenty-first century than it was in the twentieth century?

7. In what ways can a student of history better understand the nature of conflict by reading a wide variety of sources about a particular event?

8. Do you think that there is any "pomp and circumstance" that is appropriate or inappropriate when dealing with the death of a soldier? Explain.

9. Many historians agree that World War I was fought for imperialistic reasons. What documents best illustrate this point?

10. *Johnny Got His Gun* eventually became one of the banned books of the McCarthy era—and it is still banned in many school districts across the nation. Why do you think this book was, and still is in many areas, banned? Do you think it is controversial? How and why?

11. How did the voices in this chapter reinforce any of the five themes listed in "Main Points in *Voices*"?

12. Which of the voices in this chapter did you find most powerful? Least powerful? How and why?

General-Discussion Questions for *Voices* and *A People's History*

These general-discussion questions are additional questions for students who have read Chapter 14 in both books. For all questions, discussion must focus on ways the materials in both chapters help students formulate and articulate their answers.

13. Randolph Bourne wrote that "war is the health of the State." Why do you

think Howard Zinn choose this quote as the title for Chapter 14 in *A People's History.*

14. In what ways was organized labor suppressed during World War I?

15. How was class consciousness and class conflict used by antiwar advocates to illustrate the war's "true aims"?

16. What similarities do you detect between the antiwar movement during World War I and the antiwar movement prior and during the 2003 United States invasion of Iraq? Explain.

17. In what ways did the United States government sway public opinion to support the war effort? From your own perspective, was it appropriate for the government to employ such methods to build a consensus?

18. Upon passage of the Espionage and Sedition Acts, many people felt that their civil liberties were under attack as the government sought to stifle dissent. Do you think these measures were an appropriate domestic policy during a time of war? Explain.

19. What is civil disobedience? What role did it play in the antiwar movement? Do you think Emma Goldman, John Reed, and/or Eugene Debs would have supported civil disobedience? Explain.

20. How would you define our First Amendment right to freedom of speech? Do you think the Sedition Act violated that freedom? Explain. If so, how and why was it able to become law?

21. What was the Espionage Act of 1917? Do you think it was constitutional? What was the Sedition Act of 1918? Was it constitutional?

22. When Eugene Debs was in prison serving his term for violating the Espionage Act of 1917, he ran for president during the 1918 presidential election. While he was in prison, he won almost one million votes. How was that possible? What does this tell you about American society in 1918?

23. Is the right to protest protected in the United States Constitution? Explain.

24. What other voices might have been added to Chapter 14 in *Voices* that might have provided a more complete understanding of Chapter 14 in *A People's History?*

Evaluation Tools

SUGGESTED ASSIGNMENTS

These assignments can be adapted to meet any classroom need—homework, short- or long-term research projects, individual or group work. The end product should be flexible, depending on teacher interest and student abilities—papers, journals, oral reports, visual aides, and the like.

1. Learn more about the historical uses and abuses of legislation related to free speech during times of war. Be sure to focus on historical examples of curbing civil liberties, beginning with the passage of the first Sedition Act in the 1790s and ending with the passage of the 2001 PATRIOT Act.

2. Conduct biographical research on one of the people whom you met in this/these chapter(s). Be sure to read more primary documents to support your research—especially speeches, letters, articles, and so forth. What was their background? What led them to join the antiwar movement? What arguments and actions they use to support their cause? What were the consequences of their actions? Do you find their antiwar arguments convincing? How and why?

3. Watch the movie *Johnny Got His Gun*. What do you think Trumbo wanted his audience to learn from the movie? What did you take from the movie? Do you think it is still controversial in the twenty-first century? How and why? Learn more about Dalton Trumbo and what led him to become one of the so-called Hollywood Ten.

4. In January 2003, officials at the University of California at Berkeley refused to allow a fund-raising appeal for the Emma Goldman Papers, which are housed on its campus. The appeal contained a quote from Goldman about the suppression of free speech and her opposition to war. The university deemed the topics too political as the United States prepared for a possible military action against Iraq. Find out more about this controversy. Do you think the university officials acted appropriately? Why, or why not? How was the problem resolved? Can you think of any other incidents since the military invasion of Iraq in which similar free-speech issues have arisen? Explain.

5. More than two thousand people were prosecuted under both the Espionage Act and the Seditions Act, and thousands of others were intimidated into

silence. Learn as must as possible about both acts. Was there congressional and/or public opposition to the legislation? How and why was the federal government able to pass such legislation?

6. The Selective Service Act of 1917 allowed the United States government to raise an army after entering into World War I. Unlike previous draft laws, the new act placed conscientious objectors (COs) under military authority *before* they obtained religious exemptions, thus making them subject to military justice. Who were COs? What was their historical role in exemption from military service? How were they treated during World War I?

7. In 1919, the Supreme Court heard the case of *Schenck* v. *U.S.* in which the defendant challenged the constitutionality of the Espionage Act. Learn more about the case and the Supreme Court's decision. How has this case continued to influence the question of free speech during times of war?

8. In 1919, the Supreme Court heard the case of *Abrams* v. *U.S.* in which the constitutionality of the Sedition Act was challenged. Learn more about the case and the Supreme Court's decision. How has this case continued to influence the question of free speech during times of war?

9. Read W. E. B. Du Bois's article, "The African Roots of War," published in the *Atlantic Monthly* in May 1915. What were his primary points? Do you agree with his beliefs about capitalism, democracy, imperialism, international rivalry? Explain. What do you think Du Bois might have added to the article if he had attempted to rewrite it in 1920?

10. Learn more about the American Protective League. What were its primary purposes and accomplishments? How was it supported by the federal government? What impact did it have on the public?

SUGGESTED ESSAY QUESTIONS

1. Using copies of the Bill of Rights, the Sedition and Espionage Acts, and the speeches by Eugene Debs, discuss in an essay whether you believe that Debs's opposition to the war justified his arrest and imprisonment.

2. Was the antiwar movement during World War I effective in its opposition to United States policy? What were its strongest and most credible arguments? Which were the least credible? Explain with citations from *Voices*.

3.   What overall themes were present in the antiwar movement that parallel themes from earlier periods in United States history?

4.   The measures which the United States government employed to build consensus among the public for the war were extensive and in many cases intrusive. From your understanding of the time, how important do you think it was for the United States to use these measures?

5.   Define patriotism. In your view, were Helen Keller and John Reed more or less patriotic than United States soldiers who fought in the military during the war? Explain.

6.   What voices of resistance in Chapter 14 in both *Voices* and *A People's History* were of most interest to you? How and why? Which did you find most compelling and why? Least compelling?

7.   Imagine you are a worker in a West Virginia coal mine in 1918. You have just been drafted. Eugene Debs has just given a speech near your hometown. Is it your patriotic duty to go and fight? Why, or why not?

8.   Howard Zinn writes that in the pre-World War I years, "there was worry about the health of the state" (*People's History*, p. 359). What were the worries? What do you think the federal government had to worry about? Did any of these worries lead us into war? How did they influence the course and outcomes of the war?

SIMULATIONS AND OTHER CREATIVE APPROACHES

1.   Hold a town-hall meeting in the classroom in which students become characters in the documents. Invite school faculty, students, and parents to this meeting to question the characters about their antiwar positions.

2.   Have students work in small groups to create Venn diagrams that compare and contrast themes of the World War I antiwar movement and the antiwar protests sparked by the United States invasion of Iraq in 2003.

3.   Write a letter to Eugene Debs in prison. In this letter you should outline your opinions on his antiwar stance. In addition, be sure to discuss your thoughts on the Espionage and Sedition Acts.

4.   Create a movie poster for *Johnny Got His Gun*. Posters should not have any

text with the exception of the title. Students should focus on the power of imagery and the techniques propagandists use to get a particular message across to a wide audience.

CHAPTER FIFTEEN

From the Jazz Age to the Uprisings of the 1930s

In most of our textbooks, the 1920s and the 1930s are the most mythologized years of the twentieth century. While it is true that 1920s were a "roaring" good time for some people, it is equally true that the decade was bleak for many others. The reality is that the 1920s was a decade of sharp contrasts, in which social liberalism was counterbalanced by social conservatism, conspicuous consumer consumption was also characterized by materialistic excess, and corporations and skilled workers became increasingly prosperous at the same time that unskilled workers and farmers plunged into poverty and despair. There were plenty of social, political, and economic warning signs that all was not well, but those in power ignored them until the economic realities exploded into the stock market crash and the Great Depression.

The 1930s are also mythologized in our traditional discussions of the era. Indeed, while we see the government come to the aid of many Americans during this period, we must also note that Franklin Delano Roosevelt's (FDR) New Deal largely focused on recovery and relief measures—measures that helped corporations, labor unions, and organized farm groups, but did little to meet the needs of ordinary hard-working Americans. As Howard Zinn points out, FDR made the Depression bearable for some, but he did not make it go away. When our students listen carefully to the voices from the 1920s and 1930s, they hear tragic stories of desperate and angry people who have experienced broken dreams and hearts, have been dispossessed of all they hold dear, and have resisted conservative government responses at a time when radical measures were needed. And when they hear these voices, our students break through the mythology of the era and gain a more balanced understanding of these troubled times.

176 - CHAPTER FIFTEEN

Document-Based Questions

F. SCOTT FITZGERALD

1. F. Scott Fitzgerald describes the "flimsy structure" of the 1920s as "the most expensive orgy in history" and as an era that existed in "borrowed time." What does he mean, and how does he support these assertions?

2. Do you agree with Fitzgerald that it was premature to write about the Jazz Age in 1931? Do you think this article lacks perspective? When does an event or an era become history?

3. What does Fitzgerald think about the federal government's reactions to the May Day riots of 1919 and its subsequent Red Scare activities? Why does he believe that most Americans did little to question governmental responses?

YIP HARBURG

1. Why do you think Roosevelt made this the theme song for his presidential campaign? Do you think it was a successful campaign tactic? Explain.

2. What do the lyrics of this song tell you about ordinary working Americans during the Great Depression? What had they done for the United States, and what did they expect?

3. Were the expectations of the people for whom the song was written fair during a time of deep economic depression?

PAUL Y. ANDERSON

1. Do you think Paul Anderson's coverage of the Bonus March was balanced and fair? Explain.

2. What was the government's explanation for its response to the Bonus March? Do you think the Bonus Marchers posed a threat to the government or the public good?

3. What is your opinion about the government's response to the Bonus Marchers? Was the government's response to the Bonus Marchers "one of the deadliest boomerangs in political history"? Explain.

MARY LICHT

1. Why do you think the Communist Party was a leading force in the defense of the Scottsboro "boys"? How do you think the Party's involvement may have influenced the outcome of the case?

2. Why do you think that the parents agreed to have the International Labor Defense (ILD) rather than the National Association for the Advancement of Colored People (NAACP) represent their sons? Might the outcome of the case have been any different if it had been conducted by the NAACP? Explain.

3. How did continuous resistance to southern racism and agitation in regard to the Southern legal system influence the lives of the Scottsboro "boys"? What might have happened to them without these voices of resistance?

NED COBB ("NATE SHAW")

1. Why did Ned Cobb stay in the South, even though he knew "I was in a bad way of life here"? Do you think he was typical of many black southern sharecroppers? Why, or why not?

2. According to Cobb, what were the most effective means used to get him, as well as other black sharecroppers, to join in the Sharecroppers Union? Why were he and others willing to risk their lives by becoming involved?

3. Describe the various divide-and-conquer strategies that Cobb explains were used by the white men. Why do you think they no longer held any power over Cobb?

BILLLIE HOLIDAY

1. Do you think Abel Meeropol's poem would have been as successful if Billie Holliday had not recorded it as a song? Explain.

2. Why do you think Holliday's record company refused to allow her to record this song in 1937?

3. Why do you think Holliday's recording remains so powerful today? Do you think that the song would have an equally powerful effect if it were re-recorded by a contemporary singer? Explain.

LANGSTON HUGHES

1. These two poems were written six years apart. Are the topics and tones any different in the poem written in 1934 and that written in 1940? Explain.

2. What is the difference between Roosevelt, the landlord, and the police? Were any of the three more likely than the others to listen to Hughes's voice? Why, or why not?

3. Both poems are riddled with a sense of futility. Why, then, do you think Langston Hughes continued to write? When do you think people began to listen to him? Explain.

BARTOLOMEO VANZETTI

1. Why do you think Bartolomeo Vanzetti was found guilty and sentenced to death? If he had been arrested for a similar crime ten years earlier or ten years later, do you think the outcome would have been the same? Explain.

2. Vanzetti challenges his listeners in the courtroom to ask themselves if the war brought about greater "moral good," "spiritual progress," "security of life," "respect for human life." Were these things promised to Americans when we entered World War I? Explain. Do you think most Americans believed that these promises were met by the war's end? Why didn't Vanzetti believe that they were met?

3. Why do you think that Vanzetti ends his statement by saying that he would "live again to do what I have done already"? What has he "done"?

VICKY STARR ("STELLA NOWICKI")

1. Many Americans would describe Vicky Starr's experience with the Young Communist League (YCL) as brainwashing. Would you agree? Why, or why not? If you were in her situation, might you have been persuaded to join the YCL? Why, or why not?

2. Do you think people should be guaranteed the right to organize in a union? Why was it so important to workers like Starr—so important that they risked their lives to defend their right to organize? Do you think union organization is as important to most workers today? Why, or why not?

3. What role is Starr play in her union? Do you think women play similar roles today?

SYLVIA WOODS

1. Why did Sylvia Woods get in trouble for refusing to sing "The Star Spangled Banner" or recite the Pledge of Allegiance? Do you think her reasons were valid? Explain. Could and should this happen to a child in school today?

2. How do Sylvia Woods's experiences with work and labor unions compare and contrast with those of Vicky Starr? What accounts for the disparities?

3. How does Woods "sell" the union to non-union members? What were her goals as a union steward? Why was her union able to keep the workers together two years after the plant had closed down? Why do you think she was so effective in her role? How do her attitudes change as she continues her involvement in the union?

ROSE CHERNIN

1. What do we take for granted today that working-class Americans did not have in the 1930s?

2. How and why could Chernin have been "happy" during a time filled with so much misery? Is there any time in your life when you felt the same—happy in the face of great misery?

3. As an organizer, Chernin told the unemployed that they were asking the government to either give them jobs or support them in some way. Was this Socialism? Explain.

GENORA (JOHNSON) DOLLINGER

1. Genora Dollinger compares working inside General Motors to slavery. Do you think she substantiates this comparison? How and why? How might the other voices in this chapter respond to such a comparison?

2. What constitutional violations does Dollinger describe in her recollections? What violations against humanity does she describe?

3. How did the authorities of Flint use divide-and-conquer strategies to break the strike and to rationalize their response to the strikers?

JOHN STEINBECK

1. Why do you think *The Grapes of Wrath* resonated with so many Americans? Do you think it was controversial when it was first published? How and why?

2. How does Tom's explanation about his soul reflect what many of the union members and organizers in the chapter explained about the power of organization? Do you agree? Explain.

3. Do you think Tom and Casy are dreamers or realists? What drives them to take the actions they do? How are their choices similar to the choices made by the other people you read about in this chapter?

WOODY GUTHRIE

1. Why do you think this l song—which was quite critical of the nation in the 1930s—became one of the greatest symbols of American patriotism?

2. What is Guthrie's message?

3. What is Guthrie's vision of social justice? What role does private property play in his vision?

Main Points in *Voices*, Chapter 15,
"From the Jazz Age to the Uprisings of the 1930s"

After reading Chapter 15 in *Voices*, students should be encouraged to identify what they believe to be the main points therein. Following are five possible main points.

1. The 1920s and 1930s were decades of sharp economic, social, and political contrasts between the very rich and the very poor.

2. During this twenty-year period, the Communist Party, IWW, and other organizations were actively involved in resisting racist economic, political, and social practices across the nation.

3. Racism, nativism, sexism, and extreme patriotism permeated the atmosphere of post-World War I America.

4. Union membership, no matter how risky, offered workers hope for better working conditions.

5. The New Deal ushered in a period of unprecedented reform—reform that was largely brought about by widespread political resistance.

Main Points in *Voices*, Chapter 15, "From the Jazz Age to the Uprisings of the 1930s," and in *A People's History*, Chapter 15, "Self-Help in Hard Times"

If your students are also reading *A People's History*, they should be encouraged to identify what they believe to be the main points in Chapters 15 in both books. Following are five additional points to be stressed when *Voices* and *A People's History* are used together.

6. The 1920s were characterized by strong government control: the Red scare had rooted out Socialists and destroyed the IWW, the economy was stable enough to prevent mass rebellion, and a burst of nativist legislation and racist activities had disenfranchised immigrants and people of color.

7. The New Deal's organization of the economy sought first to stabilize, and second to give "enough help to the lower classes to keep them from turning a rebellion into a real revolution" (*People's History*, p. 393).

8. FDR's goals for the New Deal were "concessions" that did not solve the problems of the Depression but instead created "an atmosphere of progress and improvement" (*People's History*, p. 403) that restored the faith of many Americans in the economic and political system.

9. New Deal legislation was not responsible for recovery from the Depression because FDR did not spend enough money to generate rapid economic growth; that growth occurred only with the outbreak of World War II.

10. Throughout the 1920s and 1930s, prosperity was concentrated at the top of American society, while ordinary Americans without effective voices or political clout—African Americans, Mexican workers, women, sharecrop-

pers, and small farmers—suffered dramatic economic, social, and political losses.

General-Discussion Questions for *Voices*

While the following questions are designed for classroom discussion about all the voices read in Chapter 15, they can also be rewritten and included as evaluation tools.

1. What visions immediately come to mind when you think about the so-called Roaring Twenties? How do these visions contrast with the voices you have read in this chapter?

2. Where is the Lower East Side of New York City? What historic role has it played, and continues to play, for new immigrants to America?

3. Many of the voices you have heard in this chapter were Communists, Socialists, Anarchists, or people who sympathized with these views. Does knowing this change your opinion about their role as political dissidents? Explain.

4. Mary Licht wrote that circumstances "were hard in the North" but they were "desperate in the South where the Depression had really begun in 1927." Why were things so much worse, and why did the desperation begin so much earlier, in the South?

5. What is a sharecropper? When, how, and why did the sharecropping system begin? Why was it largely confined to the South?

6. What examples do you find in this chapter of strategies used by those in power to divide-and-conquer others? Which were especially effective and ineffective? Why?

7. What was the Harlem Renaissance? What are the most enduring legacies of this period?

8. What is nativism? What is xenophobia? Why were nativism and xenophobia large components of the 1920s?

9. Is it illegal to be an Anarchist? To verbally oppose war? Why, or why not? Explain.

10. What is blacklisting? Do you think it common in the factories during this period? Do you think blacklisting should be legal? Do you think it is still used in workplaces? Explain.

11. What do you think are the primary grievances of United States workers in the twenty-first century? How do they compare and contrast with the grievances of workers in the 1930s?

12. How widespread were evictions during this period? How did the various people you read unite in order to help those who were evicted? Does eviction continue to be a major problem among the working poor? How and why?

13. Under the First Amendment, people have the right to peaceably assemble and to freedom of speech. How, then, could people be fired for union membership or support in the 1930s?

14. How did the experiences with labor organization compare and contrast between male and female union members?

General-Discussion Questions for *Voices* and *A People's History*

These general-discussion questions are additional questions for students who have read Chapter 15 in both books. For all questions, discussion must focus on ways the materials in both chapters help students formulate and articulate their answers.

15. Why was it difficult to achieve unity among union members about whether or not to go on strike during the Great Depression?

16. Why does Anna Louise Strong, the author of the poem printed in the *Seattle Union Record*, believe that the "SMILING SILENCE" is what businessmen do not understand? Why is it a "weapon"?

17. Why do you think the federal and state governments acted so severely against the strikers? Do you think the strikers posed a real threat to society?

18. What are some examples from the 1920s that support the belief that the age was full of prosperity and fun? Was this belief accurate?

19. What were the primary causes of the Great Depression? Why do you think

that most politicians "did not know what had happened, [and] were baffled by it"?

20. Why were the policies of Franklin Delano Roosevelt called a New Deal for Americans? Do you think they really did offer a new deal? Explain.

21. What investments had ordinary people—the people about whom Yip Harburg wrote in "Brother, Can You Spare a Dime?"—made in the United States? What were the dividends they expected? Did they have a right to expect such dividends? Why, or why not?

22. Why do you think most traditional textbooks do not discuss the Bonus March?

23. What kinds of "self-help" took place during the Great Depression?

24. What role did racism play in keeping the unions from really uniting?

25. What is the difference between a sit-down strike and a walk out? Which was more effective during this period? How and why?

26. How did the Wagner Act aid union organizing?

27. What ways of "controlling direct labor action" developed in the 1930s? How successful were such efforts? How did the coming of World War II weaken "the old labor militancy of the thirties"?

28. Why do you think that only the radicals—the Socialists, Communists, Anarchists, and labor leaders—tried to break the racial barriers that existed in the 1930s?

Evaluation Tools

SUGGESTED ASSIGNMENTS

These assignments can be adapted to meet any classroom need—homework, short- or long-term research projects, individual or group work. The end product should be flexible, depending on teacher interest and student abilities—papers, journals, oral reports, visual aides, and the like.

1. By 1932, a jobless army of men and women were "hoboing" or riding the

rails, even though the practice was dangerous and illegal. To find out more about this phenomenon, see the PBS *American Experience* production of "Riding the Rails" or read the transcripts available at www.pbs.org/wgbh/amex/rails/filmmore/transcript/transcript1.html. Who rode the rails and why? What were the consequences of riding the rails? Why were teenagers so attracted to "hoboing"? What efforts were made to decrease hitching rides by rail, especially within the teenage population? Were these efforts successful? Explain.

2. Read more about the Bonus March of 1932. Be sure to read some first-hand accounts and perspectives from the marchers themselves, as well as reports by representatives from the military and the federal government. How do these views compare and contrast with the view of journalist Paul Anderson? Does your research tend to support or refute Anderson's belief that the government's response was "deliberately conceived" for the political purpose of making the leading issue of the campaign "Hoover versus radicalism"? Explain.

3. Read *The Great Gatsby* by F. Scott Fitzgerald. Why do you think many Americans believe that this book is essential reading for understanding the 1920s? What did you learn about the era that you did not previously know? Did you like the book? The characters in the book? Explain. What part of America is not examined in *Gatsby*? Does the book support the mythological belief in the Roaring Twenties, the decade-of-contrasts thesis, or both? Explain.

4. Learn more about Prohibition. What were the political maneuverings that preceded the passage of Prohibition? Who supported it, and why? Who opposed it, and why? Why did it take more than seventy years for such a law to pass? Why did it finally pass when it did? When and why was the amendment repealed? What were the short- and long-term consequences of Prohibition?

5. Learn more about immigration and the 1924 immigration Act. What was the impetus for imposing immigration quotas? What did the act entail? How did the political, economic, and social atmosphere in America during the 1920s contribute to the passage of this Act? Do we still have immigration quotas in America? What current immigration laws aim to limit immigration? Do you agree with our current immigration laws? What are the political impli-

cations of the decision made in 2003 to transfer the Immigration and Naturalization Service (INS) to the Office of Homeland Security?

6. Examine the role of union organization in the 1920s and 1930s. Why were unions so important to workers? Was it true that most unions and union leaders were socialists? What was the relationship between unions and socialism during the period? When and how did workers gain the right to organize? To strike? Under what conditions? What do you think the upper classes felt about union membership—and why did they feel as they did? How are unions viewed today? Would you join a union? Under what circumstances?

7. See the movie *Roger and Me* by Michael Moore. Then compare and contrast the experiences of Genora Dollinger in the 1930s with those of the workers in Flint, Michigan, in the 1990s.

8. Examine one of the strikes that occurred in the 1930s in great detail. Use a combination of primary and secondary documents to answer the following questions about the strike: What were the causes of the strike? What union was involved in the strike, and what was its role throughout? How did management respond? What assistance did management receive from local, state, and federal governments? How was the strike eventually broken? What were the short- and long-term consequences of the strike on the strikers? On the union? How did the primary documents you read broaden your understanding of this strike?

9. Learn more about the air-traffic controllers strike during the presidency of Ronald Reagan. How and why did the federal government respond to the strike? How did Reagan's response compare and contrast with the response by the federal government to strikes that occurred in the 1930s? What were the consequences of the air-traffic controllers strike for the strikers? On the strikebreakers? How are strikes in the twenty-first century similar to and different from those of the early and late twentieth century? What rights do today's strikers have that those of the 1930s did not?

SUGGESTED ESSAY QUESTIONS

1. What historical myths surrounding the 1920s and 1930s does Howard Zinn reexamine? Which myths do you feel are most in need of reexamination?

2. Rose Chernin begins her essay with this statement, "The things we take for granted now, part of the American way of life, these were revolutionary ideas when we began to demand them in the thirties." Using examples from the reading, explain the revolutionary ideas and actions that took place in the 1930s. How and why were they revolutionary? What things do we take for granted today that American workers did not have more than seventy years ago?

3. What were the advantages and disadvantages of union membership in the 1920s and 1930s? If you had been a member of the working-class, would you have joined a union? Why, or why not?

4. This period abounds with racism, sexism, and nativism. Using your reading as a guide, provide some examples of these maladies. Why were these characteristics so pronounced in the social, political, and economic lives of Americans between the two world wars? What role do these problems play in American life in the twenty-first century?

5. Rose Chernin wrote of her union involvement, "Life changes when you are together in this way, when you are united." Using examples from the reading, support this statement by showing the type of organizing that truly united people during this period and how it changed their lives. In what way did such organization change the dynamics between employer and employee?

6. How is the phrase quoted by Genora Dollinger, "Once you pass the gates of General Motors, forget about the United States Constitution," illustrated in the other voices of people you learned about in your reading? How did those who resisted such unconstitutional treatment change this situation? More than seventy years later, what remains to be done in terms of protecting our constitutional rights in the workplace?

7. Why do you think the words of such great authors, poets, and songwriters as John Steinbeck, Langston Hughes, Billie Holliday, F. Scott Fitzgerald, and Woody Guthrie resonated with some Americans but not with others? Using examples from the readings, explain how their messages were both similar and different. What common themes were especially descriptive of the 1920s and 1930s?

8. Using examples from your reading, describe the federal government's reac-

tion to strikers across the nation during the Great Depression. Why do you think the federal government acted so severely against the strikers? Do you think the strikers posed a real threat to society? Explain.

9. Using examples from your reading, support the belief that the 1920s was a period of sharp contrasts. Do you think the 1930s could also be characterized by such sharp contrast? Explain.

10. What economic warning signs existed prior to the stock-market crash? Why do you think they were generally ignored? How did the federal government initially respond? How and why were FDR's policies designed to respond to the Great Depression referred to as a "New Deal"?

11. Using examples from the reading, support or refute this statement by Howard Zinn, ". . . the New Deal's organization of the economy was aimed mainly at stabilizing the economy, and secondly at giving enough help to the lower classes to keep them from turning a rebellion into a real revolution." Do you agree with Zinn that when FDR came to office, a real rebellion was occurring? Why, or why not?

12. Provide plentiful examples to support Howard Zinn's statement that "only the radicals made an attempt to break the racial barriers" during the 1930s. Do you think this statement is fair given the work that the NAACP, as well as other African American self-help groups, was undertaking? Explain.

13. Describe the role of women in the labor movement of the 1930s. How did their roles differ from those of men? Would the unions have been as powerful without the organizing influence of women? Explain.

SIMULATIONS AND OTHER CREATIVE APPROACHES

1. Stage a trial of President Herbert Hoover in which several Bonus Marchers have charged him with violating their First Amendment rights to freedom of speech, assembly, and petition.

2. Impanel a jury for the trial of Sacco and Vanzetti. Each juror must examine the case from every possible angle and make a statement to the whole jury about each individual decision. Afterward, the jury must reach a conclusion about the guilt or innocence of the accused and must recommend a sentence to the court.

3. Imagine what it must have been like to be a working-class teenager during
    the Great Depression. Your father has lost his job, your family is at risk of
    losing your home, and none of you—your parents and five brothers and sis-
    ters—has enough to eat or enough clothing to keep you warm during the
    winter. You decide to leave home so that your parents will have one less
    person to take care of. You promise your parents to write often while you
    are gone, and to tell them where you are, what you are doing, and how you
    are managing to keep yourself alive. Compose your letters for the duration
    of your time away from home.

4. Organize a union meeting that takes place in the 1930s. The leaders have a
    wide variety of issues to discuss with members, and members have many
    subjects they wish to discuss with the leaders. Conduct the meeting and make
    some decisions about actions that will be taken in the immediate future, as
    well as ways that leaders and members will sell union involvement to non-
    members.

5. Write a letter to your representative in Congress in which you discuss one
    of the largest problems for working people across America in the twenty-first
    century—lack of health care. Explain the problem, how it affects you and
    your family, and what you think should be done to alleviate the situation.

CHAPTER SIXTEEN

World War II and McCarthyism

Was World War II the "good war"? In the twenty-first century, young people increasingly wonder if war can ever be "good." As they examine the wars of the twentieth century, the rhetoric used to propel us into war, and the bloody consequences for the world at large, many students have become increasingly skeptical about the "benefits" of war in general and about the so-called humanistic motivations behind World War II in particular.

In order to encourage such critical analysis of the policies that led us into World War II, it is essential that our students hear as many voices as possible. All too often, the only voices they have heard are those supporting, and often glorifying, the war. But there are ample first-hand accounts of Americans who opposed America's involvement in World War II, the horrific manner in which we ended the war through the introduction of nuclear weapons, and the domestic and international consequences of the war effort. When our students hear these voices, it gives power to their own questions about war, their own desires to oppose war, and their own fears of and implications about what being in a war means to them as young men and women.

Document-Based Questions

PAUL FUSSELL

1. What evident does Paul Fussell provide to support his statement, "As the war went on, 'precision bombing' became a comical oxymoron relished by bomber crews with a sense of black humor"? Why didn't the "home folks" recognize this fact?

2. How and why was the accuracy of "precision bombing" used as a propaganda tool during the war? How and why was it finally exposed as inaccurate?

3. Do you agree or disagree with Fussell's contention that the faith in area bombing "led inevitably . . . to Hiroshima and Nagasaki"?

YURI KOCHIYAMA

1. Why did the FBI immediately imprison all the men who had anything to do with fishing? Why did the next wave of arrests include all "those who were leaders of the community"?

2. What were the federal justifications for the curfews, the 9066 evacuation orders, the placement in relocation camps, and freezing Japanese assets?

3. Why did Yuri Kochiyama think that what happened to her and other Japanese Americans was so "unbelievable"? How and why did her attitude change?

YAMAOKA MICHIKO

1. How are Yamaoka Michiko's personal experiences at Hiroshima different from textbook accounts of the dropping of the bomb?

2. Why did the United States government oppose bringing the so-called Hiroshima Maidens to the United States for medical assistance? Do you agree or disagree with the reason for such opposition? Why would the government oppose such action but later, in 2003, support bringing some child victims of the war in Iraq to the United States for treatment? How are the two situations similar and dissimilar?

3. What kind of education do we receive in most history textbooks about atomic bombs? Do you think that Michiko would approve of such education? Why, or why not?

UNITED STATES STRATEGIC BOMBING SURVEY

1. What is the overall tone of this report? How does it compare with Yamaoka Michiko's report of the effects of the atomic bomb?

2. Years after the dropping of the two atomic bombs, is it true that "there are no indications that radioactivity continued after the explosion to a sufficient degree to harm human beings"?

3. How do you think the United States public responded to the dropping of the bombs on Hiroshima and Nagasaki? Do you think the public's opinion changed after the release of this report? Explain.

ADMIRAL GENE LAROCQUE

1. Admiral Laroque stated that being stationed at Pearl Harbor "sounded romantic." What do you think he meant? How is romantic imagery used to recruit people to join the military?

2. How would you compare Larocque's post-World War II beliefs with those of the Vietnam Veterans for Peace?

3. How have we "institutionalized militarism" since World War II? Do you think that the military continues to run our foreign policy? What would be the effect on our economy today without the military industrial complex?

KURT VONNEGUT

1. Why do you think Howard Zinn included this excerpt from *Slaughterhouse Five* in this chapter? What new information about war does it contribute?

2. What does Kurt Vonnegut mean when he describes both the people of Dresden and the American prisoners of war by writing, "Here were more crippled human beings, more fools like themselves"? How were both the Germans and Americans crippled, and what made them fools?

3. Why do you think Vonnegut describes the march through town as a "light opera"?

PAUL ROBESON'S UNREAD STATEMENT

1. Do you think the reasons provided by the State Department lawyers were sufficient to prohibit giving Robeson a passport, free movement, and access to public exposure? Why, or why not?

2. How do you think the white American public would have responded if this speech had been given? The black American public? Do you think Robeson should have been allowed to present his speech? Why, or why not?

3. Why do you think Robeson's speeches and songs were welcome through-out the rest of the world but not in the United States?

PETER SEEGER

1. What do you think accounted for the anti-Communist hysteria that occurred at Peekskill? Why didn't the police intervene in the violence?

2. Why did some people think that Peekskill "was the beginning of fascism in America"?

3. Why didn't Peter Seeger see the actions at Peeksill as fascist? Do you think his beliefs about ordinary Americas were realistic or unrealistic? Explain.

I. F. STONE

1. Why do you think so many people—Senators, the President, famous Americans, and ordinary folks—were afraid to challenge Joseph McCarthy?

2. Support or refute Stone's question, "If there is indeed a monstrous and dia-bolic conspiracy against world peace and stability, then isn't McCarthy right?"

3. What is the "Bogeyman Theory of History"? Does the McCarthy era qual-ify? Can you think of other times in our history that would also qualify for this description?

ETHEL AND JULIUS ROSENBERG

1. Do you believe that Ethel and Julius Rosenberg could have received a fair and impartial trial during the McCarthy era? Why, or why not?

2. How does one "defeat the executioner"? Did Ethel and Julius accomplish this?

3. Why do you believe they were so confident that "others would carry on after us"?

Main Points in *Voices*, Chapter 16, "World War II and McCarthyism"

After reading Chapter 16 in *Voices*, students should be encouraged to identify what they believe to be the main points therein. Following are five possible main points.

1. Even though World War II was the most popular war the United States ever fought, it was not simply a "good war."

2. Despite widespread American support for World War II, there were many Americans who opposed the war.

3. In the fifty years after World War II, most historians glorified and romanticized the reasons for American involvement in the war, our conduct during and after the war, our decision to use the atomic bomb to end the war, and its domestic and international consequences.

4. The use of the atomic bomb to end World War II continues to be surrounded in controversy.

5. Although it was dangerous to speak out against the hysteria of the McCarthy hearings, many Americans risked their lives and careers to oppose the challenges McCarthyism posed to our civil liberties.

Main Points in *Voices*, Chapter 16, "World War II and McCarthyism," and in *A People's History*, Chapter 16, "A People's War?"

If your students are also reading *A People's History*, they should be encouraged to identify what they believe to be the main points in Chapter 16 in both books. Following are five additional points to be stressed when *Voices* and *A People's History* are used together.

6. The wartime policies of the United States at home and abroad did not reflect the democratic values for which the nation claimed to be fighting.

7. Before the war's end, the administration was planning a new international

economic order that relied upon a partnership between big business and the federal government.

8. The dropping of the atomic bombs in Japan was the first shot in the Cold War with Russia.

9. After World War II, the United States was in a position to dominate much of the world and to create conditions to effectively control unrest on the home front.

10. The anti-Communist hysteria was so pervasive during the 1950s that many Americans believed that anti-Communism was heroic and patriotic, while those who opposed any effort to root out Communism were seen as unpatriotic.

General-Discussion Questions for *Voices*

While the following questions are designed for classroom discussion about all the voices read in Chapter 16, they can also be rewritten and included as evaluation tools.

1. Can war ever be "good"? How and why?

2. Do you think it was inevitable that a great deal of "hysteria" arose about Japanese Americans after Pearl Harbor? Was there anything the federal, state, and local governments could have done to discourage such hysteria? Why wasn't something done? What role does the promotion of hate and fear play in convincing people to go to war?

3. Find examples to support Yuri Kochiyama's statement, "Historically, Americans have always been putting people behind walls." Why do you think this is part of our history?

4. After the attacks in New York City on September 11, 2001, many Americans compared anti-Arab thoughts and actions with anti-Japanese thoughts and action after the attack on Pearl Harbor. Do you think they are comparable? If so, what should we do to prevent any further erosion of the human and civil rights that should be afforded to Arabs and Arab Americans?

5. Do you think the United States was determined to use the atomic bomb regardless of any realistic or unrealistic expectations? Is this argument

similar to the one raised in 2003 that the administration of George W. Bush was determined to go to war with Iraq, regardless of any real proof of weapons of mass destruction and Iraqi involvement in the events of September 11, 2001?

6. What is romantic about joining the military? About fighting a war? Should romantic imagery be used to recruit for military enlistment? Why, or why not?

7. Do you agree with Admiral Larocque's statement that "Old men send young men to war"?

8. What is "subversive" activity? Do you think the Hollywood Ten were involved in subversive activity?

9. Arthur Miller wrote his famous play *The Crucible* at the height of the McCarthy hearings. How and why did his play, written about the Salem witchcraft trials in 1692, speak to the McCarthy hearings in the late 1940s and early 1950s?

10. What was the "reckless irresponsible 'brink of war' policy" of John Foster Dulles?

General-Discussion Questions for *Voices* and *A People's History*

These general-discussion questions are additional questions for students who have read Chapter 16 in both books. For all questions, discussion must focus on ways the materials in both chapters help students formulate and articulate their answers.

1. Do you find it troubling that the United States fought for the freedom of Europeans during World War II at the same time that it denied many American of color their own freedoms? How and why?

2. Do you agree or disagree with Howard Zinn's statement that "Roosevelt was as much concerned to end the oppression of Jews as Lincoln was to end slavery during the Civil War" (*People's History*, p. 410)? How does he support this assertion?

3. Do you agree or disagree with Assistant Secretary of State Archibald MacLeish's statement that the peace that followed World War II would be

"a peace of oil, a peace of gold, a peace of shipping, a peace, in brief . . . without moral purpose or human interest"?

4. Describe various racist policies and actions that legally discriminated against African Americans during the war years both at home and abroad in the military.

5. Do you think the placement of Japanese into relocation camps was a mistake or a policy entirely consistent with "a long history of racism"?

6. Was World War II an example of what Howard Zinn has called a war that benefited the wealthy elite?

7. Why do you think that proportionally, there were three times more conscientious objectors (COs) in World War II, the so-called "good war," than in World War I?

8. Do you think COs should be imprisoned for refusing to go to war on the basis of their own spiritual beliefs? Why, or why not?

9. What does Howard Zinn mean by the statement that "A few voices continued to insist that the real war was inside each nation" (*People's History*, p. 420)? What was the "real war" that existed within the United States?

10. What credence do you give to the belief that the United States was eager to drop the atomic bomb in order to prevent the Russians from entering the war with Japan? Why was it so important to Harry Truman that Stalin not be allowed to enter the war?

11. Why do you think the Korean War is often called "the forgotten war"?

12. What did it mean to be "soft on Communism" in the 1950s? How did the fear of being so perceived influence politics at the federal level? What happened to those who were willing to take such a risk? Did anyone in power choose to do so? Why, or why not?

13. Why do you think Congress supported HUAC for such a long period of time? Why was there so little opposition to HUAC's?

14. What were the political and economic motives of the Marshall Plan? When George Bush announced in 2003 that he wanted to extend a new Marshall Plan to Afghanistan, what did he mean? Do you think this was an appropriate aim for our foreign policy? Why, or why not?

Evaluation Tools

SUGGESTED ASSIGNMENTS

These assignments can be adapted to meet any classroom need—homework, short- or long-term research projects, individual or group work. The end product should be flexible, depending on teacher interest and student abilities—papers, journals, oral reports, visual aides, and the like.

1. In his book *Brothers in Arms* (New York: Broadway Books, 2004), Kareem Abdul-Jabbar concludes that the 1.2 million African American veterans of World War II returned to America questioning "whether the first fully democratic nation on paper would fulfill its promise" (p. 253). Such questioning of the real meaning of the Declaration of Independence and the Constitution, he contends, "developed into the American civil-rights movement." Learn more about the role of African Americans in World War II and support or refute Abdul-Jabbar's contention.

2. View the PBS production of *The Good War*. If you cannot locate the movie—or after you have finished viewing the movie—visit the PBS website www.pbs.org/itvs/thegoodwar. Learn as much as you can about the role of Conscientious Objectors and other pacifists in World War II. What have been the role of COs and other pacifists in previous wars? In wars since World War II? How is the experience of the COs in World War II different from and comparable to the experiences of COs in other wars? In general, how has the American public responded to the needs and actions of COs and other pacifists in time of war?

3. View at least three (out of a total of eight) episodes of the HBO production of *Band of Brothers*. If you cannot locate the movie—or after you have finished viewing the movie—visit the HBO website www.hbo.com/band/landing/currahee.html. How did this movie bring home the realities of war? Is there anything romantic in this portrayal of war? Why do you think producers Tom Hanks and Steven Spielberg felt that this story was so important that it must be told?

4. In her book *Stubborn Twig* (New York: Random House, 1993), Lauren Kessler argues that the decision of the federal government to place 120,000 Japanese into "relocation camps" during World War II was a logical outcome

given almost 100 years of federal and state anti-Japanese policies and actions (especially in California, Oregon, and Washington). Learn as much as possible about these policies and actions, as well as the wartime Supreme Court decisions in regard to the camps, and then support or refute Kessler's contention.

5. In the movie *Rabbit in the Moon*, the director Emiko Omori states that the camps for the Japanese were not relocation camps but rather concentration camps. Yuri Kochiyama makes the same point in *Voices*. Learn as much as possible about the camps and then support or refute this contention. Do you think the Supreme Court cases about the constitutionality of the camps, as well as subsequent actions of the federal government, lend credence to this belief? Explain.

6. Some critics felt that in his academy-award-winning movie *On the Waterfront*, director Elia Kazan made a bold statement defending his decision to "name names" during the Hollywood "witch hunt" of the McCarthy era. Watch *On the Waterfront* and then learn more about Kazan, his decision, and his testimony. Then compare the decision of Marlon Brando's character to name names with that of Kazan's decision. How do you think his colleagues in Hollywood accepted Kazan after his testimony?

7. Watch the movie *The Best Years of Our Lives*. At the beginning, the movie's three main characters are on their way home after surviving the war and are discussing their plans and dreams for the future. What are their dreams? How do you think their dreams were shaped by their wartime experiences? Might they have been different had they not gone to war? Do they achieve their dreams? How and why? How do their lives and story illustrate the ongoing search for "the American Dream"? How do you think the dreams of the World War II veterans compare and contrast with those of veterans from the twenty-first-century wars in Afghanistan and Iraq?

8. Learn more about the fire bombings of Dresden and Tokyo. Why don't we hear much about these events in our textbooks?

9. In 1995, the Smithsonian Institute released preliminary plans for an exhibit that would mark the fiftieth year anniversary of the dropping of the atomic bomb. The planned exhibit, "The *Enola Gay*," named after the airplane that carried the bomb dropped over Hiroshima, was not well received by American veterans of World War II or by Congress. Learn more about the

initial exhibit plans, the resulting controversy, and the opening of the final exhibit. If you had been a member of Congress, how would you have responded? Explain. Do you think Congress should determine what is and is not history?

10. Read *Catch-22* by Joseph Heller. What is a Catch-22? Why do you think twenty-five publishers refused to publish the book? Why did it resonate with so many Americans? How does what you learned about the war in *Catch-22* compare and contrast with what you have read about World War II in these chapters?

11. Learn more about Peter Seeger and his folk-singing career. Listen to some of his songs and carefully read his lyrics. What can you learn about the post-war period in American history from his music? What other people were writing and singing about the same things? Pick one of Seeger's songs that you feel is especially relevant to the period under study and share it with your class.

12. Learn more about recent information concerning the involvement of Ethel and Julius Rosenberg in passing military secrets to the Soviet Union. How does this new information serve to support or detract from the Supreme Court's decision to allow them to be executed?

13. Explore the causes and consequences of the Korean "war." What did we achieve after several years of fighting? What did we lose? Describe the peace. Then learn as much as possible about the early twenty-first century relationship between North and South Korea and between the United States and the two Koreas. How did the Korean conflict during the Cold War shape the political realities and foreign policies of the twenty-first century?

14. Learn more about the life and political career of Joseph McCarthy. What was his background? How and why did he become involved in politics? What led to his success and ultimate failure with HUAC? What are the most important lessons Americans must learn from McCarthy's rise to power and his control over HUAC? Do you think any other personality has since arisen in Congress that comes close to rivaling the power of McCarthy? Explain.

SUGGESTED ESSAY QUESTIONS

1. The only real organized opposition to placing Japanese in relocation camps came from the Quakers and the American Civil Liberties Union. Remembering the voices you have read from American society in the 1920s and 1930s, why do you think more people did not oppose the relocation policy?

2. Comment on Yuri Kochiyama's statement that "[t]he more I think about, the more I realize how little you learn about American history. It's just what they want you to know." Do you agree or disagree? Be sure to use examples from all of your reading in *Voices* (and *A People's History*) to support your answer.

3. Support or refute Admiral Gene Larocque's statement that "we have to compete with communism wherever it appears. Our mistake is trying to stem it with guns"? How does it compare with I. F. Stone's statement that, "There can be no real peace without a readiness for live-and-let-live, i.e. for coexistence with Communism"? Do you think the Admiral and Stone would support or be critics of the twenty-first-century "war on terrorism"? Explain.

4. I. F. Stone claimed that the United States "will destroy itself now unless and until a few men of stature have the nerve to speak again the traditional language of free society." Drawing from what you have read in both *Voices* and *A People's History*, challenge his assertion that "men of stature" must step forward. What role have ordinary men and women played in not only speaking the language of freedom, but also putting their lives on the line for such freedom? In the twenty-first century, how would you define the language of freedom? Do you use such language? Why, or why not?

5. Why do you think there was very little organized opposition to World War II? What types of opposition arose?

6. Howard Zinn indicates that after World War II, the two victors—the United States and the Soviet Union—began "to carve out their own empires of influence." In so doing, they eventually controlled "the destinies of more countries than Hitler, Mussolini, and Japan had been able to do." What are the implications of this statement? Do you agree or disagree with this assessment? How and why?

7. Many historians have criticized President Truman for creating an atmosphere of crisis and fear in which the Soviet Union was portrayed as an immediate and evil threat to democratic peoples everywhere. Using information from the readings, support or refute this critique of Truman. This accusation is similar to that aimed at President George W. Bush during the 2004 presidential election—except his "axis of evil" was centered in Iraq. How do the policies of Truman and Bush compare and contrast?

8. Many people have argued that the October 2001 passage of the PATRIOT Act is the most recent chapter of many efforts by the federal government to encroach upon the civil liberties of ordinary Americans. Using examples from your reading, explain how civil liberties for ordinary Americans were violated during the 1930s, 1940s, and 1950s. Why do you think there was so little opposition during these years? Do you think the PATRIOT Act similarly violates our civil liberties? Is there opposition to the Act today?

9. Using ample examples from the reading, demonstrate the success of the "liberal-conservative coalition in creating a national anti-Communist consensus" in terms of both domestic and foreign policies.

10. Howard Zinn argues that in the fifteen years after World War II, the "liberal-conservative" coalition worked hard to destroy the legislative effects of the New Deal and to eliminate the opposition from radicals and Communists. Do you agree or disagree with this assessment? How and why? In the early twenty-first century, what are the remnants of the New Deal? How had various administrations since 1960 worked to either eliminate or salvage various New Deal policies?

11. Using examples from the readings, explain how the Cold War grew directly out of the consequences of World War II. Do you think there was anything that could have been done by our government to avoid the Cold War? Explain.

SIMULATIONS AND OTHER CREATIVE APPROACHES

1. Write a children's book that tells the story of the Conscientious Objectors and other pacifists who refused to fight during past American wars.

2. Interview a member of the local Veterans for Peace organization in your community. Develop a series of questions that will give you good information

about how and why he or she joined the military service, the war in which he or she fought, the reasons for becoming active in Veterans for Peace after he or she left the military, and what he or she feels about the efforts in the early twenty-first century to recruit young people for military involvement in the wars in Afghanistan and Iraq. If he or she is willing, issue an invitation to speak to your entire class.

3. Create a conversation between George W. Bush, Harry Truman, and Franklin Delano Roosevelt that takes place in mid-2004. President Bush is deep into sleep when his dreams are interrupted by a visit from former President Harry Truman. Truman feels it his duty to convince Bush to "stay the course" as he did in World War II, when he worked to convince the American people that the Soviet Union posed a real threat to democracy. Roosevelt, however, feels it essential for Bush to remember that nations can peacefully coexist. Both former presidents draw from their extensive experiences with the Soviets to help Bush think about his current problems. Document this three-way conversation and then present it to your class.

4. Draw three large maps—one of Europe and the Ottoman Empire before World War I, the second of Europe and the Middle East after World War I, and the third of Europe after World War II. Present these maps to the class and explain the geographical, political, and economic shifts that occurred as a result of war and shifting boundaries. Be sure to explain how these maps help us to better understand the geo-political realities of the twenty-first century.

CHAPTER SEVENTEEN

The Black Upsurge Against Racial Segregation

by Natalia Boettcher

In her classic protest song of the 1960s, Janis Joplin sang, "Freedom's just another word for nothing left to lose." In 1950, about two percent of all African Americans in the southern states were registered to vote, black children attended schools with few of the basic amenities needed to create a true learning environment, and all southern blacks were forced to use separate and unequal public facilities; indeed, they had "nothing left to lose." In was in these circumstances that the civil-rights movement began.

Any classroom discussion of the civil-rights movement must either begin or end with the question, "Is the movement over?" It is important that students understand that the effects of the civil-rights movement can still be seen today in socio-economic segregation and racism—and that various people in American society are still fighting for their civil rights. The best way to begin that conversation is through the voices of those who can convey the conviction, the exhaustion, the frustration, and the passion of the movement as it unfolded in the 1950s and eventually exploded in the 1960s. In so doing, our students learn to recognize the roots of current problems in the United States.

Document Based Questions

RICHARD WRIGHT

1. Do you think World War I had an influence on African Americans and their migration to the North? How? Why do you think the migration slowly dramatically after 1928?

2. What does Richard Wright's description tell you about the experience of moving from the South to the North? How do you think the African American migrants felt? What were some of the challenges in attempting

to create a better life? What were some of the differences between southern and northern life?

3. What were working and living conditions like in the North? Did it appear
   to be a better life? How? How was the treatment of blacks in the North
   and South similar? How was it different?

LANGSTON HUGHES

1. In the sixth line, whose feet do you think the author is talking about? What
   are they doing?

2. What do the narrator's inner feelings appear to be? What is his outward
   persona? What does the poem tell you about the life of the narrator?

3. In "Harlem," what are the essential two outcomes of a dream deferred?
   Which do you think unfolded? Do you think Langston Hughes had a feeling about the nature of the future?

ANNE MOODY

1. How does this document exemplify the planning involved in the civil-rights
   movement?

2. What did non-violent demonstrators have to endure? What qualities do
   you think the demonstrators had? Do you think they had any special skills
   or training? Who were the different people who sat at the counter? What
   do these facts tell you about the movement?

3. Why do you think the police did not intervene? Do you think they had an
   obligation to do so? What does this tell you about the role of much of the
   local law enforcement during this time? Was this fair?

JOHN LEWIS

1. What part of the speech do you think the other civil rights leaders wanted
   John Lewis to change? Why? Do you think it was a wise idea?

2. Why do you think John Lewis did not support the civil-rights bill? What
   issues did it not address? What examples does he use to make his point?

3. John Lewis asked, "I want to know, which side is the Federal Government on?" Which side do you think the government was on? Did it this change? Cite evidence to support your opinion.

MALCOLM X

1. What is the overall message delivered by Malcolm X?

2. Do you think Malcolm X makes a strong argument against the justification of violence against blacks? What examples does he cite?

3. How did Malcolm X attempt to unite African Americans in his speech?

MARTHA HONEY

1. How does Martha Honey describe her experience as an activist? What is different about her experience compared to that of black activists?

2. What does Honey's letter tell you about the state of Mississippi?

3. Is Honey proud of her contributions? Why, or why not?

FANNIE LOU HAMER

1. What makes someone a first-class citizen? Why? What is so important about being able to vote?

2. What risks did African Americans face when attempting to register or after they registered?

3. Was Fannie Lou Hamer's arrest justifiable? What was the treatment of her like?

RITA L. SCHWERNER

1. How were Rita Schwerner and her husband treated because they were white activists? Would you say they faced discrimination? Give examples.

2. According to Schwerner, how did police use fear and intimidation? What would you do if you were an activist facing these tactics?

3. Why did Schwerner go to see the governor? What was his response? Why do you think he responded the way he did?

ALICE WALKER

1. Which section of the poem most struck a chord with you and why?

2. What did the poem tell you about African Americans' view of themselves?

SANDRA A. WEST

1. Why would African Americans riot and burn their own neighborhood? What was being expressed? Do you think rioters had a goal?

2. Why did families who were fearful not leave their neighborhood?

3. Do you think rioting was an effective form of protest? Why, or why not?

MARTIN LUTHER KING, JR.

1. How does King describe black socio-economic conditions? How are conditions for blacks today similar to or different from King's description of black society in 1967?

2. What role does King's religious faith and his "audacious faith" play in his speech?

3. In 1967, King stated, "Now, when I say questioning the whole society, it means ultimately coming to see that the problem of racism, the problem of economic exploitation, and the problem of war are all tied together. These are the triple evils that are interrelated." Can you apply this statement to issues today? How?

Main Points in *Voices*, Chapter 17, "The Black Upsurge Against Racial Segregation"

After reading Chapter 17 in *Voices*, students should be encouraged to identify what they believe to be the main points therein. Following are five possible main points:

1. Fear, violence, and death were used to control African Americans and intimidate civil-rights leaders of all colors.

2. Freedom is never achieved without a struggle.

3. Not all civil-rights leaders agreed to use non-violent civil disobedience as means to achieve freedom.

4. The slow action and the inaction of the federal government influenced the evolution of the movement over many years.

5. Despite the abuse and violence many African Americans experienced during the civil-rights movement, many were not daunted in their efforts to bring about change.

Main Points in *Voices*, Chapter 17, "The Black Upsurge Against Racial Segregation" and in *A People's History*, Chapter 17, "Or Does It Explode?"

If your students are also reading *A People's History*, they should be encouraged to identify what they believe to be the main points in Chapter 17 in both books. Following are four additional points if using both books:

6. The roots of the civil-rights movement are firmly grounded in over 350 years of oppression of African Americans.

7. The civil-rights movement was a well-planned and organized effort, not a spontaneous uprising.

8. All who participated in the movement had to overcome enormous obstacles, often at great personal risk.

9. The issues of racism, war, and economic injustice are interrelated.

General-Discussion Questions for *Voices*

While the following questions are designed for classroom discussion about all the voices read in Chapter 17, they can also be rewritten and included as evaluation tools.

1. Why do you think the end of World War I led to such a huge migration of African Americans from the South to the North?

2. How would to compare and contrast the views on Martin Luther King, Jr., and Malcolm X concerning the civil-rights movement? How did each want to achieve his goals? Did they have the same goals? In your opinion, which was more effective? Explain.

3. Why do you think Rosa Parks's action set off such a chain of events? Do you think it was planned or spontaneous?

4. What made the 1960s—rather than the 1950s—the time to seek change? What gave the movement momentum, and what things were in place that contributed to its success? Why do you think violence escalated over time?

5. How did World War I, and particularly World War II, influence the way United States society dealt with racism? Why do you think the United States government took steps toward the integration of the military after World War II?

6. Several of the documents discuss the fact that blacks could not and would not vote. Why do you think it was made so hard for African Americans to vote? Why do you think many chose not to attempt to register? Why do you think the movement focused on registering blacks? What is the power in voting? Are there any limits to this power?

7. How was the Million Man March in October 1995 a legacy of the voices you heard in this chapter?

8. Why do you think so many southerners were so vociferously and violently opposed to equality for African Americans?

9. How would you define a revolution? Do you think the civil-rights movement was a revolution? Why, or why not?

10. Do you believe the social and economic justice Martin Luther King, Jr., and others sought has been served? Why, or why not? Give examples.

11. How did the voices in this chapter reinforce any on the five themes listed in "Main Points in *Voices*"?

12. Which of the voices in this chapter did you find most and least powerful? How and why?

General-Discussion Questions for *Voices* and *A People's History*

These general-discussion questions are additional questions for students who have read Chapter 17 in both books. For all questions, discussion must focus on ways the materials in both chapters help students formulate and articulate their answers.

13. Why do you think Howard Zinn entitled Chapter 17 in *A People's History*, "Or Does it Explode"? Do you think the title is well supported by the chapter's contents? Explain.

14. What was the Scottsboro Boys incident? Why was mention of the incident included in Chapter 17?

15. What is the NAACP? What did people hope to gain by associating the actions of the NAACP with Communism? Were they successful in their aims? How and why? What role did the NAACP play in the civil-rights movement?

16. What was the immediate impact of *Brown* v. *Board of Education*? What was the long-term impact? How well has desegregation met the goals and expectations of the champions of *Brown*?

17. Considering that the federal government had authority to enforce aspects of justice and equality in society, why did the government refrain form getting involved in the evolving conflict in the southern states? How and why did the federal government get involved when it did?

18. What were some of the tactics used by civil-rights activists? What tactics were used by their opponents? How are they similar and different? Which do you think was more successful?

19. Affirmative action is a current controversial issue that has arisen from the civil-rights movement. What is affirmative action? What are its goals? Why would such a system be used? Do you think it is an effective way to right socio-economic injustice?

20. What does happen "to a dream deferred"? What dreams did African Americans have to defer in the years leading up to the civil-rights movement? Which dreams might continue to be deferred in the twenty-first century?

21. What other voices might have been added to Chapter 17 in *Voices* that

might have provided a more complete understanding of Chapter 17 in *A People's History*?

22. Young people—including thousands of pre-teens and teenagers—formed the core of the civil-rights movement. Knowing the risks, why do you think they got involved? Why do you think their parents allowed them to become involved?

23. Was the civil-rights movement confined to the United States' South? Was racism, segregation, and disenfranchisement of the African American community confined to the South?

24. How did the FBI help undermine the civil-rights movement? What role did it play in discrediting the Black Panthers?

Evaluation Tools

SUGGESTED ASSIGNMENTS

These assignments can be adapted to meet any classroom need—homework, short- or long-term research projects, individual or group work. The end product should be flexible, depending on teacher interest and student abilities—papers, journal, oral reports, visual aides, etc.

1. Using a search engine of choice, find a web site that includes primary documents about the civil-rights movement. A good source is the United States National Archives and Records Administration (KARA) at www.archives.gov/digital_classroom/. What does the document tell you about the civil-rights movement?

2. Explore personal experiences by reading a biography of a civil-rights activist. (Two suggestions are *Coming of Age in Mississippi* by Anne Moody and *Warriors Don't Cry* by Melba Patillo Beals.) How did this person's experiences compare and contrast with those of the voices you read in this/these chapter(s)? Which was most compelling and why? What new information did you learn about the civil-rights movement from the book? Would you recommend it to a friend? Why?

3. Learn more about the origins of the organizations that worked to achieve the goals of the civil-rights movement: the National Association for the Advancement of Colored People (NAACP); Congress for Racial Equality (CORE); Southern Christian Leadership Conference (SCLC); Student Nonviolent Coordinating Committee (SNCC). (Be sure to reference the relevant sections of Chapter 18 in *Voices* when researching these organizations.) How were their origins and goals similar and dissimilar? What do you think were the greatest achievements of these organizations?

4. Watch a feature-length movie that depicts part of the civil-rights movement. Some suggestions are *Mississippi Burning, Ghosts of Mississippi, Malcolm X, Boycott, Men of Honor, Four Little Girls.* Which parts of the readings did it reinforce? Do you believe the movie is historically accurate? Research the film's accuracy to prove your position.

5. Watch the documentary series *Eyes On The Prize.* How does the documentary bring the writing in *A People's History* and *Voices* alive? What is the importance of having images of history? What part of the readings did it visually reinforce?

6. Learn more about the role of religion and song in the civil-rights movement. Investigate their significance and the spiritual motivation they inspired.

7. Research any two of the following historical legislative acts and judicial decisions related to the movement including: the Thirteenth, Fourteenth and Fifteenth Amendments; the 1896 Supreme Court decision in *Plessey* v. *Ferguson*; the 1954 Supreme Court decision in *Brown* v. *Board of Education*; the 1964 Civil Rights Act; and the 1965 Voting Rights Act. What were the strengths and weakness of each? How were the acts carried out? Who enforced them?

8. Learn more about the historical origins and beliefs of the Nation of Islam (NOI). How did these beliefs influence the civil-rights movement? How did Malcolm X influence the movement? How has the NOI evolved?

9. Using a search engine of choice, investigate the history of lynching. What was the role of lynching? Who participated? Was their any organized opposition to lynching? Does lynching continue to occur in contemporary American society?

10. Learn more about Martin Luther King, Jr., and Malcolm X. Explore how their views compared and contrasted.

11. Research the history of the Ku Klux Klan. What influence did it have on the South prior to and during the civil-rights movement? What social and occupational arenas did it enter? Did it have an effect on the way southern officials dealt with African Americans? What role does the Klan play in contemporary American society.

12. View art collections about the civil-rights movement. Norman Rockwell created some exemplary pieces. What do they tell you about the movement? What do they tell you about the individuals involved? Why would art be created to express the civil-rights movement?

SUGGESTED ESSAY QUESTIONS

1. It is argued that one cannot understand the civil-rights movement unless one understands the institutions of slavery and Jim Crow. Do you agree or disagree? Why?

2. Do you think the civil-rights movement was purely a black movement? Use evidence in the readings to support your answer.

3. Do you think Martin Luther King's dream to one day say, "We have overcome! We have overcome! Deep in my heart, I did believe we would overcome," has been achieved? Do you think King would be disappointed today? Use examples from the readings and from contemporary society to support your answer.

4. How has black consciousness changed since the civil-rights movement? How was it expressed then? How is it expressed today? Provide examples.

5. The evolution of federal involvement in matters concerning the rights of African Americans was very slow. Why do you think the federal government neglected to enforce civil-rights laws for so long?

6. What were the different strategies used as the civil-rights movement progressed? Why do you think it started to quiet down in the late 1960s?

7. Howard Zinn writes that the black revolt of the 1950s and 1960s should not have come as a surprise to people of the United States. Support this statement with historical evidence.

8. How is the civil-rights movement a contemporary example of the historical debate over federal versus states' rights?

9. Is the civil-rights movement over? Carefully explain your answer, using historical and contemporary examples.

10. Martin Luther King, Jr., wrote, "And so we still have a long, long way to go before we reach the promise land of freedom." What criteria do you think King used to define freedom? How do you define freedom? Do you think African Americans were free in 1967? Are they free today?

11. How has reading chapter 17 in *Voices* broadened your understanding of the civil-rights movement?

12. What voices of resistance in Chapter 17 in both *Voices* and *A People's History* were of most interest to you? How and why? Which did you find most compelling and why? Least compelling and why?

SIMULATIONS AND OTHER CREATIVE ACTIVITIES

1. Imagine that you are Martin Luther King, Jr., and you are in jail in Birmingham, Alabama. Before you write your famous "Letter from a Birmingham Jail," write a letter to Henry David Thoreau in which you discuss your feelings about the successes and failures of civil disobedience over a hundred years later.

2. Create a panel of veterans from organizations that worked to achieve the goals of the civil-rights movement: the National Association for the Advancement of Colored People (NAACP); Congress for Racial Equality (CORE); Southern Christian Leadership Conference (SCLC); Student Nonviolent Coordinating Committee (SNCC). Imagine that these veterans of the movement have gathered in the early twenty-first century to discuss with their audience (class members) how their goals for freedom and equality in the 1960s have and have not been met over forty years later.

3. Stage a debate that might have been held in 1967 between Martin Luther King, Jr., and Malcolm X about the goals and anticipated outcomes of the struggle for civil rights.

4. Write a poem or song or create a work of art that expresses the goals of any

contemporary group of United States residents who currently experience political, social, and/or economic injustice.

5. Hold a town meeting in your classroom in which the residents (students) come prepared with a list of contemporary civil-rights issues that have arisen within the community at large and within your school environment. Discuss the similarities and differences of the issues that arise, whether they are issues that are typical or atypical of other communities, and any possible solutions that could be enacted both within the larger community and in the school community.

6. Write a new section to be added to your history textbook's coverage of the civil-rights movement that is entitled, "The Civil Rights Movement in the Twenty-first century."

CHAPTER EIGHTEEN

Vietnam and Beyond: The Historic Resistance

by Mike Benbow and Robin Pickering

In the 1960s, while the United States intensified its military intervention in Vietnam, the domestic antiwar movement grew in both size and seriousness. Poor and minority citizens were among the first to recognize that the goals of the United States government in Vietnam were contrary to their own goal of social justice within United States society. Disenfranchised by literacy tests, poll taxes, and intimidation, many were still seeking true democracy within the United States. The alleged fight for democracy and freedom in Vietnam seemed a cruel reminder to those still fighting for voting rights and equality within their own nation that their government did not hold these priorities. Many also noted that because of college deferments and the lack of economic and educational opportunity within poor neighborhoods, poor members of United States society were disproportionately being sent to fight and die in Vietnam. Some criticized the lack of a defined goal; others criticized what they believed to be the true imperialist goal of the United States government to control Vietnam's rich natural resources and to maintain a secure and stable chain of military bases in East Asia to both protect United States interests and isolate Communist China.

Almost unanimously, protesters decried the damage and horror wrought upon the Vietnamese people and landscape. Though each individual had different reasons and goals for protesting the war in Vietnam, the resistance movement steadily gained power and unity and was influential in bringing United States intervention in Vietnam to an end. The documents in this chapter are necessary supplements to our classroom discussions about Vietnam. They illustrate poignant arguments against fighting the war in Vietnam, provide examples of different forms of resistance, and bring a balanced perspective to the overall discussion of the war. While examining these documents, students can debate what it means to be an active and responsible citizen in a democracy, as well as the efficacy of United States military and political actions in Vietnam.

Document-Based Questions

MISSISSIPPI FREEDOM DEMOCRATIC PARTY

1. Why might African Americans not be eager to fight in the Vietnam War?

2. With which of the five reasons presented in this document do you most agree? Why?

3. What was the Mississippi Freedom Democratic Party? What were its goals?

MARTIN LUTHER KING, JR.

1. For what reasons did Dr. Martin Luther King oppose the Vietnam War?

2. What did Dr. King mean when he said, "We must rapidly begin . . . the shift from a thing-oriented society to a person-oriented society"? Why did he feel that such a shift was so crucial to the success and progress of the United States?

3. Explain the sentence "A time comes when silence is betrayal" and what it means in the context of Dr. King's speech.

STUDENT NONVIOLENT COORDINATING COMMITTEE

1. For what reasons did the Student Nonviolent Coordinating Committee (SNCC) oppose the war in Vietnam? Which reason, if any, did you find most convincing or relevant? Why?

2. What was the Student Nonviolent Coordinating Committee? What was its role in both the civil-rights movement and the antiwar movement?

3. If you had been alive during the antiwar movement, might you have been tempted to join SNCC? Explain.

BOB DYLAN

1. What lyrics did you find most effective? Why?

2. What role did music play in the Vietnam War—both for the soldiers and those involved in the antiwar movement? What songs were especially influential?

3. Who are the "Masters of War" in this song? What is the significance of that title?

MUHAMMAD ALI

1. Why did Muhammad Ali refuse to participate in the Vietnam War? For what reasons did Ali say he would willingly enter war?

2. Was it fair and just that he lost his boxing title?

3. Would you go to war if you were drafted by the United States military? Would the nature and cause of the war influence your decision? Why, or why not?

JONATHAN SCHELL

1. How did the people of Ben Suc feel about being moved into the camps?

2. Why do you think they were placed in the camp? Was this a just or unjust action by the United States?

3. What was the purpose of demolition teams? Were they necessary to the war effort?

LARRY COLBURN

1. What happened in the small village of My Lai? What reason did Larry Colburn give for the actions of the soldiers responsible for the massacre? Does it justify their actions? Why, or why not?

2. What would you do if you were in Colburn's situation? Explain.

3. Should military personnel follow all orders? Or should individuals be able to determine which orders to follow? What kind of military would we have if soldiers didn't follow all orders? What legal precedents have been established regarding the issue of "following orders" as a defense against war crimes?

HAYWOOD T. "THE KID" KIRKLAND

1. Why might the military try to dehumanize the enemy?

2. What would be the hardest thing about coming home from Vietnam for Kirkland? Why?

3. Do you think other veterans felt the same way that Haywood did? Why, or why not?

LOUNG UNG

1. According to this document, what was it like to live under the Khmer Rouge in Cambodia?

2. Can you think of any past or contemporary governments with similar policies and ideologies to the Khmer Rouge?

3. Which groups and/or individuals "disappeared"? Why? Explain the statement, "Disappearance mixed hope with horror. It was psychologically unbearable."

TIM O'BRIEN

1. What do you believe Tim O'Brien was trying to convey with this piece? How did it make you feel?

2. O'Brien repeats many of the same phrases and images throughout this piece. Why? Is the device effective?

3. Who did Tim kill? How was Tim affected by killing him? What do you think would be the hardest part about killing another human being?

MARIA HERRERA-SOBEK

1. Compare the two poems. What do they have in common? How are they different? What lines were most effective? How and why?

2. Maria Herrera-Sobek uses color in her imagery in the poem "Untitled." Why?

3. Who/what do these poems criticize? Who/what do these poems praise?

4. Are these poems hopeful or cynical? Why?

DANIEL ELLSBERG

1. For what reasons did Daniel Ellsberg leak the Pentagon Papers? Do you agree with Ellsberg's decision to make secret documents public? Why, or why not?

2. Under what circumstances should a government official leak information to the public?

3. What information in the Pentagon Papers would the government not want the American public to know about and why?

Main Points in *Voices*, Chapter 18, "Vietnam and Beyond: The Historic Resistance"

After reading Chapter 18 in *Voices*, students should be encouraged to identify what they believe to be the main points therein. Following are five possible main points:

1. The war in Vietnam was wrong for several reasons: it was fought for imperialist purposes, it ravaged the civilians and landscape of Vietnam, funds were diverted to military ventures rather than support programs for the poor, and American soldiers were sent to fight and die in a war that had no moral justification.

2. The people of the United States had a responsibility to curb the actions of their government in Vietnam.

3. Because United States policymakers understood neither the Vietnamese struggle nor the mood of Americans at home, their actions eventually alienated the civilian population and encouraged antiwar resistance.

4. Many African Americans and other disenfranchised people did not want to fight a war to allegedly promote freedom in Vietnam when it still eluded them at home.

5. Racial conflict, so prevalent within American society, permeated the military as well.

Main Points in *Voices*, Chapter 18, "Vietnam and Beyond: The Historic Resistance," and in *A People's History*, Chapter 18, "The Impossible Victory: Vietnam"

If your students are also reading *A People's History*, they should be encouraged to identify what they believe to be the main points in Chapter 18 in both books. Following are five additional points to be stressed when *Voices* and *A People's History* are used together.

6. The United States, like the colonial powers before it, wished to control the valuable natural resources of Vietnam, such as rice, tin, rubber, and oil.

7. The success of the National Liberation Front (NLF) was due to the fact that it brought significant and much-needed social change; the Viet Cong recognized and understood the needs of the peasantry and provided land and improvements in daily life.

8. Civil-rights leaders recognized and illustrated the connection between the war in Vietnam and the "war" on workers and the poor in United States society.

9. Opposition and resistance to the Vietnam War was so widespread throughout United States society that it eventually became an influential factor in ending the war.

10. The greatest technological and military power in the world was defeated by a third-world nation of well-organized and passionate peasants.

General-Discussion Questions for *Voices*

While the following questions are designed for classroom discussion about all the voices read in Chapter 18, they can also be rewritten and included as evaluation tools.

1. How do these voices illustrate the ways the Vietnam War affected poor Americans?

2. How have journalists changed the nature of war? How does journalism coverage of Vietnam compare with the journalistic coverage of the War in Iraq?

3. Some people have argued that racism played a big role in the Vietnam War. Do you believe racism was a key element in the Vietnam War? Why, or why not?

4. How would you compare and contrast the documents of Schell, Ung, and Colburn? How do you think their experiences compare and contrast with those of an ordinary Vietnamese citizen during the war?

5. The issue of responsibility for the actions of one's government as well as oneself is raised within these selections. Who is responsible for the actions of the United States government? For the actions of individual soldiers? For bringing war to an end?

6. Which groups and individuals are represented in these voices? Which groups or individuals are missing from this selection?

7. The current war in Iraq has been a divisive issue within the United States. Which arguments in *Voices* could also be used to protest the war in Iraq? Have those arguments been successful? (What is "successful"?)

8. The selections in Chapter 18 cover a variety of media—songs, poetry, fictional and non-fictional literature, essays, speeches, and so forth. How is the basic message of each entry enforced or shaped by the medium through which it is expressed? Do you feel that one medium was more powerful than the others during this time period? How and why? Which of these media do you believe is used most commonly by resistance movements today? Why?

9. What is the responsibility of the news media during times of war? Is the contemporary news media fulfilling that responsibility?

10. How did the voices in this chapter reinforce any of the five themes listed in "Main Points in *Voices*"?

11. Which of the voices in this chapter did you find most powerful? Least powerful? Why?

General-Discussion Questions for *Voices* and *A People's History*

These general-discussion questions are additional questions for students who have read Chapter 18 in both books. For all questions, discussion must focus on how the materials in both chapters helped students formulate and articulate their answers.

12. In looking at Chapter 18 in both *Voices* and *A People's History*, what United States actions alienated the civilian population of Vietnam?

13. What was the aim of the Vietminh in Vietnam? What was the aim of the United States?

14. How were United States soldiers affected by their experiences in the Vietnam War? What actions did they take to bring it to an end?

15. In *A People's History*, Howard Zinn discusses the many different elements in United States society that opposed the war. Which of these elements are reflected in *Voices*? Which are not represented?

16. Zinn argues that the antiwar movement in the United States was instrumental in bringing the Vietnam War to an end. Do you agree? Why, or why not?

17. Senator Ted Kennedy and others have called the invasion of Iraq "another Vietnam." Why? What similarities and differences do you see in the two conflicts? Do you agree or disagree with the comparison? Explain.

18. What evidence do you find in both *Voices* and *A People's History* that soldiers, leaders, and the United States public were encouraged to dehumanize the Vietnamese population? Do you believe this was necessary? What is the outcome of dehumanization? Do you feel dehumanization is still a large part of contemporary warfare? Explain.

19. What was the United States strategy in Vietnam? What were the strengths and weaknesses of this strategy? Why was it ultimately unsuccessful?

20. Why is Chapter 18 in *A People's History*, entitled ""The Impossible Victory"? Why was victory impossible? For whom?

21. How would you describe the FBI's treatment of the antiwar protesters? Do you think such treatment was justified? Explain. How does the federal government respond to antiwar protesters in the early twenty-first century? Are there any comparisons between the two responses?

22. What is guerrilla warfare? What other examples of guerrilla warfare are evi-

dent in United States history?

23. What specific actions did the NLF and Vietminh take to gain support of the Vietnamese civilian population?

Evaluation Tools

SUGGESTED ASSIGNMENTS

These assignments can be adapted to meet any classroom need—homework, short- or long-term research projects, individual or group work. The end product should be flexible, depending on teacher interest and student abilities—papers, journals, oral reports, visual aides, and the like.

1. Interview someone who experienced the Vietnam War—a soldier, a protester, a supporter, and the like—and write a paper that describes what you learned and share it with the class.

2. Locate a primary voice of resistance not included in Chapter 18 of *Voices* that would be beneficial to further your understanding of the Vietnam War and the antiwar movement. What new information does this voice provide? How does it build on the other voices in the chapter? What does it contribute to your overall understanding of the Vietnam War?

3. Research the role of the news media in Vietnam. Compare news coverage of the war in Vietnam to that of the current war in Iraq. What words, phrases, scenarios are similar and different?

4. Find five images of the Vietnam War that you feel illustrate the struggle and write a paper that explains why you chose those specific images.

5. Research and write an essay about the Vietminh and the National Liberation Front—their strategy, goals, methods by which they gained the support of Vietnamese civilians, leaders, experience, and so on.

6. Read *The Things They Carried* by Tim O'Brien. Then answer the following questions: What more did you learn from reading the entire book versus reading the singular passage in *Voices*? While the book is considered a work of fiction, what do you believe is fictional about this story and what is nonfiction? Does its truth or fiction affect the power of O'Brien's mes-

sage? How does this book change your understanding of the Vietnam War?

7. Research and write a biography on a specific personality that influenced the Vietnam War—Ho Chi Minh, Lyndon B. Johnson, John F. Kennedy, Diem, Robert McNamara, and the like.

8. The War in Vietnam has had a lasting effect on United States society, and especially on the nation of Vietnam. Research the conditions that exist in Vietnam today and the effects of the war.

9. Research the history of draft resistance within the United States through the present day.

10. What was the Khmer Rouge? How did United States involvement in Vietnam influence its rise to power? What could be done to stop the Khmer Rouge's reign of terror? What would happen to people who might speak out against it? What is the responsibility of the international community in protecting citizens from their own governments?

11. There are many different views regarding Ho Chi Minh. Compare and contrast the ways this significant figure is represented in three different sources.

12. Watch the movie *Fog of War*. Who was Robert McNamara, and what role did he play in the Vietnam War? Why do you think McNamara agreed to be interviewed for this film? What new information did McNamara bring to light in this movie as well as in his 1995 book *In Retrospect*? What do you think he meant by the title of his book?

ESSAY QUESTIONS

1. Take a position for or against the Vietnam War, using strong evidence from your reading to support your position.

2. What is the domino theory? How did it influence United States involvement in Vietnam?

3. Explain the events leading up to United States intervention in Vietnam and how those events influenced the struggle between the Vietnamese and United States military.

4. What different groups made up the antiwar movement? What different

grievances did they have regarding United States policy in Vietnam?

5. Discuss the controversy of the Vietnam War Memorial in Washington, D.C. Do you feel that it is an appropriate and effective memorial? Why, or why not?

6. How did journalists affect the outcome of the Vietnam War? What is the responsibility of the news media during times of war? Are the contemporary news media fulfilling that responsibility?

7. Discuss at least three mistakes the United States government made in Vietnam that resulted in defeat.

8. Thousands of Americans fled the country to avoid being drafted. Do citizens have the right and/or responsibility to break a law that they believe is unjust? Why, or why not?

9. Howard Zinn refers to "the gap between the internal government discussion about Vietnam and the reality that was well understood by those in Washington" (*Voices*, p. 450). What does this mean? Using evidence from *Voices* and *A People's History*, discuss this "gap."

10. Ellsberg states, "I was not wrong, either, to hope that exposing secrets five presidents had withheld and the lies they told might have benefits for our democracy that were worthy of the risks." Do you agree or disagree? What other individuals have taken similar actions? Why?

11. Is the selective-service system, or draft, necessary for the safety of a nation during times of war?

12. Define patriotism. Are the voices of resistance included in this chapter those of patriots?

SIMULATIONS AND OTHER CREATIVE APPROACHES

1. Write a story from the point of view of a United States soldier in Vietnam that addresses the soldier's goals and experience. Write a story from the point of view of a Vietnamese civilian or NLF guerrilla that does the same.

2. Create a political cartoon that clearly illustrates one of the arguments for or against the war in Vietnam.

3. Assign different roles to students and conduct a debate regarding the

Vietnam War and other social issues of the 1960s. (Which characters should be represented could be an interesting class discussion.)

4. Compose a song or poem that expresses an emotion associated with the Vietnam War.

5. Stage a debate on the following topic: There are strong parallels between United States intervention in Vietnam and intervention in Iraq.

CHAPTER NINETEEN

Women, Gays, and Other Voices of Resistance

by Jack Bareilles

In most of our classrooms, discussions of movements of the 1960s generally focus on those big endeavors—civil rights and the antiwar efforts—that are discussed in the traditional textbooks. Yet this approach, as Howard Zinn reminds us, omits an essential topic for discussion—the emergence of a counterculture with "radically different ideas about how people should live their lives." Indeed, "The United States experienced a general revolt in the culture against oppressive, artificial, previously unquestioned ways of living. This revolt touched every aspect of personal life," Zinn suggests. Certainly the civil-rights movement and the Vietnam Era protests affected us all, but our lives were also changed forever by the poetry, literature, speeches, and protests of women who demanded their liberation, gays and lesbians who "came out of the closet," native peoples who launched the Red Power movement, and prisoners who questioned their rights as incarcerated Americans.

As teachers, it is important to bring the voices of the counterculture to our students. And in so doing, we must remain ever mindful that to our students, this revolt has colored and textured the only history they have known. Indeed, in their eyes, today is the way the world has always been. It is imperative, then, that we give our students the tools to understand the events leading up to this transformation, the voices that shaped it, and the way in which it changed the American social landscape.

Document-Based Questions:

ALLEN GINSBERG

1. In his introduction to "America by Allen Ginsberg," Howard Zinn states that the poem "gives voice to his critique of the nation's Establishment." What are Ginsberg's criticisms of the establishment?

2. How many of those criticisms from 1956 are still relevant today?

3. Why do you think Ginsberg wrote this poem? What was his motivation? What point was he trying to convey?

MARTIN DUBERMAN

1. What were the short- and long-term causes of the Stonewall Riot?

2. Later, when talking about the night in general and perhaps the "chorus line of mocking queens," Sylvia said that "Something lifted off my shoulders." What do you think Sylvia meant?

3. Why should we care, many decades later, about what happened at Stonewall?

WAMSUTTA (FRANK B.) JAMES

1. Wamsutta James says "Sometimes we are arrogant but only because society has pressured us to be so." What do you think he means?

2. What does James say was "perhaps our biggest mistake"? How do you think the citizens of Plymouth would have felt about this statement?

3. Why do you suppose the "officials who checked the speech" suppressed it?

ADRIENNE RICH

1. Why do you think Adrienne Rich's work was called *Of Woman Born*?

2. Rich writes, "I know of no woman . . . for whom the body is not a fundamental problem." What does she mean?

3. Re-read the last two paragraphs, which start, "We need to imagine a world." What future do you think Rich envisions for womankind?

ABBEY LINCOLN

1. What are Mark Twain's three steps toward enslaving a people, as paraphrased by Abbey Lincoln? Does Lincoln believe that all three of these steps had been accomplished? How and why?

2. What does it mean to revere something or someone? What does Lincoln mean when she asks, "Who will revere the black woman?" What does Lincoln say is the role of black men in their own oppression and that of black women?

3. Reread the last paragraph of Lincoln's essay. Whom is she calling to step forward? Do you believe that end has been accomplished in the last forty years?

SUSAN BROWNMILLER

1. According to Susan Brownmiller, what was the reality for most women who experienced unwanted pregnancies prior to the legalization of abortion?

2. What tactics did pro-abortion advocates adopt from the protest movements of the 1960s?

3. Why do you think Brownmiller chose to include the story of St. Louis debutante Jane O'Reilly?

ASSATA SHAKUR (JOANNE CHESIMARD)

1. What do you think Assata Shakur means when she writes, "There are no criminals here at Riker's Island Correctional Institution for Women . . . only victims."

2. Why would Shakur deliberately misspell the word America throughout her essay, as in the sentence, "One thing is clear: amerikan capitalism is in no way threatened by the women in prison on Riker's Island."

3. Some of the prisoners seemingly believe that a stint in Riker's is a "vacation." How could they justify that view, and what does that belief say about their conditions outside?

KATHLEEN NEAL CLEAVER

1. What was, in Kathleen Cleaver's words, "the first order of business" in the early to mid-1960s?

2. After pointing out that a 1969 survey showed that two-thirds of the Panthers were women, Cleaver asks, "why isn't this the image that you have

of the Black Panther Party?" What is her answer? What does Cleaver feel to be distinctive about gender relations within the Black Panther Party?

3. Based upon your reading of Shakur and Cleaver, which is the greatest challenge—to be black, poor, or a woman?

Main Points in *Voices*, Chapter 19, "Women, Gays, and Other *Voices* of Resistance"

After reading Chapter 19 in *Voices*, students should be encouraged to identify what they believe to be the main points therein. Following are five possible main points.

1. Throughout history, those in power used a long-standing practice of "divide and conquer" to keep marginalized groups of ordinary people from demanding their rights.

2. The voices of resistance from the 1960s are the direct consequence of historical social, political, economic, and ideological oppression.

3. A counterculture comprised of persons and groups who are ignored and marginalized by society profoundly influenced United States politics in the 1960s and 1970s.

4. Many of the counterculture social movements saw issues of oppression as being interlinked.

5. An ideology of social control and punishment has dominated United States incarceration practices, rather than a philosophy of rehabilitation.

Main Points in *Voices*, Chapter 19, "Women, Gays, and Other *Voices* of Resistance" and in *A People's History*, Chapter 19, "Surprises"

If your students are also reading *A People's History*, they should be encouraged to identify what they believe to be the main points in Chapter 19 in both books. Following are five additional points to be stressed when *Voices* and *A People's History* are used together.

6. The political, economic, and social ferment of the 1960s created a positive environment for the growth of the counterculture movement.

7. Women of the 1960s united in many ways to give voice to their desire for liberation: demanding equality; legally challenging the right to make decisions about their own bodies; joining consciousness-raising women's groups; and frankly discussing sex and sexual roles.

8. Within the myriad liberation efforts of the 1960s, many people expressed a desire to unite against the "common oppression . . . of control and indoctrination."

9. Because the United States prison system was "an extreme reflection of the American system itself," it was in need of the same dramatic reforms that the counterculture demanded for United States society as a whole.

10. During the 1960s and 1970s, there was a "loss of faith in big powers" and a corresponding "stronger belief in self."

General-Discussion Questions for *Voices*

While the following questions are designed for classroom discussion about all the voices read in Chapter 19, they can also be rewritten and included as evaluation tools.

1. Who or what were the Wobblies, Tom Mooney, the Spanish Loyalists, Sacco and Vanzetti, and the Scottsboro Boys, discussed in earlier chapters? What role do they play in understanding the voices in this chapter?

2. Why do you think the gay-rights movement has placed such emphasis on the Stonewall Riot?

3. "To seek visions, to dream dreams, is essential, and it is also essential to try new ways of living, to make room for serious experimentation, to respect the effort even where it fails." With this line Adrienne Rich begins her afterword in the paperback edition of her book *Of Woman Born*. How might the other voices in Chapter 19 feel about this line?

4. How do you think the activists of the 1960s might measure the changes achieved by the beginning of the twenty-first century?

5. How important is the fact that the authors of the last five excerpts in Chapter 19 are all women? Does their womanhood make all three topics they write about secondary to the question of where women fit into this society?

6. How does each document support Howard Zinn's assertion that "With the loss of faith in big powers—business, government, religion—there arose a stronger belief in self, whether individual or collective"? How do the documents illustrate this belief in individual or collective self-worth and the desire to be treated equally?

7. Did any of these four movements arise independently of the others and the more general civil-rights and Vietnam War movements? How and why?

8. How is rage and indignation expressed by the various authors of the eight documents? Do you think these feelings were justified?

9. Why did Black activists feel the need for a new movement—a Black Power movement—after fighting a two-decade battle for civil rights?

10. Why do you think many people left SNCC and joined the Black Panthers?

11. Do you think any of the voices in this chapter reinforce any of five themes listed in "Main Points in *Voices*"?

12. Which of the voices in this chapter did you find most powerful? Least powerful? How and why?

General-Discussion Questions for *Voices* and *A People's History*

These general-discussion questions are additional questions for students who have read Chapter 19 in both books. For all questions, discussion must focus on ways the materials in both chapters help students formulate and articulate their answers.

13. Why do you think Howard Zinn entitled Chapter 19 of *A People's History* "Surprises"?

14. What is feminism? How did the movement begin? What achievements have feminists made? What gains remain to be made?

15. The voices and stories in these chapters are representative of groups that have

historically been marginalized. Are the voices of representatives of these groups commonly heard in the United States today?

16. What is the spark that sets off each of the movements in this chapter? Do similarities exist among the sparks that ignite the different movements?

17. What are the similarities between the women's rights, gay rights, prisoners' rights, and Native American rights movements? How are they interconnected?

18. Why do you think all these movements arose at approximately the same time? What was it about the 1960s that allowed, and even encouraged, protest?

19. What do you think about the uprising at Attica? What were the goals of the prisoners? Did their conditions justify the uprising? Do you think prison conditions have changed in the last three decades? Should they change?

20. Should prisoners be allowed to organize in prison? What do you think the role of the prison should be—rehabilitation or punishment? What are the pros and cons of each position?

21. What issues surrounding treaties formed the basis for the early civil-rights movement among Native peoples? Why are some Indian Nations allowed to have year-round fishing and hunting rights in areas where non-natives must get seasonal permits?

22. Do you think the Indians of All Tribes were justified in their occupation of Alcatraz? Why, or why not?

23. How are American Indians portrayed in your textbook? In the movies? Is this portrayal accurate? Why, or why not?

24. Where is Pine Ridge Reservation? What conditions led to the American Indian Movement (AIM) confrontation at Pine Ridge? Do you think the actions of the AIM activists were justified? Why, or why not?

25. What other voices might have been added that might have provided a more complete understanding of Chapter 19 in *A People's History*?

Evaluation Tools

SUGGESTED ASSIGNMENTS

These assignments can be adapted to meet any classroom need—homework, short- or long-term research projects, individual or group work. The end product should be flexible, depending on teacher interest and student abilities—papers, journals, oral reports, visual aides, and the like.

1. Using a search engine of choice, find out how the *New York Times* and other New York City newspapers reported the Stonewall Riot. Then search for journalistic and eyewitness accounts of the riot. How do these accounts of the goals, accomplishments, and consequences of the riots compare and contrast with Duberman's version of events? Compare accounts of the event from 1969 to accounts written on the twenty-fifth, thirtieth or thirty-fifth anniversary of the event.

2. Wamsutta James concludes the speech he was not allowed to give by saying, "We are determined, and our presence here this evening is living testimony that this is only the beginning of the American Indian, particularly the Wampanoag, to regain the position in this country that is rightfully ours." Earlier, he asked, "Has the Wampanoag really disappeared?" Using a search engine of choice, see if you can answer James's question. Then try to determine whether or not in the years since 1970, American Indians have regained "the position in this country that is rightfully ours."

3. Read Angela Davis's book *Angela Davis: An Autobiography* (New York: International Publishers, 1989). How does it compare and contrast with the information you learned about African American resistance in both Chapters 17 and 19 in *Voices* and *A People's History*. What new information does her voice add to your understanding of the civil-rights movement and the women's movement? What can you find out about her life since the book was written? How and why do you think she has become so involved in the movement for prisoner's rights?

4. Using a search engine of choice, gather statistics of violence against women from all ethnicities and socio-economic groups in the United States over the last three decades. What major conclusions did you reach after examining

the statistics over time? Prepare a statistical chart that demonstrates what you found.

5. In *Voices*, Howard Zinn calls Abbey Lincoln "one of the nation's greatest jazz singers." Using a search engine of choice, find lyrics of her songs and the songs themselves. Are they what you would have expected? Learn more about other jazz singers of the 1960s. How do their lyrics compare and contrast with those of Lincoln? What did their music contribute to the movement?

6. Learn more about the poets of the 1960s. Who else was writing poetry, and how did their messages compare and contrast with those of Allen Ginsberg? How influential was their poetry to the social movements of the time? Compare and contrast the resistance poetry of the 1960s with resistance poetry of the early twenty-first century. Which poems and poets from which generation most resonate with you? Explain.

7. *Roe* v. *Wade* remains perhaps the most controversial Supreme Court decisions of the past few decades. Using a search engine of choice, learn more about the case—its origins, its findings, and its consequences. Read what newspaper editorials wrote about the decision in 1973. Then trace the history of the decision from 1973 forward. What other court cases have dealt with the abortion issue? Have these decisions undermined *Roe*? How and why? What do you think is the future of the decision?

8. Susan Brownmiller claims that prior to *Roe* v. *Wade*, one million women underwent abortions each year. Now that abortion is legal, how many women undergo abortions each year today? How accessible are abortions to women across the nation? Has accessibility increased or decreased since the Roe decision? Explain.

9. Learn as much as possible about COINTELPRO. What were its historical origins, and who were its targets? What were some of its most famous activities? What led to its demise? Under the guidelines of the PATRIOT Act, do you think it is possible that a program similar to COINTELPRO could re-emerge? Explain.

10. Find the latest crime statistics and incarceration statistics for Riker's Island or the New York State Penitentiary System. Be certain to check for the number of women and the socio-economic data of the prisoners. Then compare them to the statistics from your state or local prison system.

11. Learn more about the historical origins, goals, and activities of the Black Panther Party. How many of its goals was it able to achieve? How were its growth and actions influenced by white public opinion? By the FBI? What happened to the party? To some of its best-known members? What other groups have been involved in an organized black-power movement during the latter decades of the twentieth century? What have been their goals and accomplishments?

12. Abbey Lincoln wrote, "Maybe if our women get evil enough and angry enough, they'll be moved to some action that will bring our men to their senses." Learn more about the goals and actions of the Million Man March that was held in Washington, D.C., in 1995. Do you think that the marchers may have been responding in some way to Lincoln's hope? Explain.

13. Learn as much as possible about how the struggle for gay liberation has changed since the Stonewall Riot. You may want to start by watching the documentaries *Before Stonewall* and *After Stonewall.* What were the goals of the movement in the late 1960s, and how do they compare with contemporary goals? How has the AIDS crisis influenced the course of the movement? Which issues surrounding gay liberation have found their way into the national political arena? How and why?

14. Learn more about the prison-reform movement. You may want to begin with *Are Prisons Obsolete* by Angela Davis (New York: Seven Stories Press, 2003). What are the major issues surrounding prisons and imprisonment in the United States today? What are the current racial and gender-related issues related to the American prison system in the twenty-first century? How have corporate prisons changed prisons and prison culture?

15. Learn more about Indian activism in the last several decades. What were the goals, actions, and accomplishments of AIM, and how have they changed over the past four decades? What are the issues surrounding the efforts of today's Indian Nations to regain greater tribal sovereignty?

SUGGESTED ESSAY QUESTIONS

1. What are the similarities between the excerpts in Chapter 19 of *Voices?* Taken as a whole, what do they tell you about life in the United States before the 1960s? About the counterculture movement of the 1960s?

2. What rights (both civil and social) were all the authors of the eight documents demanding? In your opinion, which of these civil and social rights have been achieved? Which do you think will not be achieved until well into the twenty-first century?

3. Adrienne Rich wrote, "We need to imagine a world in which every woman is the presiding genius of her own body. In such a world, women will truly create life, bring forth not only children (if we choose) but the visions, and the thinking necessary to sustain, console, and alter human existence—a new relationship to the universe." What achievements have women made toward this end? What obstacles still remain?

4. In 1999, Susan Brownmiller wrote, "Abortion is a woman's right." Using information from both chapters to back up your response, as well as your own understanding about the issue, support or refute Brownmiller's premise.

5. Why did all of these movements arise at approximately the same time? What was it about the era we call the Sixties that allowed (some would say encouraged) protest?

6. How was the long-standing sstrategy of "divide and conquer" used by elites to keep the groups in Chapter 19 from demanding their rights? In which documents is this strategy particularly exposed? How and why?

7. Assata Shakur wrote that the women who are incarcerated at Riker's Island "come from places where dreams have been abandoned like the buildings." Where are these places, and what are these dreams? How do they compare and contrast with the places in your life and your dreams? What do you believe should be the goals of United States prisons? Do you feel they are achieving such goals?

8. How has listening to the voices in Chapter 19 broadened your understanding about the protest groups of the 1960s and 1970s?

9. Since the 1960s, annual Thanksgiving Day protests have been staged across the nation. What are the goals of American Indian people involved in such efforts? Do you think non-Native people understand these goals? How and why should non-Native people be aware of the events that occurred in the almost 400 years since the first Thanksgiving?

10. As you read these voices, decades after the events in them occurred, how do they relate to the world today?

11. At the end of "Surprises," Howard Zinn writes, "Never in American history had more movements for change been concentrated in so short a span of years." Using examples from both chapters, support or challenge this statement. Do you think it could also be said that these movements made more progress in the decade than had resistance movements in the past? Explain.

SIMULATIONS AND OTHER CREATIVE APPROACHES

1. Compose a protest song or poem on a contemporary topic/issue about which you are committed. In your composition, be sure to provide clues about what you are protesting, why you are committed to this topic, and how you think things should be changed. Present your composition to any group that will listen.

2. Write a speech to be given at the Four-Hundredth Anniversary of the Pilgrim's landing at Plymouth. While writing it, think about how Wamsutta James might have responded to your comments. Be prepared to present your speech to you classmates.

3. Invite the five women in *Voices* to a town meeting to be held in the early twenty-first century. The two topics for discussion are: the similarities and differences of the role and treatment of black and white women in the 1960s; the ways in which the role and treatment of black and white women have changed in the early twenty-first century.

4. Organize a discussion to which you will invite some of the female freedom fighters Kathleen Cleaver identifies in her essay (including the historical figures Sojourner Truth, Harriet Tubman, and Ida Wells Barnett). At the party, be sure that the women discuss their various roles as freedom fighters—the goals they hoped to accomplish, the actions they undertook, their achievements. Have them compare their gains and losses, as well as discuss what still needs to be achieved. After their initial discussion, invite some of the male freedom fighters she identified to join the party. How will their inclusion change the discussion? How are the goals of male and female activists similar and different?

CHAPTER TWENTY

Losing Control in the 1970s
by Jennifer Rosebrook

Students continue to feel the effects of the 1970s in their everyday lives. The twin catastrophic events early in the decade—the tragic ending of the Vietnam War and the scandals of Watergate—shocked the nation and rocked the foundations of our fundamental belief in government. To many Americans—including the parents of many of our students—whatever had happened previously seemed distant and simple compared to the events of this period. Frustration and cynicism characterized the attitudes in many homes across the nation.

In addition, our students have had to confront modern scandals—Iran-Contra, savings and loans, Monica Lewinsky, Enron, Abu Ghraib—scandals that suggest that perhaps not much has changed. The voices in this chapter reflect the frustration and cynicism that resulted from the scandals of the 1970s, and in so doing, suggest that we may have opened a Pandora's box that, for good or bad, may be impossible for us to close.

Document-Based Questions

HOWARD ZINN

1. Howard Zinn argues that "Our problem is civil *obedience*." What examples does he provide to support this?

2. Zinn suggests that the rule of law "regularized and maximized the injustice that existed before the rule of law." What does this mean? What example does he provide to support this?

3. How do you think the establishment viewed Zinn's speech? What might have been the response to Zinn's arguments about civil disobedience?

GEORGE JACKSON AND BOB DYLAN

1. George Jackson's letters provide insight into the lives of many African Americans in prison. What are some of their complaints or areas of concern?

2. What role did economics play in Jackson's complaints? What similarities or connections with the past history of African American can be made?

3. In Bob Dylan's song "George Jackson" he sings, "some of us are prisoners and some of us are guards." Which one do you identify with more? What conditions do you share with George Jackson? Explain.

ANGELA DAVIS

1. What role does Angela Davis claim prisons play in our society? Is her conclusion accurate in your view?

2. Davis writes that many prisoners (especially blacks, Chicanos, and Puerto Ricans) feel as though they are "political prisoners." What is a political prisoner? In what ways are their feelings justified? Do you believe that white prisoners could claim the same? Explain your response.

3. Davis writes, "The prison is a key component of a state's coercive apparatus." What does this mean? Do you agree or disagree? Do you think Davis adequately supports this statement? How do any of the other readings in this chapter support this statement?

ELLIOT JAMES ("L. D.") BARKLEY AND FRANK "BIG BLACK" SMITH

1. What did the Attica prisoners demand? Which demands seem reasonable, and which seem unreasonable? What was their greatest fear?

2. What conditions existed in Attica, according to Frank Smith? What kind of response would you have to those types of conditions? Is there any instance in which a riot would be justifiable?

3. How do these two writings by Barkley and Smith compare and contrast with the essay written by the scholar Angela Davis? Which is/are the most compelling and why?

LEONARD PELTIER

1. The title of the demonstration Leonard Peltier describes was Trail of Broken Treaties. How was the ending of the demonstration an ironic twist on this title?

2. How can a demonstration like this one be beneficial or harmful to a movement?

3. What do you think the government's response should have been to this situation? Explain your response.

SELECT COMMITTEE TO STUDY GOVERNMENTAL OPERATIONS

1. Describe the relationship between ITT and the CIA.

2. The information in this document was a surprise to some but not to others. One of the themes is that no telling of history is neutral or objective. Apply that theme to this document.

3. What role did corporations play in shaping United States foreign policy toward Chile? Do corporations have a similar influence today?

NOAM CHOMSKY

1. What do you think is meant by "the engineering of consent"? Explain your answer by citing examples from Noam Chomsky's article and providing one of your own.

2. What connection does Chomsky make between the FBI's activities and Watergate? Do you feel that these two items are connected? If so, what might be the implications? If not, explain why.

3. What does Chomsky mean when he writes, "The FBI casts a wide net"? Why does he see this as problematic?

Main Points in *Voices*, Chapter 20, "Losing Control in the 1970s"

After reading Chapter 20 in *Voices*, students should be encouraged to identify what they believe to be the main points therein. Following are five possible main points:

1. A wide variety of people in the United States began to distrust the government in the 1970s.

2. The 1970s establishment was unsure and fearful of changes in United States society.

3. After the Vietnam War, Americans became increasingly unhappy with, and more vocal about their criticisms of, United States foreign policy.

4. Because so many people were reluctant to intervene with military force abroad, the government turned to covert methods to expand its power overseas.

5. The federal government responded to protests of the 1960s and 1970s by investigating, harassing, and infiltrating groups it believed to be a threat to the social, political, and economic status quo.

Main Points in *Voices*, Chapter 20, "Losing Control in the 1970s," and in *A People's History*, Chapter 20, "The Seventies: Under Control?"

If your students are also reading *A People's History*, they should be encouraged to identify what they believe to be the main points in Chapters 20 in both books. Following are five additional points to be stressed when *Voices* and *A People's History* are used together.

6. Watergate, which was a serious blow to the establishment, caused those in power to turn inward.

7. After the end of the Vietnam War, United States leaders quickly looked for opportunities to re-establish their worldwide supremacy.

8. The establishment, sensing serious threats to the status quo, closed ranks, conducted public investigations, and expelled culprits, but left the political and economic system fundamentally the same.

9. The United States public's increasing feelings of uncertainty and alienation lead to a substantial decline of optimism about the future.

10. The problems of governability of the 1970s had its roots in the social movements of the 1960s.

General-Discussion Question for *Voices*

While the following questions are designed for classroom discussion about all the voices read in Chapter 20, they can also be rewritten and included as evaluation tools.

1. The title of Chapter 20, "Losing Control in the 1970s," suggests that someone or something once had control. If that is the case, who lost control, and why?

2. Who are "independents" in terms of the electorate? Why do you think that more people began to vote independent in the 1970s?

3. Do you believe that citizens have the right to practice civil disobedience as Howard Zinn explains it? How does Zinn's explanation of civil disobedience compare with the theory developed by Henry David Thoreau? (See the discussion in Chapter 8.)

4. What might be some of the consequences of civil disobedience? Conversely, what might be some of the consequences for citizens if they practice civil obedience?

5. Why do you think the system "could not hold the loyalty of the public" in the 1970s?

6. Is it against the law to be a Communist in the United States? If not, how does the government justify harassing people who are openly involved with or sympathetic to Communism?

7. Why did Congress investigate the CIA and FBI in the 1970s? What did Congress find?

8. Howard Zinn writes that "We've never had justice in the courts for the poor people, for black people, for radicals." How do the voices in this chapter reinforce his statement?

9. How did the voices in this chapter reinforce any of the five themes listed in "Main Points in *Voices*"?

10. Which of the voices in this chapter did you find most powerful? Least powerful? How and why?

General-Discussion Questions for *Voices* and *A People's History*

These general-discussion questions are additional questions for students who have read Chapter 20 in both books. For all questions, discussion must focus on ways the materials in both chapters help students formulate and articulate their answers.

11. What do these chapters tell you about the sanctity of the law? How, why, and by whom are our laws changed?

12. Given the political, economic, and social conditions of the 1970s, why do you think the people of the United States had become so disillusioned with the "establishment"? Cite examples from both chapters.

13. If you could retitle the chapters, what would you title them? Explain why. How would the readings support your new title?

14. If the establishment was "losing control," in what ways could it reassert its control? Are these means legitimate?

15. The role of media in public knowledge has changed since the 1970s. What was the media's role in the 1970s? What do you think the media's role should be today? What benefits do the media provide to people in a democracy? What might be some negative outcomes of this situation?

16. Why were so many people reluctant to use military intervention abroad in the 1970s?

17. Why did President Nixon resign? What happened to him after his resignation?

18. What does Howard Zinn mean by this statement, "The word was out: get rid of Nixon, but keep the system" (*People's History*, p. 546)? Do you think this is what happened?

19. Who is Henry Kissinger? What role did he play in the Nixon and Ford administrations?

20. What was the *Mayaguez* affair? Why was the United States so quick to attack? How did the press handle the attack?

21. Should our government have the power to assassinate foreign leaders? Is such assassination ever justifiable?

22. What is the "human side of capitalism" to which former Secretary of Treasury William Simon referred?

23. What is "an excess of democracy"? Do you believe there can ever be "too much" democracy? Why, or why not?

24. What were the recommendations of the Trilateral Commission? Do you agree with these recommendations? Why, or why not?

Evaluation Tools

SUGGESTED ASSIGNMENTS

These assignments can be adapted to meet any classroom need—homework, short- or long-term research projects, individual or group work. The end product should be flexible, depending on teacher interest and student abilities- papers, journals, oral reports, visual aides, and the like.

1. Examine the evolution of prisons in the United States. How have prisons changed over the past 200 years? How have they remained the same? What are some of the current issues related to prisons? How do they compare and contrast with the issues you read about in this/these chapter(s)? Reread the words of those who were imprisoned in the 1970s. Then using a search engine of choice, read some contemporary primary documents from those who have been or are imprisoned in the twenty-first century. How do their experiences compare and contrast? What do you think needs to change?

2. Read several of the primary sources related to Watergate, such as the Articles of Impeachment for Richard Nixon (1974), Nixon's Watergate Investigations Address (1973), Nixon's White House Impeachment Departure Speech (1974), *United States* v. *Nixon* (1974). Explain how these documents are influential in the writing of history for this time period. What other primary sources or documents or voices would provide a balanced view of the time period?

3. Research a local or regional juvenile or adult detention facility. When and why was it created? What type of population does it serve? Try to get an interview with an administrator or an inmate (only under direct supervision, and only with parental approval) to ask about conditions in the facility. Create

a presentation to give to your class. Relate the documents from *Voices* to that presentation.

4. Using a search engine of choice, research a social movement, leader, or issue that was active in the 1970s. What were this person's or movement's philosophies, goals, tactics, and accomplishments? Is the movement still alive? If so, how have its goals and tactics changed? If not, what led to its demise? Focus on what items have changed and what items have stayed the same in the last thirty years. What might account for this?

5. Choose a modern issue about which you feel strongly. Find several songs and/or poems that address this topic. How is the issue portrayed in the words/lyrics? What attracted you to these compositions? How do they contribute to your understanding of the issue?

6. Research the habits of voters in United States presidential elections in the 1960s, 1970s, 1980s, and 1990s. What trends can be seen? What might account for these trends? Were there any significant changes in these trends in the 2000 and 2004 presidential elections? Explain.

7. Watch a feature-length film that deals with the topics discussed in Chapter 20 in both *Voices* and *A People's History*. Three possible choices might be *All the President's Men*, *Attica*, and *Thunderheart*. How did the movie(s) reinforce or refute the voices that you learned about in these chapters? What parts of the film do you feel were historically accurate? Inaccurate?

8. Many people first became aware of governmental abuses in the 1970s. Part of this new awareness was due to the Freedom of Information Act of 1974 that allowed public access to a number of previously classified government records. Research how to access and use this source. Present one declassified document that you examined to the class. Explore how this new information can be a positive or negative force in public opinion about the government.

9. The issue of corporate personhood has become the subject of increasing discussion in the twenty-first century. What is corporate personhood? Research the Supreme Court decision that granted Fourteenth Amendment rights of personhood to corporations. How did other late-nineteenth- and early-twentieth-century court decisions reinforce corporate personhood? Do you think corporations should have the same rights as people? What resistance actions challenging corporate person-

hood have begun to take place across the nation? Do you support these actions? How and why?

10. Find out more information about the election of Salvador Allende to the presidency of Chile. What role did the CIA play in his assassination? Do you think that United States involvement was justified? Explain. Watch the movie *Missing*, which is a fictionalized version of the events before, during, and after the Allende era. What do you think was historically accurate about the movie? Inaccurate? What have been the short- and long-term consequences of United States involvement with the Chilean government in the 1970s?

SUGGESTED ESSAY QUESTIONS

1. Watergate has left a permanent stain on the office of the president. Discuss other major effects of Watergate on the American political, economic, and social landscape.

2. Social change is never easy or quick. Do you believe that the 1960s and 1970s were the beginning of or the end of a social-change movement? Explain your point of view by citing examples from the readings. Explain how the 1980s fit into your analysis.

3. The role of corporations has increasing come under scrutiny in United States politics. Discuss the history of the rise of corporations and their influence on government. What should be the role of corporations in United States society?

4. Howard Zinn raised the question of civil obedience or disobedience. Explain which course of action you believe was best, given the climate and issues of the 1970s. Are there any conditions under which you would alter your opinion? Explain.

5. In 1976, the United States celebrated its two hundredth birthday. In what ways had the country grown, and in what ways had it remained the same? What ideals that were expressed two hundred years ago have survived? What has been altered? What do you believe will be the case in another two hundred years?

6. Howard Zinn argued that resistance movements of the 1970s were motivated by "the principles and aims and spirit of the Declaration of Independence."

Explain what he meant. What do you believe to be the principles, aims, and spirit embodied in the Declaration? Do you feel that any of these have been compromised in the early twenty-first century? How and why?

7. Many of the voices in this/these chapter(s) talk about racism within the criminal-justice system. Provide specific examples from the readings of such racism. Do you think this situation has changed over the past 30 years? How and why?

8. What voices of resistance in Chapter 20 in both *Voices* and *A People's History* were of most interest to you? How and why? Which did you find most compelling and why? Least compelling?

9. What do you think are the government's rights and responsibilities? Should these change if a political or economic crisis occurs? Explain. What are our rights and responsibilities as citizens? How do they compare and contrast with those of the government? How do the voices in this/these chapter(s) better help you understand the issue of rights and responsibilities?

10. Howard Zinn quotes Samuel Huntington, a writer of a portion of the Trilateral Commission Report "The Governability of Democracies," as stating that the United States had developed "an excess of democracy" and that there might be "desirable limits to the extension of political democracy" (*People's History*, p. 560). Given the events of the late 1960s and early 1970s, is this a valid statement? Use specific examples from the reading to defend your response.

11. Some have said that the United States was on the verge of a domestic revolution in the early 1970s. What evidence can be seen from the readings? If a revolution had occurred, where and with what group do you believe it would have begun? Explain why.

12. Howard Zinn writes, "Corporate influence on the White House is a permanent factor of the American system" (*People's History*, p. 547). Defend or refute this statement using materials from the reading. How was this particularly true during this 1970s—or was it?

13. Howard Zinn writes that the effort behind the 1976 bicentennial celebration "suggests that it was seen as a way of restoring American patriotism." Defend or refute this observation. What events, if any, do you believe similarly galvanized American patriotism in the late twentieth and early twenty-first centuries?

250 ~ CHAPTER TWENTY

SIMULATIONS AND OTHER CREATIVE APPROACHES

1.   Convene a session of the committee that investigated COINTELPRO. Your committee has called J. Edgar Hoover to testify. Using primary documents you found online, question Hoover about the FBI's actions in regard to one issue surrounding the controversial operations of the COINTELPRO program. After Hoover's questioning, decide whether or not the committee will recommend to the president that he be fired or retained.

2.   Watch the movie *Fog of War*, in which former Secretary of State Robert McNamara retrospectively reflects upon the role of the United States in Vietnam. Imagine that you are writing the script for a similar retrospective analysis of the 1970s in which you will be interviewing former President Richard Nixon and his secretary of state, Henry Kissinger. What will you call the film? What specific questions will you ask Nixon? What will you ask Kissinger? How do you think they will answer? Preview your script with the class, or actually stage the video with your classmates.

3.   Imagine that you are responsible for the two hundred and fiftieth anniversary of the signing of the Declaration of Independence in 2026. Using information about centennial and bicentennial celebrations, as well as the historical eras in which they were held, create a week-long agenda for the celebration. Whom will you invite to speak? What will be the issues discussed at the celebration? Where will it be held? Who do you think might boycott the celebration? Who might hold a countercelebration?

4.   Invite four of your favorite Founding Fathers to a discussion hosted by four powerful figures of the 1970s. The twentieth-century leaders want some advice about the loss of confidence they are feeling in the United States public. Stage that conversation. At another discussion, invite four ordinary post-Revolutionary United States citizens to a conversation hosted by four ordinary people of the 1970s. The twentieth-century participants want some advice about the growth of big business and corporate control as well as about their feelings that the government is out of control. Stage that conversation. Then compare and contrast the issues raised and discussed in both conversations.

CHAPTER TWENTY-ONE

The Carter–Reagan–Bush Consensus

by Ron Perry

Chapter 21 in *Voices*, "The Carter–Reagan–Bush Consensus," provides readers with a perspective that allows them to better understand present-day America. Historians often mistakenly dismiss the importance of the recent past as less than history, merely current events. Certainly the era from 1976 to 1992 is clearly connected to the current challenges facing the United States today. *Voices* provides students with a window through which to look back just far enough to recognize important trends in United States society and challenges them to act on them today.

The policies and priorities of Presidents Carter, Reagan, and George. H. W. Bush illustrate the growing gulf in power and wealth between the poor and the rich in the United States—a gulf that continues to widen today. Despite the end of the Cold War, the military-industrial complex continued to have a stranglehold on the federal budget and on foreign policy. Though new drugs greatly improved the quality of life for people with AIDS, the virus continued to ravage much of the world, as well as people who could not afford expensive medical care in the richer countries. Although the United States continued to dominate the world economy, its workers still struggled to earn a fair wage. By presenting these disturbing patterns in our society, *Voices* illustrates the need for ordinary citizens to speak out and take action to address the injustices and skewed governmental priorities in America.

Document-Based Questions

MARIAN WRIGHT EDELMAN

1. What new information did you learn about how the United States government spent tax dollars during the 1980s? Do you agree with Marian Edelman's assertion that these policies are tantamount to "theft" from the nation's poor?

2. What choices does Edelman present to her audience? Identify and explain the most compelling piece of evidence presented by Edelman.

3. Edelman challenges her audience by stating, "Democracy is not a spectator sport." What actions can ordinary citizens take to address the inequities Edelman describes?

CÉSAR CHÁVEZ

1. How does César Chávez describe the life of the migrant farm worker? What evidence makes the most compelling case that Mexican Americans in the United States are second-class citizens?

2. How does Chávez define the United Farm Workers (UFW)? Describe his goals for farm workers. Why is the UFW a civil-rights organization as well as a trade union?

3. What two major trends does Chávez say "give us hope and encouragement"? From a twenty-first century perspective, do you believe his hopes were met? How and why?

TESTIMONY OF ISMAEL GUADALUPE ORTIZ

1. What does this passage teach us about the United States government's actions in Puerto Rico?

2. According to Ortiz, what crimes has the United States committed in Vieques? Why did Ortiz choose to "fight" the United States Navy?

3. Do you think Ortiz's actions were justified? Why, or why not?

LOCAL P-9 STRIKERS AND SUPPORTERS

1. How did working conditions change in the Hormel meat packing plants during the 1980s? What actions did workers take in response to these changes?

2. What risks did workers at Hormel assume when they took action to demand fair wages and safe working conditions? What risks did workers face if they didn't advocate change? If you had been working at the Hormel plant, would you have stood with the strikers? Explain.

3. In the next passage in *Voices*, Douglas Fraser writes, "The Republican Party remains controlled by and the Democratic Party heavily influenced by business interest." How does the Hormel strike support or undermine this view?

DOUGLAS A. FRASER

1. What reasons did Douglas Fraser give for resigning from the committee? What evidence does Fraser present to justify his position?

2. Fraser states "I am convinced there has been a shift on the part of business community toward confrontation, rather than cooperation." Does the evidence presented by Fraser prove his point? Do you feel the account of workers at the Hormel plant prove Fraser's point? Explain.

3. What is the "new flexing of business muscle" that Fraser discusses? Do you think he presents enough evidence to prove that it is a danger?

VITO RUSSO

1. How does this reading change your understanding of the fight against AIDS?

2. In "Why we Fight," Vito Russo asserts that "I'm dying from homophobia. If I'm dying from anything, I'm dying from racism." In your opinion, what is the meaning of Russo's statement?

3. How far has the struggle for AIDS in the United States come since Russo spoke these words in 1988?

ABBIE HOFFMAN

1. What evidence does Abbie Hoffman present to show that the CIA cannot be trusted? Which piece of evidence do you find most compelling?

2. What did Hoffman mean when he said that Thomas Paine was "talking about this spring day in this courtroom" when he wrote about the American Revolution?

3. How does Abbie Hoffman describe the attitude of people in the United States today? Do you agree with Hoffman's analysis?

PUBLIC ENEMY

1. In your opinion, what message is Public Enemy conveying in their song "Fight the Power"? Who is their audience?

2. What evidence in "Fight the Power" can you find that the traditional approach to examining history fails to reach significant portions of United States society?

3. What statement does Public Enemy make about traditional United States heroes? Who might Public Enemy consider a true hero? Why?

Main Points in *Voices*, Chapter 21, "The Carter–Reagan–Bush Consensus"

After reading Chapter 21 in *Voices*, students should be encouraged to identify what they believe to be the main points therein. Following are five possible main points.

1. The large corporations and the wealthiest individuals in the United States have encouraged belief in the American Dream as a way of preventing a critical mass of individuals from demanding fundamental change.

2. In terms of foreign policy, there is little discernible difference in the positions of the two major parties in the United States: both parties have placed military spending over the needs of the poor.

3. The needs of people who are not powerful are often entirely overlooked in our society, especially in times of economic downturn.

4. During the 1970s and 1980s, United States unions, facing aggressive efforts by big business to increase profits, lost ground in the fight for a fair wage.

5. While AIDS decimated significant portions of the gay population, the reaction of government and the media revealed an unwillingness to fully address the scale of the problem.

Main Point in *Voices*, Chapter 21, "The Carter–Reagan–Bush Consensus," and in *A People's History*, Chapter 21, "Carter–Reagan–Bush: The Bipartisan Consensus"

If your students are also reading *A People's History*, they should be encouraged to identify what they believe to be the main points in Chapter 21 in both books. Following are five additional points to be stressed when *Voices* and *A People's History* are used together.

6. By maintaining Cold War levels for military spending, the United States revealed that its foreign policy was based on a compulsion to maintain ideological, economic, and physical domination throughout the world.

7. During the Cold War, the United States continued to support dictators around the world, despite knowledge of their blatant institutional human-rights violations.

8. The energy policies of the 1970s and 1980s demonstrated a shortsighted determination to expand the economy that flew in the face of scientific evidence.

9. "The Iran-contra affair was only one of the many instances in which the government of the United States violated its own laws in pursuit of some desired goal in foreign policy" (*People's History*, p. 588).

10. The United States government carefully manipulated the media during the course of the Persian Gulf War in 1991 to prevent reports from impacting United States public opinion negatively, as it did during the Vietnam War.

General-Discussion Questions for *Voices*

While the following questions are designed for classroom discussion about all the voices read in Chapter 21, they can also be rewritten and included as evaluation tools.

1. Marian Wright Edelman asks, "How do you want to spend scarce national resources?" Using passages from *Voices* answer Edelman's question.

2. How do the passages from César Chávez and the workers from Hormel change your perception of the purpose of unions and the challenges they face?

3. What does the testimony of Ismael Ortiz reveal about the ways the United States military impacts the rest of world and its opinion of the United States? Does it reflect a legacy of imperialism? Explain.

4. What is a boycott? How have boycotts been used throughout United States history? How do you think the UFW boycott differed in substance and accomplishments from other historical boycotts?

5. What do you think is the "unfinished struggle of farm workers for justice" in the twenty-first century?

6. Do you think Puerto Ricans were justified in their resistance to the bombing at Vieques?

7. Why do you think it is so difficult to "forge 'cooperation' between workers and employers"? Under what circumstances do you think the task might be less difficult?

8. Do you think rap music is an appropriate agent of protest? Is it representative of many voices, or only of the voices of African American rappers?

9. What do the voices in this chapter have in common? How are they different? Which, if any, do you think were most and least effective in getting people to understand the features of the Carter–Reagan–Bush "consensus"?

10. What is homophobia? How does it influence the lives of gay people? How does it influence your educational and social environment?

11. How did the voices in this chapter reinforce any of the five themes listed in "Main Points in *Voices*"?

12. Which of the voices in the chapter did you find most powerful? Least powerful?

General-Discussion Questions for *Voices* and *A People's History*

The general-discussion questions are additional questions for students who have read Chapter 21 of both books. For all questions, discussion must focus on ways the materials in both chapters help students formulate and articulate their answers.

13. What does Reagan's treatment of the striking air-traffic controllers reveal about the United States government's attitude toward organized labor? What evidence from *Voices* reinforces your conclusion? What do you think about unions? Would you join a union?

14. In your opinion, what lessons does the Iran-contra affair teach us about the Reagan presidency? What evidence from the chapters supports your conclusions?

15. How has the tax structure in the United States changed since 1945? How does the changing tax structure illustrate the influence corporations and the rich in United States politics?

16. What is an epidemic? What is a pandemic? How did AIDS move from an epidemic to a pandemic?

17. Who were the Braceros and why were they brought to the United States?

18. How do the voices and stories of protest in Chapter 21 compare and contrast to the voices of protest and stories in Chapter 19? Are there any "surprises" in Chapter 21?

19. From your reading of these chapters, what do you think were the various strengths and weaknesses of the Carter, Reagan, and Bush administrations?

20. Was there any issue raised during the period in these chapters that you would be willing to fight for? How and why?

21. In these chapters, Howard Zinn discusses several "fundamentals of foreign policy" during the three presidencies. What were they?

22. What is OSHA? Did it protect workers during the terms of these three presidents? Does it protect United States workers today? Explain.

23. Was Reagan able to make good on his promise to balance the budget through tax cuts that would stimulate the economy and produce new revenue?

24. What other voices might have been added to Chapter 21 in *Voices* that might have provided a more complete understanding of Chapter 21 in *A People's History*?

Evaluation Tools

SUGGESTED ASSIGNMENTS

These assignments can be adapted to meet any classroom need—homework, short- or long-term research projects, individual or group work. The end product should be flexible, depending on teacher interest and student abilities—papers, journals, oral reports, visual aides, and the like.

1. The selections from Chapter 21 in *Voices* point illustrate the importance of those individuals who had the courage to take a stand, to take action. Brainstorm a list of all the issues, problems, and conditions in your school, community, state, nation, and world that should be changed and challenged. Discuss the question, "Why have these problems not been solved?" Select one issue. In a formal letter addressed to the community or to someone who has the power to affect the situation, identify and explain the problem and suggest a solution.

2. In describing "Fight the Power" by Public Enemy, Howard Zinn writes that the song "offered an uncompromising message of protest." What musical artists offer a voice of protest today? Using the search engine of your choice, examine and explain lyrics from a song critically commenting on today's society.

3. Passages from *Voices* illustrate the struggles of the working-class to secure a living wage. Using the search engine of your choice, research the arguments for and against raising the minimum wage. In your opinion, what is a fair minimum wage? Justify your answer.

4. In "Why We Fight," Vito Russo argues that America's slow response to the AIDS virus provided clear evidence of the existence of two Americas. While AIDS had ravaged gay Americans, drug users, and the poor for years, the general alarm in America did not sound until the disease entered the ranks of the mainstream population. Using a search engine of your choice, research the impact AIDS has had on Africa. Analyze the United States government's response to AIDS in Africa. How does the federal government's response to the crisis in Africa mirror its early reaction to the AIDS impact on its own population?

5. Chapter 21 in *Voices* and *A People's History* provide evidence of the influence

of big business on the Democrats and the Republicans. Using a search engine of your choice, research the platforms and policies of these two parties during the 2004 presidential election. What were the differences? Do you think America would benefit from another viable politician option, such as a labor party? Explain.

6. Learn more about the United States government's role in Puerto Rico. How and why did the United States gain control over Puerto Rico? Why do you think the United States continues in this role? How has the effort for Puerto Rican independence evolved over the years? What are the goals and actions of those who are fighting for independence? Do you think the United States should retain its current political control of Puerto Rico or change it? How and why?

7. Learn more about the International Conference on AIDS held in Malaysia during the summer of 2004. What were some of the key national and international statistics pertinent to the AIDS pandemic? How do they compare with statistics of the 1990s? What did the members of the conference propose should be done to fight the pandemic? Why do you think most Americans are not concerned about this rapidly growing disease?

8. Read Abbie Hoffman's book *Steal This Book* and/or view the movie *Steal This Movie*. What are the primary messages of the book and/or the movie? How does this source add to the understanding of Hoffman that you gained by reading his "Closing Argument"? Are Hoffman's messages relevant to the early twenty-first century? How and why?

SUGGESTED ESSAY QUESTIONS

1. According to Public Enemy, "Elvis was a hero to most / but he never meant shit to me you see." In your opinion, what statement is being made in "Fight the Power"? Who are the true heroes in American society today?

2. What voices in Chapters 21 in both *Voices* and *A People's History* were of most interest to you? How and why? Which did you find most compelling and why? Least compelling?

3. What actions did the UFW and workers at Hormel take to make their point for improved working conditions and wages? Which do you feel were most effective? How and why? Do you think unions are necessary in

contemporary United States society? What role should union's play in our future?

4. Howard Zinn states that the Carter, Reagan, and Bush administrations "clearly illustrated Hofstadter's thesis" that the men of power in American political parties have, in Hofstadter's words, "accepted the economic virtues of capitalist culture as necessary qualities of man" (*People's History*, p. 563). Using the voices and examples from the chapter(s), support or challenge the statement. How do the entries in *Voices* demonstrate that these qualities may not be the ones valued by many ordinary Americans?

5. What are the arguments against spending so much money on the United States military put forward in this/these chapter(s)? Do you agree or disagree with these arguments? How and why?

6. In "Carter–Reagan–Bush: The Bipartisan Consensus," Howard Zinn quotes a Republican analyst as saying, "It was the truly wealthy, more than anyone else, who flourished under Reagan . . . . The 1980s were the triumph of upper America . . . the political ascendancy of the rich, and a glorification of capitalism, free markets, and finance" (*People's History*, p. 580). What is the most compelling evidence Zinn provides in both chapters to prove this point?

7. In *Voices*, Howard Zinn writes that the Local P-9 strike "was a classic example of how employer power is used to break unions and maintain their profits." How does this/these chapter(s) support this statement? How are strikes handled in contemporary society? Has the employer response changed? Do you think you might ever join in a strike? Explain.

8. Using examples in the reading, as well as knowledge you have of other historical eras, discuss why you think it was so difficult to "forge 'cooperation' between workers and employers" in the 1970s and 1980s. Is it any less difficult today? Explain. Under what circumstances do you think it might be less difficult?

9. In the final line of his address, Chávez writes, "And on that day, our nation shall fulfill its creed—and that fulfillment shall enrich us all." For Chávez, what was this creed? In the time since this statement was made, have farm workers experienced significant changes in their lives and working conditions in the United States? Explain.

10. Abbie Hoffman states, "I grew up with the idea that democracy is not something you believe in, or a place you hang your hat, but it's something you do. You participate." Do you agree or disagree with this view? Explain. What do you think are the weaknesses and strengths of United States democracy today?

SIMULATIONS AND OTHER CREATIVE APPROACHES

1. Create a list of all the national resources that would be available to you as president of the United States. Then convene a meeting with your presidential advisers and begin a dialog about how you feel these should be spent. Once you reach some sort of consensus, ask members from the opposition party to join your discussion. How will the allocations change, based on this new dialog?

2. Design a stamp honoring a deserving individual or a group of unsung heroes who have yet to be honored. Keep in mind Public Enemy's statement that "Most of my heroes don't appear on no stamps." What other figures from United States history have been honored by having their images placed on a stamp? Are most of these people the important figures in United States history, or are they ordinary folks like ourselves? Bring some of these images to class on the day that you share your new stamp and explain how and why your stamp is different from the others in origin and substance.

3. Develop a policy report for the president of the United States about the actions he should take to address the AIDS pandemic both in the United States and in the world.

4. Stage an AIDS awareness event. Be sure to clearly state the facts and make your goals clear.

CHAPTER TWENTY-TWO

Panama, the 1991 Gulf War, and the War at Home

by Robert Standish

Whenever I tell my students that I was in the military, they just stare at me in disbelief; my pacifist leanings are well known within the tiny community where I teach. However, when I tell them that I joined in order to afford the cost of college, there is a unanimous nod of understanding. The financial worry of college is heavy on their eleventh grade minds, and the idea of four years of service doesn't sound too bad when the recruiter waves $50,000 in their faces. As odd a match as I was to the military, I soon found that I wasn't alone. Among the reasons why my peers joined, none included such patriotic declarations as "to serve my country" or "to defend Democracy." Instead, the reasons were, more often than not, simply financial. We were mostly just working-class kids looking for any chance at a real opportunity. Indeed, Alex Molnar's letter to President Bush was the letter all of our parents wanted to write and the letter no politician wants to answer, because it picks at the scab of class issues in the military.

As a soldier, I was part of the massive public affairs machine during the 1991 Gulf War, doing "Hi, Mom"s for the troops as my commander escorted media pools to sanitized "events" so that the journalists could file enough copy and capture enough footage to earn their day's pay. It was disheartening to see how the journalists responded—unquestioningly, and thankfully. I was never quite sure if they were massively incompetent or if they understood our sleight of hand, but didn't mind as long as the show was entertaining. The lesson was clear: there is a serious vacuum in our Fourth Estate, and it has become part of the class problem in this country. The selections in Chapter 22 are a vital tool for showing students the darker side of United States military intervention and the role the media play in keeping it secret. It is a side we won't see on TV but will hear about from the ordinary soldiers and citizens like those in this book.

Document-Based Questions

ALEX MOLNAR

1. In what ways does Alex Molnar use the word "vacation" to make his point about his opposition to the Gulf War of 1991?

2. What part of the "American way of life" does Molnar criticize? What consequences of this lifestyle does he present?

3. How might. Molnar's opinion have been different if the United States had at least appeared to exhaust all diplomatic options before engaging our troops in the Middle East?

EQBAL AHMAD

1. What two post-World War II realities does Eqbal Ahmad suggest we face today? How do these contribute to the betrayal of the world's hope for an end to war?

2. Ahmad directly asks the reader, "What happens now?" Do you think we are on the verge of a New World Order? If so, what will it be like, who will benefit, and who will not benefit?

3. What does Ahmad suggest are the real reasons for why the United States went to war with Iraq in 1991? Are these valid reasons for declaring war? Explain why or why not.

JUNE JORDAN

1. Read June Jordan's first paragraph out loud. How does she effectively appeal to our emotions? Is emotional appeal a valid technique for discussing the Gulf War of 1991? Explain why or why not.

2. Why do you think Jordan argues that the Gulf War of 1991 was a racist war? Do you agree or disagree with her assessment? Explain.

3. How does Jordan portray the decision of President Bush, Colin Powell, and Dick Cheney to disregard the agreement that Iraq signed with Russia? Why do you think they were not interested in a peaceful resolution on the eve of the ground war?

YOLANDA HUET-VAUGHN

1. What credentials does Yolanda Huet-Vaughn list in the introduction to her letter? How do these credentials give validity to her refusal to participate in the Gulf War of 1991?

2. Describe some of the medical and environmental consequences of war that Huet-Vaughn discusses. Were her warnings merited?

3. What do you think were the positive and negative results of the Gulf War of 1991? Was the war worth the costs to Iraqis and to people in the United States?

INTERVIEW WITH CIVILIAN WORKER

1. What are some things the civilian worker mentions that indicate the United States military was not solely interested in capturing Manuel Noriega?

2. What do you think were the effects of using twenty-year-old soldiers in the invasion of Panama? How might veteran troops have acted differently?

3. How were civilians treated in the invasion of Panama? How did the results of this investigation differ from how the government and media portrayed the invasion?

MIKE DAVIS

1. In what ways did the Los Angeles riots of 1992 showcase the problem of poverty in the United States? Do you think the riots would have been as violent if there wasn't as much poverty in Los Angeles? Why, or why not?

2. Why were undocumented immigrants especially vulnerable during the riots?

3. How does Mike Davis compare the Rodney King trial to the Dred Scott decision of the Supreme Court? Do you think it is as historically important? Why or Why not?

MUMIA ABU-JAMAL

1. What is meant by David Kairys statement, "Law is simply politics by other means" How might Mumia Abu-Jamal's situation verify this statement?

2. What percent of the United States population is living below the official poverty line? Is this an acceptable percentage for a first-world nation?

3. What kind of "rebellion of the spirit" do you think Abu-Jamal envisions that the poor must undertake? Do you think this would help reduce poverty in the United States? Why, or why not?

Main Points in *Voices*, Chapter 22, "Panama, The 1991 Gulf War, and The War at Home"

After Reading Chapter 22 in *Voices*, students should be encouraged to identify what they believe to be the main points therein. Following are five possible main points:

1. United States foreign policy has historically been and continues to be militaristic, with profound domestic and international social consequences.

2. "Supporting our troops" does not mean blindly accepting the idea that poor and working-class soldiers be put in the line of fire, no matter what the alleged reasons for the war.

3. The United States government has increasingly used humanitarian causes to justify its wars abroad, as in Panama and Iraq.

4. The 1989 invasion of Panama and the 1991 invasion of Iraq helped to define a new role for the United States military as the Cold War with the Soviet Union came to an end.

5. Although largely ignored or demonized by mainstream media, a "permanent adversarial culture" has developed in the United States that seeks the possibility of a more equal, more humane society.

Main Points in *Voices*, Chapter 22, "Panama, The 1991 Gulf War, and The War at Home," and in *A People's History*, Chapter 22, "The Unreported Resistance"

If your students are also reading *A People's History*, they should be encouraged to identify what they believe to be the main points in Chapter 22, "The Unreported

Resistance." Following are five additional points to be stressed when *Voices* and *A People's History* are used together.

6. The military-industrial complex has so much influence that both Republican and Democrat leaders have sacrificed social reform in favor of military strength.

7. Elected party officials tend to ignore their constituents who, when polled, often express beliefs that are contrary to those of the Republican and Democrat Parties.

8. Contemporary contributors to the "permanently adversarial culture" include priests, farmers, doctors, soldiers, teachers, mothers, scientists, laborers, children, and other sectors of United States society.

9. The United States invaded Iraq in 1991, claiming that a big country (Iraq) could not be allowed to invade a small country (Kuwait); yet two years earlier, the United States had invaded Panama, a much smaller country.

10. Because many teachers of United States history are currently teaching with more candor and honesty than in the past, their academic approach has been variously interpreted; many in power see such education as a threat, while others see it as a sign of progress.

General-Discussion Questions for *Voices*

While the following questions are designed for classroom discussion about all the voices read in Chapter 22, they can also be rewritten and included as evaluation tools.

1. What evidence do the voices presented in Chapter 22 give to support the opinion that the 1991 Gulf War was "an immoral and unspiritual diversion . . . a blatant evasion of our domestic responsibilities"?

2. What is "the American way of life"? Does it have anything to do with the American Dream? How many people in the United States currently enjoy this way of life or the American Dream?

3. Do you think there could have been a diplomatic solution to the Gulf crisis in 1991—a solution that might have avoided war? How and why?

4. Comparing June Jordan's entry to that of Mumia Abu-Jamal's, what factors do you think contribute to a disproportionately high number of African Americans in both the armed services and prisons in the United States? Why might these facts make it understandable that African Americans were also disproportionately opposed to the Gulf War of 1991?

5. Many of these entries offer criticisms of United States foreign policy in the Middle East. What are some examples? What are some solutions?

6. How does the 1991 Los Angeles riot compare and contrast with earlier riots you have learned about in this/these book(s)?

7. If, as some of these voices suggest, the mainstream media, universities, and Congress have all failed to discuss the legitimacy of United States military actions, then who should take on this role? How and why?

8. After the 1989 invasion of Panama, there were no governmental investigations into alleged violations of the laws of war. Should investigations be required when such allegations arise? Why, or why not?

9. How do the voices in this chapter support the idea that the United States continues to pursue imperialistic aims at home and abroad?

10. Do the voices in this chapter sound as if the speakers hate the United States? How and why? Do they make a distinction between the people of the United States and the policies of the United States government? Explain.

General-Discussion Questions for *Voices* and *A People's History*

11. These general-discussion questions are additional questions for student who have read Chapter 22 in both books. For all questions, discussion must focus on ways the materials in both chapters help students formulate and articulate their answers.

12. What evidence is presented in both chapters that suggests corporations play a significant role in shaping United States foreign and domestic policy? What negative effects do the authors suggest might arise as a result of this?

13. In what ways did the Vietnam War change people's opinions of United

States military actions? What evidence is provided in both books to suggest that United States military actions have or have not changed?

14. If the media were to provide an open forum for dissenting voices in the United States, do you think that opportunity would cause more problems or help to solve the ones we already have? Explain why or why not.

15. What common values do you think the dissenters presented in both chapters share? Why do you think these values appear to be lacking in those who shape United States foreign and domestic policy?

16. What ways might the United States government respond to the "permanently adversarial culture" that Howard Zinn describes?

17. What is the "military-industrial complex?" How, why, and when did it become a reality in the United States?

18. What were the causes and consequences of the Gulf War?

19. Do you think most people in the United States respect the voices of dissent in the early twenty-first century?

20. Who are the loudest voices of dissent in the United States today? What are the reasons for their discontent? Do you believe these voices will bring about change? Explain.

21. How would you change the media's presentation of the news in a way that would make you want to pay attention to the daily news?

22. How well informed are you as a consequence of using any or all of the following news sources: television news, online news, radio news, and newspapers? Which do you prefer? Why?

23. Prison construction in America became a growing industry in the 1990s. What does this fact say about America's socio-economic health?

Evaluation Tools

SUGGESTED ASSIGNMENTS

These assignments can be adapted to meet any classroom need—homework, short or long-term research projects, individual or group work. The end product should be flexible, depending on teacher interest and student abilities—papers, journals, oral reports, visual aides, and the like.

1. Using the Internet, investigate the various reports on the number of people killed, on both sides, in the Panama invasion of 1989. Prepare a table that lists the different totals and indicate the possible accuracy and credibility of each estimate. In a report or a PowerPoint presentation, address the disparity in the counts and the possible reasons for them. Include in your investigation the accusation that the United States military dug several mass graves in Panama to hide the true number of casualties. In your conclusion, state whether or not you recommend an investigation into possible war crimes committed by the United States.

2. Compare several different media sources and how they report a particular day's international news stories. Be sure to include independent, non-profit, and non-United States media. List the headlines of each. Note similarities and differences of the stories. What did they include and exclude? Could you note any bias or agenda? Is there a way to get trustworthy news?

3. Invite combat veterans in your community to a panel discussion. Possible topics may include dissent among troops, Gulf War Syndrome, personal opinions of United States foreign policy, and the experiences of war.

4. Create a display board that highlights the voices of Iraqis. Visit several non-United States websites (such as the BBC at http://www.bbc.co.uk/ and Al Jazeera at http://english.aljazeera.net/HomePage) to discover how the Gulf War of 1991, the subsequent embargo on Iraq, and the Iraq War of 2003 have affected Iraqis.

5. Write an opinion piece on "The War on the Poor . . . Is it Real?" Research the relationship of poverty to crime in the United States. What are the correlations between crime and education level? What are the differences between the ways white-collar crime is treated and crimes committed by the poor?

6. Write a letter to your member of Congress expressing your opinion of United States foreign policy and telling how it affects your life. Ask your representative to answer specific questions you have about where he or she stands on foreign-policy issues.

ESSAY QUESTIONS

In her entry in *Voices*, Yolanda Huet-Vaughn asks, "What is the worth of all this death and destruction?" Using examples from the reading, how would you answer her question?

1. Using examples from your reading, explain what led up to the Gulf War of 1991. What were the voices of opposition to the war? Why were they ignored? What were the consequences of the war? Do you think war could have been avoided? Why, or why not?

2. Some people believe that the unfinished business of the Gulf War led to the 2003 invasion of Iraq. Using examples from the reading, as well as your own research, support or refute this belief.

3. Support or refute Howard Zinn's contention that United States foreign policy historically has been and continues to be militaristic. Do you agree or disagree with the current direction of foreign policy? Explain.

4. Using various examples from the reading, support Howard Zinn's belief that the United States government appears to be waging war on America's poor.

5. Using specific examples from the reading, describe the "permanent adversarial culture" that has arisen in the last several decades. Does one exist? If so, what is it? What are the roots of its origin? What are its goals? What has it achieved? Do you think the existence of such a culture is a benefit or a detriment to American society?

6. What do the voices in this chapter have in common? How do their issues compare and contrast with the issues of those who dissented in earlier generations?

7. Do you think the Gulf War was worth fighting? How do the goals and accomplishments of this war compare to those of the Vietnam War? With the 2003 war in Iraq?

8. Drawing examples from the reading, explain whether or not you think it is important for the United States public to support troops during wartime. Must public support be unconditional? Explain.

SIMULATIONS AND OTHER CREATIVE APPROACHES

1. Create an imaginary non-profit organization to help alleviate the problems of poor kids and to direct them to a hopeful, non-criminal life. Make a logo. Draw up a charter. Plan your first fundraising event. Explain how the money will be used to reach the goals of your charter.

2. Select several committees that will provide policy recommendations for the United States president in the early twenty-first century on one of the following topics: meeting United States energy demands; improving United States relations with third-world countries; reducing poverty in the United States; dealing with the growing prison population. Then use all your persuasive powers to present your recommendations to the president (the teacher or a designated student.)

3. Hold a Socratic seminar revolving around the question, "Should people be allowed to make a profit from weapons of mass destruction?" Use Chapter 22 as the reference text.

4. Write and illustrate a children's book on the origins, goals, and consequences of the Gulf War. Be sure you provide a balanced understanding of the war that includes a discussion of the antiwar movement. Your book should include maps that help the reader to understand the geo-political realities of the war. When you are finished, read the book to an elementary-school class. Ask the students for their comments and critiques.

5. Write an editorial on an international conflict or issue in which the United States is currently involved. Be sure to use the information about the media in this chapter as a guideline for your well-researched and informed editorial.

6. Stage a debate that you imagine might have been held in your community in 1991 on the following topic: It is imperative that the United States intervene in the conflict between Kuwait and Iraq.

CHAPTER TWENTY-THREE

Challenging Bill Clinton

During the final days of the 2004 presidential election and after his recuperation from heart surgery, Bill Clinton triumphantly joined the John Kerry campaign. Everywhere he went, he was greeted as an American hero—the Comeback Kid who spoke with the ease and eloquence that so many Democrats yearned to hear again. Earlier in the year, another former president was lauded as he was laid to rest. But were Ronald Reagan and Bill Clinton heroes during their presidencies, and if not, why do we remember them as such?

The voices in this chapter speak to the opposition that arose to many of the domestic and foreign policies of the Clinton administration. They remind us that in a democracy, it is important that the people be vigilant and vocal when examining the leadership of their sitting presidents. And we must be equally as inquisitive about their legacies. Under the Clinton presidency, whom did the North American Free Trade Agreement (NAFTA) really serve? How and why did the number of prisoners in America double? What are the contemporary consequences of our foreign policies with Afghanistan and Iraq? Why did the United States continue to impose the Cuban and Iraqi embargoes? While it will be years before historians have enough distance to provide any definitive answers to these questions, our students can begin to address them by listening to the voices of dissenters who dared to step forward while the policies were being made.

Document-Based Questions

BRUCE SPRINGSTEEN

1. Do you think the experiences of the people of Youngstown were typical of the 1990s? How and why?

2. How and why are the lyrics of the people in both of these songs evocative of what the Joad family experienced in John Steinbeck's novel *The Grapes of Wrath.*

3. In "Sinaloa Cowboys," the father tells his sons that "for everything the north gives it exacts a price in return." What does the North give, and what is the price for Mexican immigrants?

LORELL PATTERSON

1. Does Lorell Patterson's description of the strikes make a believable comparison to a "war zone"? Why, or why not?

2. Do you agree with Patterson that every human being has the right to the "basic essentials" of education, livable wages, decent housing, and health care? Are you willing to commit your taxes to making such essentials available to all? Why, or why not?

3. Patterson argues that the ordinary people of the United States have the power, not the politicians. What evidence for this view does Patterson provide? Do you agree? Why, or why not?

WINONA LADUKE

1. Do you think Winona LaDuke adequately supports her statement that "major party" candidates and the media neglect the most important public-policy issues? Do you agree? Why, or why not?

2. Do you think LaDuke is correct when she claims that "there is no real quality of life in America until there is quality of life in the poorest regions of this America"? Why, or why not? How do the other voices in the book support her contention?

3. What does LaDuke mean when she says that American Indians are "the only humans in the Department of Interior treated as a natural resource"?

TWO OPEN LETTERS OF PROTEST

1. What are Alice Walker's criticisms of the embargo against Cuba? Why does she feel the embargo should be lifted?

2. How are Alice Walker's and Adrienne Rich's letters similar? What common theme do they address?

3. What did Rich mean when she wrote, "But I do know that art . . . means nothing if it simply decorates the dinner table of power which holds it hostage"?

RANIA MASRI

1. Do you think the political goals and actions of the embargo of Cuba had anything in common with the embargo of Iraq? Explain.

2. Masri quotes the former chief weapons inspector who wrote in 1998 that the weapons of mass destruction that were cited as the primary reason for the embargo were "destroyed or rendered harmless." How and why do you think this information was not widely known five years later when George W. Bush declared that the war in Iraq was being waged because of the threat from Iraq's weapons of mass destruction?

3. If the "unwritten goal" of the embargo was to remove Saddam Hussein from power in Iraq, how do you think the United States government justified the fact that ordinary Iraqis, not Saddam Hussein, were the victims of the embargo?

RONI KROUZMAN

1. How does your interpretation of Krouzman's experience compare with the decision of the Seattle city authorities to call the demonstration a "civil emergency"? Was the law-enforcement response justified?

2. Do you think the World Trade Organization (WTO) demonstrators were "making history"? How was this demonstration similar to or different from earlier protests described in *Voices*?

3. The Seattle authorities used tear gas and mass arrests to break up the WTO protests. Do you think this reaction was justified? Why, or why not?

ANITA CAMERON

1. Why did builders in Denver oppose the construction of accessible housing? Do you think the civil disobedience tactics used by ADAPT members were an appropriate response to the builders' refusal to pay more attention to their demands?

2. Do you think ADAPT provides enough information to support the argument that homes should be built to provide access for people with disabilities? Why, or why not?

3. Why do you think the police arrested the ADAPT members? Do you agree or disagree with this action? Explain.

ELIZABETH ("BETITA") MARTINEZ

1. How did the goals and activities of the "blowouts" of 1968 compare and contrast with the student walkouts of the 1990s? What had changed in schools serving Latino populations? What remained the same?

2. Do you think the actions of the student demonstrators in the 1990s were justified? Why, or why not? If you had attended any of these schools, would you have been involved? Why, or why not?

3. How are these students "making history"? How do their efforts compare with those used at the WTO in Seattle and with the work of the ADAPT activists in Denver, who also claimed to be making history?

WALTER MOSLEY

1. Do you think that many people in the United States believe that survival is "reliant upon servitude"? Explain.

2. What does Walter Mosely mean when he says, "We live within the margin of profit. We are the margin of profit"? Do you agree or disagree? Explain.

3. Is Mosely arguing for revolutionary overthrow of capitalism? For the creation of a socialist system of government? Explain.

JULIA BUTTERFLY HILL

1. How is Julia Hill's act of civil disobedience similar to and different from the other acts of civil disobedience described in this chapter or in earlier chapters?

2. Agree or disagree with Hill's statement that "the best tools for dismantling the machine are the ones the mechanics are using to keep it running." What tools are the mechanics using to keep the machine running?

3. Do you think it is useful to keep "preaching to the choir," or is it more effective to preach to an uncommitted audience? Are these necessarily competing goals? Explain.

Main Points in *Voices*, Chapter 23, "Challenging Bill Clinton"

After reading Chapter 23 in *Voices*, students should be encouraged to identify what they believe to be the main points therein. Following are five possible main points.

1. The Clinton administration failed to live up to its promise to support union activists and instead served the interests of United States corporations.

2. The battle for full civil rights is still being fought in the United States.

3. In the 1990s, many came to see globalization (or "neoliberalism") as a threat to people in other countries as well as to many people in the United States.

4. As the United States population changes and becomes more diverse in its racial and ethnic composition, people of color and immigrants have been blamed—or scapegoated—for social problems that have other causes.

Main Points in *Voices*, Chapter 23, "Challenging Bill Clinton," and in *A People's History*, Chapter 23, "The Clinton Presidency"

If your students are also reading *A People's History*, they should be encouraged to identify what they believe to be the main points in Chapter 23 in both books. Following are five additional points to be stressed when *Voices* and *A People's History* are used together.

5. The Democratic Party moved closer to the right during the Clinton administration.

6. The political, economic, and social interests of the Democratic Party increasingly have less in common with the political, economic, and social interests of United States working people.

7. The Clinton administration joined the Republicans in upholding the tradition of big government support of big business.

8. During the Clinton administration, United States foreign policy was guided more by corporate interests than by human rights.

9. During the 1990s, enough people were disillusioned with the Democratic and Republican Parties to create several independent political movements.

General-Discussion Questions for *Voices*

While the following questions are designed for classroom discussion about all the voices read in Chapter 23, they can also be rewritten and included as evaluation tools.

1. What is the North American Free Trade Association (NAFTA)? The General Agreement on Tariffs and Trade (GATT)? Why did these programs seem so controversial to the people included in this chapter?

2. Do you think most United States taxpayers would be willing to commit their taxes to making the basic essentials Patterson discusses—education, decent housing, livable wages, health care—available to all Americans? Why, or why not? Would you be willing?

3. What is scapegoating? What role has it played in American society throughout our history? Do you think Americans will ever stop using each other as scapegoats? How and why?

4. Do you think the other voices in this chapter with agree with Patterson's assessment, "If you dare to struggle, you dare to win. If you dare not to struggle, you don't deserve to win"? Explain.

5. What is the seventh generation Winona LaDuke describes?

6. What are the goals of the Endangered Species Act? Why is it important to have such an act? How did Presidents Bill Clinton and George W. Bush respond to the provisions of the act?

7. What are sanctions? What is an embargo? Why did the United States initially impose an embargo on Cuba? On Iraq? Why did the Clinton administration continue both embargos? Do you think we should lift the embargo on Cuba?

8. In Alice Walker's letter to President Clinton, she refers to the Cuban strug-

gle for freedom from both Spain and the United States. How, when, and why have the Cubans had to struggle for freedom from the United States?

9. What was the United Nations' "food for oil" program in Iraq?

10. What is corporate globalization?

11. Does your school have a history of any student walkouts, blowouts, or demonstrations? If not, why do you think such actions have been avoided? If so, did any manage to change school policy?

General-Discussion Questions for *Voices* and *A People's History*

These general-discussion questions are additional questions for students who have read Chapter 23 *Voices* and *A People's History* (or 24, depending on which edition you are using). For all questions, discussion must focus on ways the materials in both chapters help students formulate and articulate their answers.

12. Why do you think President Clinton was re-elected in 1996 "with a distinct lack of enthusiasm"? Do you think this lack of enthusiasm was similar to that which characterized the presidential campaign of John Kerry in 2004? How and why?

13. How did the Democratic Party move to the right under the Clinton presidency? Do you think this move was good for the party? For ordinary people? For Bill Clinton? Explain.

14. Do you agree with criminologist Todd Clear that being tougher on crime is "dumber"? What does Clear believe to be the real reasons for crime? Do you agree?

15. Why should Americans be concerned with the plight of immigrants who enter the United States illegally?

16. What proof does Howard Zinn provide that the Clinton administration continued the "historic use of economic aid to gain political influence" (*People's History*, p. 639)?

17. Why did labor unions oppose NAFTA? Have their criticisms been proven in the years since NAFTA passed?

18. What is the "wealth tax"? Would you support such a tax? Why, or why not?

19. How powerful do you think third parties will be in the American political system of the twenty-first century?

Evaluation Tools

SUGGESTED ASSIGNMENTS

These assignments can be adapted to meet any classroom need—homework, short- or long-term research projects, individual or group work. The end product should be flexible, depending on teacher interest and student abilities—papers, journals, oral reports, visual aides, and the like.

1. Learn more about the origins of NAFTA during the Clinton administration. What were its goals? Why did Clinton support the agreement? How did other Democrats stand on NAFTA? What was the Republican position? How did the positions of both parties compare and contrast? Who opposed its passage, and why? Why do you think the voices of opposition were not widely heard or understood? Who has most benefited from the passage of NAFTA?

2. Conduct some research on the rise of the Green Party in the 1990s. What are its origins and goals? What has it accomplished since its creation? How have the Greens influenced the last three presidential elections? What do you think is the future of the Green Party in the twenty-first century?

3. Using a search engine of choice, read other primary accounts about the ways United States sanctions affected the Iraqis after 1991. Then read several government documents from the Clinton administration that explain why the United States government continued the embargo. If you had been an adviser to the president in 1999, would you have advised him to continue or terminate the embargo? Explain.

4. Compare and contrast the Chicago demonstration of 1968 at the Democratic National Convention with the Seattle demonstration in 1999 at the WTO meeting. What were the goals, activities, and short- and long-term accomplishments of each? How did the media report on both demonstrations? How did the American public respond to the demonstrators? Which of the two do you feel were most successful? What criteria did you use to measure its success? Explain.

5. Examine the archives of your local newspaper(s) to determine whether or not there have been any local demonstrations in your community over the past year. If so, learn as much as possible about the origins, actions, and consequences of the demonstration. Then interview someone who participated in the demonstration. How have the issues raised by the demonstrators been addressed? What contemporary controversial issues that might lead to demonstrations exist in your community?

6. Learn more about the money allocated to education and to prisons in your state. What is the annual expenditure per pupil? Per inmate? Do you think the money is being allocated appropriately? Explain. Compare your state's allocations to those of two neighboring states. What do you think these figures tells us about the health of democracy in the twenty-first century?

7. Learn more about the "Personal Responsibility and Work Opportunity Reconciliation Act of 1996." What were its primary provisions? How did the law reform the welfare system? How did the Clinton administration explain its backing of the law? Almost a decade after this law was passed, how has it affected the lives of poor Americans? Did it actually save the $50 billion it promised? Did it balance the budget? Why do you think Clinton was more comfortable with passing such a welfare-reform law rather than establishing new government programs to create jobs?

8. Study the origins, goals, and accomplishments of the Million Man March and the Rainbow Coalition. How do they compare and contrast? Which do you feel were most effective and why?

SUGGESTED ESSAY QUESTIONS

1. It has often been suggested that since the 1990s, there has been very little difference in Democratic and Republican policies in both Congress and the White House. Both, critics say, support the ruling elite at the expense of ordinary Americans. Using the voices from your reading throughout the book(s), support or refute this sentiment.

2. Patterson claims the existence of "a worldwide war on workers" in the mid-1990s. To counter the war, she suggests that workers "need to stand up with one voice—people of all races." Do you think this attitude is possible? Why, or why not? Do you think the WTO demonstration may have been a step

in this direction? Do the voices in this chapter give you any indication of how such a unified voice of opposition could be lifted? Explain.

3. Using examples from your reading, explain how the recent opposition to corporate globalization compares with historical opposition to corporate control over domestic workers in the late nineteenth and early twentieth centuries. What has improved for those who work for United States corporations? What has remained the same? What has become worse?

4. Many argue that the battle for civil rights is still being waged. After reading this/these chapter(s), who do you think fought for civil rights during the Clinton administration? What battles remain to be fought after the Clinton presidency? What could Clinton have done to promote civil rights? As the twenty-first century unfolds, what do you feel are the major unresolved civil rights issues?

5. Several of the voices in this chapter claim that their actions of resistance were making history. How and why do you think the resistance movements of the 1990s were different from past movements? How were they similar? Do you think they were making history? Explain.

6. In his essay, Walter Mosely states that "if the system defines you, then it owes you something too." How would the other voices in this chapter respond to this statement? Do you agree or disagree? Explain.

7. In your opinion, what are the most important messages shared by the voices in this chapter? Which were involved in the most successful effort to be heard? Which had the most impact on society? Which were least successful and had the least impact? Explain.

8. When Bill Clinton ran for a second term, he frequently invoked the name of Martin Luther King, Jr., in his campaign. When George W. Bush ran for his second term in 2004, he frequently compared his decision-making with that of Franklin Delano Roosevelt and Harry Truman. What is accurate and what is inaccurate about these comparisons? Does the United States public "buy" these comparisons? Support your answer with examples from the reading.

9. Howard Zinn claims that Clinton misread public opinion when he declared that the "era of big government is over." What does he believe the public really wanted in the early 1990s? Do you agree? Explain. How does Clinton's declaration compare and contrast with the same declaration repeatedly made by George W. Bush in his elections campaigns of 2000 and 2004?

10. Using plentiful examples from your reading of *A People's History*, support Howard Zinn's contention in Chapter 23 that "[b]ig government had, in fact, begun with the Founding Fathers, who deliberately set up a strong central government to protect the interests of the bondholders, the slave owners, the land speculators, the manufacturers" (*People's History*, p. 637). Then demonstrate how the Clinton administration joined the Republicans in keeping this tradition alive.

SIMULATIONS AND OTHER CREATIVE APPROACHES

1. Write a play about activists involved in the WTO demonstration. Base your dialog on at least one interview with a person who participated in the demonstration, as well as other accounts obtained from both primary and secondary documents. Be sure to include dialog that explains why they were opposed to corporate globalization, how they shaped the demonstration to reflect their concerns, what they hoped to gain by their resistance, and what they experienced during and after the actual demonstration.

2. Make a list of what you think you will deserve after your own lifetime of labor and ask everyone in the class to make such a list. Share the lists with your fellow students. Then discuss these questions among yourselves: What is common on everyone's list? Do most people currently have access to these things? Why, or why not? Do you think you will have access to these things within your lifetime? Why, or why not? For which of the items on your list would you be willing to fight? Would you be willing to fight for any item on the lists of your classmates? Explain.

3. Draw two maps of the United States, one that illustrates poverty across the nation during the Great Depression and one that illustrates poverty across the nation in the early twenty-first century. Where has poverty persisted? Where has it improved? Where has it increased? What progress have we made since the federal government declared a War on Poverty?

4. Stage a mock press conference of the prominent leaders of the 1990s that is attended by a diverse coalition of ordinary Americans. As the press conference progresses, have the ordinary Americans address their questions to specific leaders.

CHAPTER TWENTY-FOUR

Bush II and the "War on Terror"

Everything seemed changed in the world after the tragic events of September 11, 2001. Or was it? True, people in the United States experienced a very real fear. After all, it was the first time we were attacked on our own soil. But when we truly subject the rhetoric of the Bush administration to scrutiny, it becomes clear that much did not change. The politics of fear are part of our history. If we move backward to Salem in 1692 or move forward to McCarthyism in the 1950s, it is easy to recall the politics of fear that encouraged irrational reactions to perceived threats. Internal enemies have always threatened the status quo; they were Loyalists in the eighteenth century, Communists from the mid-nineteenth century through 1989, and today they are terrorists.

Since September 11, 2001, the balance between civil liberties and security has often tipped in favor of the latter. But this imbalance is also part of our history. Only seven years after the Bill of Rights was signed, Congress passed the Alien and Sedition Acts. During World War I, a new and more virulent rendition of these acts became law. In the wake of September 11, we saw the passage of the PATRIOT Act. The voices in this chapter recognize that we are fighting old enemies in a new political package. They ask us to listen carefully to the reasons the Bush administration gave for the wars in Afghanistan and Iraq. They ask us to learn from our past mistakes and to question governmental decisions that have lead us into new wars.

Document-Based Questions

MICHAEL MOORE

1. Do you think that Michael Moore is being fair to Bush? Is it really fair to criticize someone who was born into wealth for taking advantage of his or her position? Why does Moore think such behavior is wrong?

284 ~ CHAPTER TWENTY-FOUR

2. Why does it seem hypocritical to Moore that Bush used the federal government to back him in the voter controversy during the 2000 presidential election? Do you agree or disagree with Moore? Explain.

3. What are Moore's complaints about the Democrats? Do you agree or disagree with his criticism? Explain.

ORLANDO AND PHYLLIS RODRIGUEZ

1. Why wouldn't the parents of a young man who perished in the World Trade Center attack support the "war on terror"? Do you think their response was typical or atypical of the responses by families of other victims? Explain.

2. The Rodriguezes feel that a war of revenge will only nurture "further grievances against us." What grievances against the United States already existed in "distant lands"? Do you think we should be concerned about these grievances? Explain.

3. Do you agree that their son, Greg, was "a victim of an inhuman ideology"? How would you describe that ideology?

RITA LASAR

1. What similar themes are echoed in the Rodriguez and Lasar letters?

2. Do you agree or disagree with Lasar that September 11 "did not change the world. What it did, in is own terrible way, was invite Americans to join the world"? Why?

3. In 2002, Lasar felt that "[w]e can no longer afford a go-it-alone approach." Do you think most people in the United States agreed with her when she wrote this piece? What do people think about this unilateral approach today?

MONAMI MAULIK

1. What does Maulik say is the difference between organizing and providing services? Do you agree or disagree? Would you rather be involved in organizing or providing services? Why?

2. Do you agree that an "anti-immigrant backlash is currently being institutionalized"? How and why?

3. How is the PATRIOT Act a form of "state violence"? In what ways does the author think the PATRIOT Act encourages racism and xenophobia?

INTERNATIONAL BROTHERHOOD OF TEAMSTERS LOCAL 705

1. Why would some labor unions oppose the war in Iraq?

2. Why did the Teamsters Local 705 think that Bush planned to go to war with Iraq? Were these beliefs typical or atypical of most people? Explain.

3. How can the goal of fighting for justice be used to both defend and support the war in Iraq?

RACHEL CORRIE

1. Why are eight-year-old Palestinians "much more aware of the workings of the global power structure" than Rachel Corrie was as a young adult? Why aren't eight-year-old Americans as aware? Should they be more aware?

2. What do you find most compelling about Corrie's description of living in the Gaza Strip?

3. Why do you think the Palestinians would have concerns about the United States going to war with Iraq?

DANNY GLOVER

1. What justification do Danny Glover and the other voices in this chapter provide for the accusation that the United States government represents "the real users of weapons of mass destruction"?

2. What are the "obstacles that have been placed in our path on this journey"? What is the journey Glover describes? Do you think the obstacles were fair? Explain.

3. How and why are some people more inclined to listen to Glover's message than to messages from some of the other voices in this chapter? Who might be less inclined and why?

AMY GOODMAN

1. How do independent media sources differ from mainstream media sources? Which sources do you prefer, and why?

2. Do you think embedded reporters can provide balanced journalistic news? Why, or why not? What are Amy Goodman's criticisms of embedded reporting?

3. Do you agree with Goodman's goal "to make dissent commonplace in America"? Why, or why not? Do you agree with Goodman when she states, "Dissent is what makes this country healthy"?

TIM PREDMORE

1. Why does Tim Predmore claim that the "shock and awe" description of the war in Iraq is hypocritical? Do you agree or disagree? Explain.

2. What does Predmore believe to be the real purpose of this "modern-day crusade"? Do you agree or disagree? Explain. Why has he lost his "conviction"?

3. At the time you read this article, how many United States soldiers had died in Iraq? How many Iraqis?

MARITZA CASTILLO, ET AL.

1. How has the United States government justified sending members of the National Guard to Iraq? How has it justified extending the soldiers' military commitment in Iraq?

2. Do you think that a group of mothers who organized a hunger strike would influence military decisions in regard to the National Guard? Why, or why not?

3. Do you think it is true that the "coalition we are being told about does not really exist"? How does the Bush administration describe this coalition? Is it really a coalition? Should fighting as part of a coalition be required before a nation goes to war?

KURT VONNEGUT

1. What is Kurt Vonnegut's "dream" for America? How does it compare and contrast with yours?

2. Why do you think Howard Zinn included this particular entry in Chapter 24?

3. Do you think that "only nut cases want to be president"? What examples might Vonnegut use from United States history?

PATTI SMITH

1. This song was written in 1988. Is it still relevant today?

2. Do the "people have the power"? Do they really "rule"? Provide examples from the voices used throughout this book to illustrate your answer.

3. Why does Howard Zinn end his book with Smith's "People Have the Power"?

Main Points in *Voices*, Chapter 24, "Bush II and the 'War on Terror'"

After reading Chapter 24 in *Voices*, students should be encouraged to identify what they believe to be the main points therein. Following are four possible main points.

1. Immediate and eloquent opposition arose when President Bush declared a vengeful "war on terrorism" after September 11, including those affected by the attack, such as family members.

2. While the "war on terror" declared after September 11, 2001, opened a new chapter in United States history, it also shared continuity with earlier chapters in United States history, especially in terms of the aims, goals, and methods of United States foreign policy and of ways the United States government has sought to treat dissent and limit civil liberties in times of war or during the threat of war.

3. Since September 11, 2001, the anti-immigrant backlash in the United States has increased against those of Arab, South Asian, and Muslim descent and appearance.

4. As the occupation of Iraq continued throughout 2004, opposition to United States involvement grew within military ranks, as well as among veterans of the war and their families.

Main Points in *Voices*, Chapter 24, "Bush II and the 'War on Terror,'" and in *A People's History*, Chapter 24, "The Coming Revolt of the Guards," or Chapter 25, "The 2000 Election and the 'War on Terrorism'"

If your students are also reading *A People's History*, they should be encouraged to identify what they believe to be the main points in Chapter 24 in *Voices* and in Chapter 24 or 25 in *A People's History* (depending on which edition you are using.) Following are five additional points to be stressed when *Voices* and *A People's History* are used together.

5. In the 2000 election, there was little difference in the corporate support of the Democratic candidate, Al Gore, and the Republican candidate, George W. Bush.

6. The 2000 presidential election was both one of the most "bizarre" events and one of the closest calls in United States history.

7. Despite the claims of the Bush administration, terrorism cannot be defeated by force; rather, defeating terrorism depends on addressing the deep grievances against the United States, making fundamental changes in United States foreign policy, and changing the United States government's domestic and international funding priorities.

8. Ever since the calamity of September 11, the United States public has been "overwhelmingly supportive" of President Bush's "war on terrorism."

9. The mainstream media have failed to convey the full extent of the human catastrophe that has been caused by the wars in Afghanistan and Iraq, nor have they publicized the voices critical of current United States foreign policy in regard to Afghanistan and Iraq.

General-Discussion Questions for *Voices*

While the following questions are designed for classroom discussion about all the voices read in Chapter 24, they can also be rewritten and included as evaluation tools.

1. In looking back at the 2000 and 2004 presidential races conducted by George W. Bush, how do the two compare and contrast in style and substance?

2. What other choices might have been made after September 11 instead of declaring "war on terrorism"? Do you think people would have supported any of these alternative choices? Why, or why not?

3. What are the "roots of terrorism," according to Lasar?

4. What is the PATRIOT Act? Why did it receive overwhelming bipartisan support? What are some current criticisms of the act?

5. What is "grassroots" organizing? Do you think that this type of organizational activism is more effective than work done at the state or federal level? How and why? Have you ever been involved in grassroots organizing?

6. What is xenophobia? Is anti-immigrant sentiment new to the United States? Explain.

7. How would you describe the current Palestinian national entity? Why are most Americans ignorant of the current status of the Palestinians? What political changes do most Palestinians support?

8. How much coverage did the mainstream media give to antiwar demonstrations that began in early 2003 and continued throughout the invasion and the subsequent American occupation of Iraq?

9. Is it unpatriotic to challenge the decision of the United States government to go to war with Iraq? Explain.

10. What is "investigative" journalism? Has there been much investigative journalism conducted in regard to the wars in Afghanistan and Iraq? Explain. Do you think people want more or less investigative journalism? Why?

11. What problems arise when large corporations dominate ownership of media outlets? What do you expect from the media today? Are your expectations being met? How and why?

12. What general themes are common to all the voices of this chapter?

General-Discussion Questions for *Voices* and *A People's History*

These general-discussion questions are additional questions for students who have read Chapter 24 in *Voices* and Chapter 24 or 25 in *A People's History* (depending on which edition you are using). For all questions, discussion must focus on ways the materials in both chapters help students formulate and articulate their answers.

13. If Al Gore and George W. Bush were alike in their bids for the presidency as Howard Zinn suggests, how did they differ?

14. What was Ralph Nader's political agenda in the 2000 and 2004 presidential elections?

15. What was the role of the Electoral College in determining the 1876, 1888, and 2000 presidential elections?

16. Justice John Paul Stevens's minority opinion in *Bush* v. *Gore* (December 11, 2001) held that the real loser in the 2000 election was "the nation's confidence in the judge as an impartial guardian of the rule of law." Do you agree or disagree? Explain.

17. Why do you think the Democrats have only been able to muster a "timid opposition" to the Bush administration's "pro-big-business agenda"?

18. Do you agree or disagree with Howard Zinn that "terrorism could not be defeated by force"? Does he provide enough evidence to convince you of his position? Explain.

19. Why do you think the American public initially demonstrated overwhelming support for Bush's "war on terrorism"? Was there more or less support for the war on Iraq?

20. Do you agree with some antiwar critics that the United States government was fighting a war of revenge in both Afghanistan and Iraq? If this is the case, is revenge a good reason to wage war?

21. What are the grievances that some people in the Arab world harbor against the United States government? Are these grievances that can be mitigated

with a war on terrorism? Should the United States government address these grievances?

22. Why does Howard Zinn believe that the United States government would never make American foreign-policy changes that would change the power of the military-industrial complex?

Evaluation Tools

SUGGESTED ASSIGNMENTS

These assignments can be adapted to meet any classroom need—homework, short- or long-term research projects, individual or group work. The end product should be flexible, depending on teacher interest and student abilities—papers, journals, oral reports, visual aides, and the like.

1. Watch at least two of Michael Moore's most recent movies—*Fahrenheit 911* and *Roger and Me* would be good choices—or watch one movie and read one of his books—*Stupid White Men* and *Dude, Where's My Country?* After reading his letter to president-elect Bush written in 2000, what themes do you find consistently emerge from the letter and the movie(s), or the letter, movie, and book? Which themes do you think are most effectively presented in these three sources? Least effectively? Do you think Moore is a modern-day muckraker? Explain. Do you think Moore's style brings new converts, or does it alienate potential supporters? Use specific examples from your three sources to support your position.

2. Anti-Muslim prejudice existed in the United States long before September 11. Such watchdog organizations as the American-Arab Anti-Discrimination Committee (ADC) began reporting on anti-Muslim actions shortly after the Gulf War. Learn more about such beliefs and activities over the past decade. What is being done to protect Muslims in the United States? What is not being done? What should be done?

3. Learn more about a grassroots organization in your community that is devoted to a social-justice cause. Attend a meeting, visit its headquarters, and interview a member to learn more about its origin, goals, membership, and accomplishments. Is this an organization you might support?

Explain. Do you think it has been effective in recruiting members and accomplishing any of its goals? Explain.

4. Create an annotated chronology of anti-immigrant federal actions and legislation from the late eighteenth century on. What themes emerge from such actions and legislation? Do we see more or less actions and legislation in the twentieth century than before? Why do you think that we—a nation of immigrants—have such a long history of anti-immigration policies? Do you think this situation will change in the twenty-first century? Explain.

5. In October 2004, Ariel Sharon convinced the Israeli Knesset to vote for the withdrawal of Jewish settlers from the Gaza Strip. Learn more about the growth of Jewish settlements in both Gaza and the West Bank from 1967 on. What role have such settlements played in preventing the Israelis and Palestinians from reaching a peaceful solution to a long war? What role has the United States played in getting the Israelis and Palestinians to negotiate the settlement question? Why did a significant percentage of Palestinians oppose the procedure under which the 2004 decision to withdraw was made? Do you think the settler issue will ever be resolved? Explain.

6. Using a search engine of choice, find out more about Rachel Corrie's mission in the Palestinian territories, her death, the media's treatment of her death, and the United States government's response to her death. Do you think she died in vain? Explain.

7. Go to the *Democracy Now!* Web site (www.democracynow.org) and learn more about how and why this independent source is different from mainstream television, radio, and print media. Do you think that we need such a source to ensure, as Howard Zinn notes, that we will not "sacrifice truth for profit"? Select at least one news article from the website to illustrate how truth rather than profit has been the motive behind the report.

8. Using a search engine of choice, select a news story on any particular day that has to do with a current and controversial United States foreign policy. Read at least two articles about this story from the mainstream press and then read two others from independent news sources. Finally, read about the story from a news source outside the United States. How do they compare and contrast? Which is the most useful coverage and why? Least useful?

9. In the November/December 2004 edition of *Mother Jones* magazine, journalist David Goodman reports on a growing movement—Iraq Veterans Against the War (IVAW). Read the article, "Breaking Ranks," available online at www.motherjones.com/news/feature/2004/11/10_400.html, and then find out more about IVAW at www.ivaw.net, and Military Families Speak Out at www.mfso.org. How does their information compare and contrast with the article in *Voices* by Tim Predmore? Why are the Iraq veterans and their families "breaking ranks" with the Bush administration? What do you find most compelling about their reasons? Least compelling? Why aren't these stories covered by the mainstream press? Should they be?

10. Learn more about the origin and functions of the Electoral College in presidential elections. Then write an essay arguing that the Electoral College should or should not be abandoned and replaced by popular vote in all presidential races.

11. Conduct research on Al Jazeera, the Arab news station located in Qatar. View the film *Control Room* and visit the network's English-language Web site at http://english.aljazeera.net/HomePage. What are the origins, goals, and accomplishments of this news organization? How and why does its news coverage differ from that provided in the United States? Do you think its reporting is biased? Is it more or less biased than United States news reporting in the mainstream media?

SUGGESTED ESSAY QUESTIONS

1. In Rita Lasar's essay, written one year after September 11, she states, "We Americans have a choice." We could "go-it-alone" or accept the invitation "to join the world." Using examples from your reading, show reasons for and against each of these choices. Then make your own choice and support it.

2. Shortly after the tragic events of September 11, 2001, President Bush declared that "You are either with us, or you are with the terrorists." What is the message in this declaration? Is this a new message for a United States president? If so, how? If not, why not? Do you agree or disagree with the president? Does this message infringe your rights under the First Amendment? Be sure to provide examples with your answers.

3. What role have journalists and the media played in "selling" the wars in

Afghanistan and Iraq to the American people? Be sure to use information from the chapters to support your answer. In your opinion, have they been successful? Explain. How would you change news coverage of war?

4. Throughout 2004, much debate focused around the comparisons between United States involvement in Vietnam and in Iraq. Do you think American involvement in the two wars is comparable? Why, or why not? Be sure to use examples from both Chapter 18 and Chapter 24 to answer this question.

5. It has often been said, as Kurt Vonnegut does in Chapter 24, that "power corrupts us, and absolute power corrupts absolutely." What does this statement mean? How do the voices in this chapter support this contention? Do you believe that United States governmental policies of the early twenty-first century support or refute this statement? Provide examples from the reading within your answer.

6. Many people have argued that a vote for a third-party candidate in the 2000 and 2004 elections was a vote that hurt the Democratic Party. Using the various voices you have read, as well as other information in your books, discuss the role of third parties in the 2000 and 2004 presidential elections. Did they help define the political debate or did they detract from it? Do you think you might support a third-party candidate? If so, under what circumstances? If not, why not?

7. Using as many examples as possible from your reading, write an essay that argues that the war on terrorism—as it is presently being fought—can or cannot be won.

8. Howard Zinn closes the final chapter in *A People's History* by reminding his readers that the future of democracy depends on the actions of the United States public. What decisions have we made in the early twenty-first century that will shape the future of the United States? Are these decisions consistent or inconsistent with past decisions? Which of these decisions do you feel will have a positive effect on the next decades? A negative effect? Be sure to use examples from your reading to back up your answers.

9. In your own words, explain your understanding of the twenty-first century "war on terrorism." Then use some of the voices from your reading to answer the following questions: How and when did the war begin? How and why has it been a unilateral or a multilateral war? How and why has it

moved from Afghanistan to Iraq? How and why might it expand to other parts of the world?

SIMULATIONS AND OTHER CREATIVE APPROACHES

1. Write two letters—one to George W. Bush and the other to John Kerry—in which you discuss your feelings about the presidential race of 2004. It's important that you let them know what you thought about the campaign—the debates, what they said that you could support, and what they failed to discuss during the course of the campaign. Then tell them how you felt about the election outcome and what you predict will be the course of our nation over the next four years.

2. Create a grassroots organization that is devoted to activism on a topic important in your academic setting. Define the issue and how you propose your organization will act upon it. Arrange for a meeting and create flyers designed to get people to attend. Then hold a meeting in your classroom. Afterward, determine the degree of success you had in getting your colleagues to "buy in to" your cause. What will you have to do to maintain the organization's momentum? Do you think it would be worth the effort?

3. Imagine that you have been asked to design a fourth presidential debate for the 2004 election. You have decided to invite the five major candidates—George W. Bush, John Kerry, Ralph Nader (Reform Party/Independent), David Cobb (Green Party), and Michael Badnarik (Libertarian Party). You have also decided that the discussion will be exclusively devoted to United States foreign policy and that you will invite all twelve contributors to Chapter 24 in *Voices* to pose three questions each. The candidates will be given the questions the day before the debate. Now, stage the debate.

4. Write and illustrate a children's book on antiwar activism. Be sure to include the history of antiwar efforts in the United States, as well as antiwar efforts currently operating in the United States. When the book is completed, ask an elementary-school teacher if she or he is willing to read it in their classroom.

CHAPTER TWENTY-FIVE

War and Injustice: People Speak Out

by Jeff Coomber, Adam Crug, Nicole Sinclair, and Megan Watson

Six years have passed since the initial publication of this teaching guide. At that time, the last chapter began with a plea to listen to the voices of those who questioned our involvement in Iraq and Afghanistan, who asked us to learn from our past mistakes, and who encouraged us to question governmental decisions about committing ourselves to war. Five years later, we have included a new chapter with four voices raising similar questions and concerns. An Iraq War veteran, the mother of a son who was killed in Iraq, the brother who lost his sibling who died of "friendly fire" in Afghanistan, and the twelve-year-old daughter of lesbian parents offer clear evidence that to them and their families, injustice still exists in the United States.

Document-Based Questions

CAMILO MEJÍA

1. Mejía mentions many institutions and issues those in the antiwar movement must confront: corporations, hypocrites, etc. Which of these entities do you think requires the most difficult struggle for the antiwar movement? For whom and why? In what ways could this struggle be resolved?

2. What is your opinion on Mejía's seven-month confinement for not wanting to fight in "George Bush's war"? Is his resistance justifiable? If so, on what grounds? If not, why?

3. How do you think the United States should handle situations like Mejía's?

CINDY SHEEHAN

1. Cindy Sheehan equates the threat of communism in the 1950s to the terrorist threat in present-day America. Do you feel this is a valid comparison or not? Explain.

2. Explain what Cindy Sheehan meant when she said that 58 percent of the public was with her, and if they spoke up, they could stop the war.

3. Do you think Cindy Sheehan's plan to camp in front of George Bush's house was successful? Why or why not?

KEVIN TILLMAN

1. What does Kevin Tillman mean when he states, "Somehow, those afraid to fight an illegal invasion decades ago are allowed to send soldiers to die for an illegal invasion they started"? Agree or disagree with Tillman's statement using examples to back up your position.

2. Does Kevin Tillman's statement to the public leave you more hopeful or less so? Why?

3. In his statement, Kevin Tillman made the point that "Much has happened since we handed over our voice." What did Tillman mean by saying he and his brother handed over their voices? Why would Kevin not be able to speak out against the war before this point? Why did Pat feel that way?

EVANN ORLECK-JETTER

1. What do you think Evann Orleck-Jetter means when she says, "Vermont's Freedom to Marry can help us get back on track"? Do you think Orleck-Jetter makes an effective argument when she says that the people of Vermont have not reached the "promised land" envisioned by civil rights leader Martin Luther King as a result of not allowing same-sex marriage? Support your answer.

2. Why do you think gay marriage laws have yet to be passed in all fifty states?

Main Points in *Voices*, Chapter 25, "War and Injustice: People Speak Out"

1. The voices of religious and corporate interests play a significant role in the "democratic" process of policy making in the United States.

2. When corporations and the wealthy are allowed more say in the government, common people sacrifice their civil liberties.

3. Civil rights are not freely given but rather require protection by ordinary people.

4. In the words of Martin Luther King, "We have yet to reach the Promised Land."

5. The government of the United States is a government of the people. If you aren't happy with what it's doing, it is your right and obligation to change it.

General Discussion Questions For *Voices*

The following questions can be used to stimulate class discussion about all the voices read in Chapter 25. They could also be rewritten or designed to serve as an evaluation tool.

1. Which voices best reinforce the main idea behind this quote by Andy Rooney: "I wish we could dedicate Memorial Day, not to the memory of those who have died at war, but to the idea of saving the lives of the young people who are going to die in the future if we don't find some new way . . . that takes war out of our lives." How and why do they support Rooney's statement?

2. Whose voice do you think reaches a wider U.S. audience? Why? Whose voice do you think reaches a limited U.S. audience? Why?

3. In her speech, Orleck-Jetter mentions that she has been studying the civil rights movement. Do you think that her fight for marriage equality is part of the same movement, or is it an entirely new civil rights issue?

4. Do you think twenty-first century Americans are more apathetic about war and civil rights compared to Americans in the late twentieth century? Why or why not?

5. Mejía and Sheehan both refer to similarities between Cold War rhetoric and that which politicians use today. Who do you think makes a better argument? Why is it more effective?

6. How would you create an antiwar activity in your community? Who do you think would be the most difficult group of people in your community to get involved in this activity? Why? What would be the group most open to involvement? Why?

7. Have you ever been involved in a protest activity? If so, how and why? If not, is there any issue that might convince you to be involved in a protest action?

Evaluation Tools

These assignments can be used as any type of assessment—homework, short- or long-term research projects, group or individual work. The end product should be flexible, depending on teacher interest and student abilities.

1. Learn more about the "hot war" between the Soviet Union and the United States in Afghanistan. Do you think the current presence of U.S. troops in Afghanistan is a new conflict or a continuation from the past? Explain your answer.

2. Read a book review on *State of Denial* by Bob Woodward. Did this review give you any information about the Bush administration's handling of the war in Iraq?

3. Research the history of same-sex marriage propositions in the United States. How many times have they appeared on ballots and what seems to be the deciding factor of the outcome?

4. Create a chronology documenting same-sex marriage court cases and the significance of their outcome. Include the decision, reasoning, and end result.

5. Imagine that you are Cindy Sheehan. Then, write a letter to your congressman explaining your feelings about the war. Make sure you explain the reasons you are against it and what you expect your congressman to do about it.

6. Research at least three different antiwar movement groups that have organized within the last fifty years. What are the different tactics each group uses to initiate change? Which method do you think is most effective?

Why? Which would you choose to join and why? Which would you not choose and why?

7. Learn more about the confinement of prisoners at Guantánamo Bay. When did their imprisonment begin and upon what grounds were most people imprisoned? How many remain at Guantánamo and why are they still being held? What are the current problems related to those who remain? Based upon what you learned, write President Barack Obama a letter that supports some action about those remaining in Guantánamo.

8. Learn more about the history of corporate personhood in the United States. When did it begin and how has it evolved? What rights do corporations currently have that are the same rights to which all are entitled?

Suggested Essay Questions

1. What does Mejía mean when he writes, "No longer able to rely on the rhetoric of the Cold War, the corporate warmongers need this global terrorism to justify the spread of its empire." Agree or disagree with this statement. What were the justifications and goals of the United States during the Cold War?

2. Take a position for or against the current wars in Iraq and Afghanistan. You must use strong evidence from your reading to support your position.

3. Do you agree that "the so-called American Dream, to many poor people, is tied to the obligation to fight in a war for corporate domination"? Why or why not? Does this statement apply to previous wars? How and why? Defend your opinion with actual examples of wars for corporate domination.

4. What do you believe Camilo Mejía meant by writing the following: "Poverty and oppression around the world provide the building blocks for an empire. Poverty and oppression at home provide the building blocks to build an imperial army." Do you agree or disagree? Why?

5. Cindy Sheehan claims that she is part of the "silent majority," just as President Richard Nixon claimed his supporters were the "silent majority." In what ways are Sheehan and Nixon's silent majorities similar and in what ways are they different? Would you consider yourself a part of Sheehan's silent majority? Why or why not?

6. How would you describe America's "War on Terrorism"? Is this a war you can support? Why or why not?

Simulations and Other Creative Approaches

1. Conduct a survey in which you ask ten people four important questions: Why did the United States go to war with Afghanistan? Do you support such reasons? Why did the United States go to war with Iraq? Do you support such reasons? Then ask them their personal feelings toward the two wars. Write a paper discussing what you find.

2. Assume the role of a military recruitment officer. Based on what you know about the wars in Iraq and Afghanistan, try to persuade an eighteen-year-old high school graduate to enlist.

3. Assume the role of an antiwar protestor. Based on what you know about the wars in Iraq and Afghanistan, try and persuade an eighteen-year-old high school graduate to join your cause.

4. Stage a debate between Cindy Sheehan and George W. Bush in which Sheehan wants to bring the troops home and Bush justifies the war's cause.

5. Before the passage of same-sex marriage, Vermont was confronted with one major question: should the state grant same-sex couples the right to marry, or should it maintain a "separate but equal" policy by providing for civil unions or domestic partnerships? This "separate but equal" issue was first raised in a legal context in the landmark U.S. Supreme Court decision *Plessy v. Ferguson* (1896) and was repealed in *Brown v. Board of Education* (1954). Learn more about the court's decision on "separate but equal" in both court cases. Then, compare the decisions with the recent case of *Baker v. State of Vermont* on same-sex marriage. Create a graphic portrayal of how these three cases compare and contrast in terms of "separate but equal."

6. Conduct a classroom debate on this issue: domestic partnerships are equal to traditional marriage.

7. Stage a debate on this issue: the war in Iraq is the twenty-first century equivalent to the war in Vietnam.

OTHER HOWARD ZINN TITLES AVAILABLE
FROM SEVEN STORIES PRESS

For ordering and course adoption information visit
www.sevenstories.com/textbook

A Young People's History of the United States
Adapted by Rebecca Stefoff

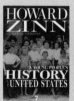

Zinn's first book for young adults retells U.S. history from the viewpoints of slaves, workers, immigrants, women, and Native Americans, reminding younger readers that America's true greatness is shaped by our dissident voices, not our military generals. The single-volume edition also includes sidebar stories of actual children who made American history, from Anyokah, who helped bring written language to her Cherokee people, to John Tinker, a high school student who fought all the way to the Supreme Court for freedom of expression at school—and won.

"In many years of searching, we have not found one history book to recommend . . . until the just published *A Young People's History of the United States*. This is the edition of *A People's History* that we have all been waiting for."—Deborah Menkart, executive director, Teaching for Change

Volume 1: From Columbus to the Spanish-American War / Paper over board 978-1-58322-759-6 $17.95 224 pages, illustrations throughout
Volume 2: From Class Struggle to the War on Terror / Paper over board 978-1-58322-760-2 $17.95 240 pages, illustrations throughout
SINGLE-VOLUME EDITION
Paper 978-1-58322-869-2 $19.95 464 pages, 50 b&w illustrations and photos
Cloth 978-1-58322-886-9 $45.00 464 pages, 50 b&w illustrations and photos

Voices of a People's History of the United States
Second Edition
Edited with Anthony Arnove

The companion volume to historian Howard Zinn's legendary best-selling book *A People's History of the United States*.

"*Voices* should be on every bookshelf. [It presents] the rich tradition of struggle in the United States, from the resistance to the conquest of the Americas in the era of Columbus through the protests today of soldiers and their families against the brutal invasion and occupation of Iraq." —Arundhati Roy

"In *Voices*, Howard Zinn has given us our true story, the ongoing, not-so-secret narrative of race and class in America." —Russell Banks

Paper 978-1-58322-916-3 $22.95 672 pages

Readings from Voices of a People's History of the United States
Edited by Anthony Arnove and Howard Zinn

Authors Howard Zinn and Anthony Arnove are joined on this audio CD by Danny Glover, Sarah Jones, Paul Robeson, Jr., Lili Taylor, Wallace Shawn, and Marisa Tomei to perform rousing words of dissent selected from the complete anthology.

Audio CD 978-1-58322-752-7 $14.95 45 minutes

Artists in Times of War

Zinn's essays discuss America's rich cultural counternarratives to war, from grassroots pamphlets to the likes of Bob Dylan, Mark Twain, E. E. Cummings, Thomas Paine, Joseph Heller, and Emma Goldman.

"The essays are all elegantly written and relate history to the great crisis of current times: war of aggression, western state terrorism, and obedience to state power under the guise of patriotism." —Tanweer Akram, Press Action

Open Media Book / Paper 978-1-58322-602-5 $9.95 160 pages

Howard Zinn on Race
INTRODUCTION BY CORNEL WEST
Howard Zinn on History 2nd edition
INTRODUCTION BY MARILYN B. YOUNG
Howard Zinn on War 2nd edition
INTRODUCTION BY STAUGHTON LYND

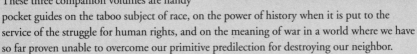

These three companion volumes are handy pocket guides on the taboo subject of race, on the power of history when it is put to the service of the struggle for human rights, and on the meaning of war in a world where we have so far proven unable to overcome our primitive predilection for destroying our neighbor.

On Race Paper 978-1-60980-134-2 $14.00 192 pages / On History Paper 978-1-60980-132-8 $14.00 192 pages / On War Paper 978-1-60980-133-5 $14.00 192 pages

Terrorism and War
Edited by Anthony Arnove

Zinn explores how truth, civil liberties, and human rights become the first casualties of war and examines the long tradition of Americans' resistance to US militarism.

"A significant number [of students] say that this and other books from a radical perspective have transformed their understanding of US society, politics, and culture." —Darrell Y. Hamamoto, University of California, Davis

Open Media Book / Paper 978-1-58322-493-9 $9.95 144 pages

The Zinn Reader

Writings on Disobedience and Democracy, 2nd Edition

The definitive collection of Zinn's writings on the great subjects of our time—race, class, war, law, means and ends—now updated with thirteen recent essays.

"A welcome collection of essays and occasional pieces by the dean of radical American historians."—*Kirkus Reviews*

Paper 978-1-58322-870-8 $21.95 752 pages

La otra historia de los Estados Unidos

"Zinn's work is a classic of revisionist history, bringing forth voices that have previously been muffled. He lets women, African Americans, working-class people, and, yes, Hispanics speak for themselves. This Spanish edition should prove popular in both public and academic libraries."
—*Library Journal*

Updated Spanish-language edition of Howard Zinn's contemporary classic, *A People's History of the United States.*

SIETE CUENTOS EDITORIAL
Paper 978-1-60980-351-3 $19.95 512 pages

THE ZINN EDUCATION PROJECT

Seven Stories is pleased to support the Zinn Education Project, a collaboration between Rethinking Schools and Teaching for Change, dedicated to introducing middle school and high school students to a more accurate, complex, and engaging understanding of United States history than is found in traditional textbooks and curricula. Visit the web site to see how you can bring Zinn's teaching into the classroom, showing students that history is made not by a few heroic individuals, but by people's choices and actions. http://www.zinnedproject.org

A People's History for the Classroom
Bill Bigelow

Activities and projects for middle school and high school classrooms, inspired by Zinn's *A People's History.* Available from The Zinn Education Project: http://www.zinnedproject.org